THE CYBERCRIME HANDBOOK FOR COMMUNITY CORRECTIONS

ABOUT THE AUTHOR

Art Bowker has 26 years experience in law enforcement and corrections. He earned an undergraduate and graduate degree in criminal justice and corrections from Kent State University. Art has completed computer forensic training through the National White Collar Crime Center (NW3C), SEARCH, the Federal Law Enforcement Training Center (FLEC), the Federal Bureau of Investigations (FBI), the American Probation and Parole Association (APPA), and the High Technology Crime Investigation Association (HTCIA). He is a lifetime HTCIA member and served in various positions on its Executive Committee, including International President in 2008. Art is also an APPA member and serves on its Technology Committee. He is an Adjunct Professor at Chancellor University (www.chancelloru.edu/) and writes a blog, the Three C's (Computers, Crime and Corrections), at corrections.com/cybercrime. He can be followed at http://twitter .com/Computerpo.

THE CYBERCRIME HANDBOOK FOR COMMUNITY CORRECTIONS

Managing Offender Risk in the 21st Century

By

ART BOWKER, M.A.

CHARLES C THOMAS • PUBLISHER, LTD.
Springfield • Illinois • U.S.A.

Published and Distributed Throughout the World by

CHARLES C THOMAS • PUBLISHER, LTD.
2600 South First Street
Springfield, Illinois 62704

© 2012 by CHARLES C THOMAS • PUBLISHER, LTD.

ISBN 978-0-398-08728-9 (hard)
ISBN 978-0-398-08729-6 (ebook)

Library of Congress Catalog Card Number: 2011039968

With THOMAS BOOKS *careful attention is given to all details of manufacturing
and design. It is the Publisher's desire to present books that are satisfactory as to their
physical qualities and artistic possibilities and appropriate for their particular use.*
THOMAS BOOKS *will be true to those laws of quality that assure a good name
and good will.*

*Printed in the United States of America
MM-R-3*

Library of Congress Cataloging-in-Publication Data

Bowker, Art.
  The cybercrime handbook for community corrections : managing
offender risk in the 21st century / by Art Bowker.
  , p. cm.
  Includes bibliographical references and index.
  ISBN 978-0-398-08728-9 (hard) -- ISBN 978-0-398-08729-6 (ebook)
  1. Community-based correction--United States--Management.
2. Probation officers--United States. 3. Parole officers--United States.
4. Computer crimes--United States--Prevention. 5. Criminals--
Rehabilitation--United States. I. Title.

  HV9304.B69 2012
  364.16'80973–dc23

                                    2011039968

FOREWORD

Digital technology is a part of all of our lives. Our cars record and adjust to our driving habits. We text, tweet, and post our daily lives. We prefer plastic over cash and frequently let the keyboard do the walking when shopping. We choose GPS over maps to get us from point A to point B and our research librarians are being replaced by Google® and Bing®. The spring of 2011 was deemed "The Arab Spring." The rise of the populous was supported, if not created, by social networks and the Web. Modern politicians are more concerned by their SNS following than mass media coverage. The TSA adjusts its policies in response to You Tube® videos. Blogs and re-tweets have replaced sound bites. Yet, for many years, we acted as if offenders were not part of the wired community. We ignored their digital behavior and failed to monitor it.

I have long held that a computer is a window into the mind of the offender. People look at what they like, they seek out and consume material which supports their beliefs. By examining what an offender seeks and views, we gain an understanding of whom we are trying to manage in the community. Moreover, we gain the ability to assist the offender in learning to appropriately utilize computers in their daily lives. Andrews, Bonta, Latessa et al. focused community corrections on "What Works" and the importance of attitudes, values, and beliefs as well as procriminal associations as factors fostering criminal behavior. Despite understanding these factors, we continued to ignore how the Web isolated offenders and provided support for illicit ideation.

In the 1990s a group of community corrections professionals (Art Bowker among them) began to question how we should address offender computer use while on supervision. Unfortunately, there were few, if any, tools available to assist us. For years we attempted to use tools designed for lab forensics in the far from sterile environment of field forensics within community supervision. In the past 10 years, tools emerged which were developed specifically for triage and field forensics. As these tools were rapidly embraced by many professionals, it became evident there was a second prob-

vi	*The Cybercrime Handbook for Community Corrections*

lem for community corrections. Officers lacked a full understanding of what they could look for, how to look for it, and how to interpret what they found.

This book attempts to resolve this second problem. Written by a man with more than two decades in the trenches of investigations and forensics, Art Bowker provides a clear outline of what we can and should do regarding the management of offender computer use. Not only does this book help community corrections professionals understand how to monitor computer use, but it helps us realize how information gained during monitoring can assist us in overall case management. The technology is now readily available to effectively manage offenders' digital behavior. Bowker's book moves us all toward a more informed use of the technology.

JIM TANNER, PH.D.
Boulder, Colorado

PREFACE

This book will take the reader through paces of managing offender cyber-risk. No advanced technology expertise or background is needed to grasp the discussed concepts or issues. This book is meant specifically for pretrial, probation, parole, and community sanction officers. It hopefully will empower them to meet the supervision challenges of the twenty-first century.

Many probation and parole officers are turning to law enforcement to obtain the technological skills needed for supervising the cyber-offender. This is great for various aspects of managing cyber-risk such as searches. However, proper management frequently requires more than just the ability to do a computer search. One example is installing computer software and reviewing the results. Therefore, community corrections officers need to be trained beyond traditional law enforcement concerns. The material presented in this text will further aid law enforcement trainers when tasked with instructing community correction officers on cybercrime investigation and management.

Many of the techniques discussed in this book obviously require computer use. However, agency computers and systems are not typically controlled or serviced directly by community corrections officers. That function is performed by the correction agency's information technology (IT) staff. This book will provide guidance to IT staff so they can effectively meet the evolving technology needs of those involved in managing cyber-risk.

There is also more to cyber-supervision than just understanding technology. There are also other nuances, such as legal concerns, pro and cons of various techniques, training, equipment needs, and so on. Therefore, anyone charged with managing a community corrections agency (supervisors, chiefs, court administrators, judges, parole commissioners, corrections directors, etc.) will benefit from reading this book. Additionally, both prosecutors and defense attorneys will be in a better position to advocate the various sentencing options, including the imposition of technological conditions, by reviewing this book's material.

This text extensively covers law applicable only in the United States. However, the covered techniques and practices in managing an offender's computer use can be adopted by any foreign jurisdiction involved in community corrections. Many of the tools discussed are openly available outside of the United States. Foreign correctional agencies will therefore gain a better understanding of the technologically possibilities for managing cyber-risk by reviewing this book.

The chapters are organized by major areas. The material presented can be read in order or the reader can jump to the topic that he or she is most interested in at the moment. Chapter 1 provides an overview of cyberspace and how it intersects in community corrections. Chapter 2 covers the pros and cons of the various options available for managing cyber-risk. Chapters 3 and 4 cover the legalities of imposing various computer restrictions as well as the enforcement of technological conditions.

Chapter 5 focuses on evaluating cyber-risk. Chapter 6 is a basic primer for understanding computer components and their relevance for supervision officers. Chapter 7 delves into the basic principles of managing an offender's computer use. Chapter 8 discusses computer searches and seizures. Chapter 9 discusses deploying computer monitoring. Chapter 10 covers online investigations by community corrections. Finally, the Appendix contains nine forms mentioned in the text which can be adopted by any community correction agency involved in managing cyber-risk.

A.B.

ACKNOWLEDGMENTS

Almost 25 years ago, when I was first a probation officer at Cuyahoga County (Cleveland, Ohio), I started looking at cybercrime literature. Later, my years as an investigator with the U.S. Department of Labor, Office of Labor Management Standards (OLMS) helped me greatly in becoming comfortable with computers as an investigative tool. Under the tutelage of District Director Jim Gearhart and Supervisor Jack Graczyk, my writing skills also developed. I truly learned the concepts of being concise, accurate, and thorough while working at OLMS.

In 1997, I became a U.S. Probation Officer and transferred those skills again to working with offender supervision. Chief Keith Koenig and later Chief John Peet, III and Supervisor Pete Hoose, encouraged me in developing practices that could be used to manage offender cyber-risk. One result of their encouragement was my seeking out contact with subject matter experts. Two of the first were Lanny L. Newville, Electronic Monitoring Specialist, Texas Western Pretrial Services and Dan Wieser, Jr., Senior U.S. Probation Officer Middle District of Florida, both of whom greatly impacted and improved my cybercrime knowledge base and offender supervision practices.

I also reached out to the High Technology Crime Investigation Association (HTCIA) and the High Tech Crime Consortium (HTCC). These two groups provided much needed information and guidance on best practices. My Ohio HTCIA Chapter friends (Diamond Boggs, Joe Corrigan, Len Drinkard, Barry Gummow, Jim Hawke, and many others) led me many times by the hand in developing some level of comport handling computer investigations. Additionally, my East and West Coast HTCIA friends, Anthony Reyes and Ron Wilczynski, respectively provided support while I worked on this project and with HTCIA. Much of what I have learned can be tied directly to attending an HTCIA conference or event or speaking with an HTCIA member.

There was also the cybercrime training through the FBI, the Federal Law Enforcement Training Center, National White Collar Crime Center, SEARCH, and the American Probation and Parole Association (APPA). I want to especially call out Jim Tanner, who teaches the APPA cybercrime course, and thank him for writing this book's Foreword. Finally, there were countless conversations over the years with federal legal experts, such as Bob Kern, Chris Stickan, and Michael Sullivan, which gave me much needed insight into the law and computer crime.

I mention these groups and individuals as they all in a real way contributed to this book's eventual creation. Without their willingness to be supportive and to share their knowledge, this book would not have been written, at least not by me.

There also were some individuals who had a more direct role in helping make this book a reality. They are Scott Brantley, Director of the Chancellor University Criminal Justice Program and former Special Agent and Chief Division Counsel for the FBI in Cleveland, Ohio; Jim Hawke, Partner with Binary Intelligence and former Special Agent with the Ohio Bureau of Criminal Identification and Investigation, Computer Crime Unit; Shawna M. Olachea, Special Offender Specialist, California Central Probation Office, and Debra A. White, Aftercare Specialist, Ohio Northern Probation Office. Their collective comments and suggestions made this book much more readable and understandable. I also want to thank Christopher Brown, Chief Technical Officer of Technology of Technologies Pathway, LLC and Todd Shipley, President at Vere Software for providing screen shots of their software (Figures 28 and 29 respectively). Also I want to thank my son Mark for taking most of the hardware pictures contained in this book. He did a most excellent job. The remaining pictures and screen shots were taken by me.

There are three people who really deserve a special mention. They are my parents, Harry and Martha, and my sister, Bonnie. My parents provided the initial loving and supportive environment to develop the desire to learn new things, including how offenders commit cybercrimes. My smarter sister provided the loving sibling rivalry to push me to do more.

I also want to mention my daughter Stephanie and granddaughter Scarlet; I owe them and my son apologies for diverting my attention to this book. Believe me though, I never diverted my love. This book hopes to provide officers guidance so they all will be better protected as they live and grow in a world ruled by computers and the Internet.

Most importantly, I want to thank my wife Kathy. She provided the needed support for a project like this, as well as the love and encouragement to make me not give up. She also kept at bay the "honey do" list until I finished it. I love you and thank you so much!

Finally, I want to thank Charles C Thomas, Publisher, Ltd. for agreeing to publish this book. Community corrections will never be the same as a result.

CONTENTS

Page

Foreword—Jim Tanner v
Preface vii
List of Illustrations xvii

Chapter

   1. DOES COMMUNITY CORRECTIONS COVER
         CYBERSPACE? 3
      Cybercrime Overview 4
         Traditional Practices 6
         Digital Age's Advent 6
         Cyber-sex Crimes 8
         Current Practices 8
      Conclusion 11

   2. UNDERSTANDING THE OPTIONS 15
      Restrictions 16
         Functional Restrictions 16
         Access Restrictions 17
         Total Computer Ban 19
      Impact 21
         Supervised Person 21
         Family/Significant Others 22
         Agency 23
      Monitoring, Searching, and Other Techniques 26
         Monitoring 26
         Computer Searches 27
         General Searches 28

          Online Investigations 29
          Polygraph 31
          Home Confinement/Location Monitoring 31
          Field and Collateral Contacts 32
          Interviewing and Records Examination 32
       Conclusion 33

 3.   CONDITION LEGALITY 35
       Federal/State Constitutions 36
          First Amendment (U.S. Const. Amend. I) 36
          Fourth Amendment (U.S. Const. Amend. IV) 36
          Fifth Amendment (U.S. Const. Amend. V) 37
          Sixth Amendment (U.S. Const. Amend. VI) 37
          Eight Amendment (U.S. Const. Amend. VIII) 37
          Fourteenth Amendment (U.S. Const. Amend. XIV) 38
          State Constitutions 38
       Statutes 38
          Federal Law 38
          State Law 39
          Interstate Compact 39
       Case Law 40
          U.S. v. Paul, 274 F.3d 155 (5th Cir. 2001) 42
          U.S. v. Lifshitz, 369 F.3d 173, 175, 190-92 (2d Cir.2004) 43
          U.S. v. Zinn, 321 F.3d 1084 (11th Cir. 2003) 44
          U.S. v. Sales, 476 F.3d 732 (9th Cir. 2007) 45
          U.S. v. Voelker, 489 F.3d 139, 154 (3d Cir.2007) 46
          U.S. v. Love, 593 F. 3d 1 (DC Cir. 2010) 47
          U.S. v. Tome, 611 F. 3d 1371 (11th Cir. 2010) 48
          In Re Hudson, (49 Cal. Rptr. 3d 74 - Cal: Court of
             Appeals, 1st Appellate Dist., 1st Div. 20, 2006 ... 49
          State of New Hampshire vs. Steven Merrill, Case No.
             2009-811 50
          People v. TR, (Cal: Court of Appeals, 4th Appellate Dist.,
             1st Div. 2010) 51
       Regulations 53
       Conclusion 53

 4.   OPERATIONAL LEGALITY 57
       Search Case Law 58

U.S. v. Tucker, 305 F. 3d 1193, (10th Cir. 2002) 59
U.S. v. Lifshitz, 369 F.3d 173, 175, 190-92 (2d Cir.2004) 63
U.S. v. Yuknavich, 419 F. 3d 1302, (11th Cir. 2005) 63
U.S. v. Herndon, 501 F. 3d 683 (6th Cir. 2007) 68
Discussion 69
Statutes 72
The Stored Communications Act, 18 U.S.C. §§ 2701-2712
("SCA") 73
The Wiretap Statute (TITLE III) 18 U.S.C. §§ 2510-2522 75
The Privacy Protection Act ("PPA"), 42 U.S.C. § 2000aa 79
Other Legal Concerns 81
Fifth Amendment Issues 81
Cyberspace Investigations 83
Privileged Materials 85
Use of WiFi Detectors 85
Use of Ultraviolet Light 87
Conclusion 88

5. ACCESSING CYBER-RISK 91
Computers and Criminal Behavior 91
Risk Assessment 94
Offender's Motivation 95
Criminal Computer Use 96
Technical Means 97
Technical Ability 99
Prior Criminal Behavior 100
Evaluating Risk 101
Cyber-Sex Offenses 103
Files Found 103
Equipment and ISP 105
Online Activities 106
Other Activities 107
Risk Level and Monitoring 107
Juvenile Texting 109
Other Risks 110
Substance Abuse 110
Gambling 111
Suicide 112
Conclusion 112

6. A "BIT" OF COMPUTER EDUCATION 116
	Two Basic Concerns 116
	Computer Basics 123
		Input and Output Devices 125
		Storage 127
		Processing, Communication, and Electrical Supply 134
		Software 136
		Other Concerns 138
	Conclusion 139

7. PRINCIPLES OF EFFECTIVE COMPUTER
		MONITORING 140
	Principle 1: Have a Plan 141
	Principle 2: Limit Access 144
	Principle 3: Actively Look for Circumvention 147
	Principle 4: Utilize A Resilient Method 148
	Principle 5: Reliability and Accuracy 149
	Principle 6: Utilize Alerts 150
	Principle 7: Review Notifications/Data 150
	Principle 8: Accessibility 151
	Principle 9: Avoid Negative Impact on Others 151
	Principle 10: Monitoring Can Be Compromised 152
	Conclusion 154

8. SEARCH AND SEIZURE 155
	Search Types 158
	Boot CD/DVD Software 161
		ImageScan 162
		TUX4N6 163
		Knoppix 164
		NTA Stealth 169
		Discussion 170
	Windows-Based Software 171
		Field Search 172
		Digital Evidence and Forensic Toolkit (DEFT) 174
			FTK Imager® 176
			WinAudit 177
			USBDeview 179
		Triage Tools 180

Advanced Computer Examination Support for Law
        Enforcement 182
    ProDiscover® 182
    Computercop 183
    Remote Examination Agents (REA) 184
  Forensic Software and Hardware 185
  Seizure 187
  Mobile Phone and Device Searches and Seizures 189
  Evidence Storage 190
  Evidence Disposal 191
  Conclusion 192

9. DEPLOYING MONITORING SOFTWARE 195
  Evolution of Monitoring Software 196
  Consumer Monitoring Software 197
    Original Focus 197
    Authority 198
    Familiarity 198
    Time/Access 199
    Volume 199
    Comparison 199
    Features 200
  The Company Approach 201
    Internet Probation and Parole Control (IPPC) 204
    RemoteCom 205
  Discussion 207
  Mobile Phones 208
  Monitoring Other Systems 209
  Conclusion 209

10. ONLINE INVESTIGATIONS 212
  Social Networking 212
    Getting Started 214
    SNS Profiles 215
    SNS Monitoring 217
  Websites 218
  Documentation 219
  Training Resources 220
  Conclusion 222

EPILOGUE 224

APPENDICES
    A. Computer Restriction and Monitoring Program
        Participant Agreement 229
    B. Computer Usage Questionnaire 231
    C. Hardware/Software Restrictions 244
    D. Computer Monitoring Release 245
    E. Computer Usage Update Questionnaire 246
    F. Authorization to Search/Seize Computer Equipment/
        Electronic Data 247
    G. Knoppix Evidence Inventory Worksheet 248
    H. Preview In Windows 249
    I. Property Receipt 250

Index 253

ILLUSTRATIONS

Figures

1. Wrist Watch Containing 2 GB USB Flash Drive
2. Ink Pen Containing 128 MB USB Flash Drive
3. CyberRisk Factors
4. Various Modems
5. Desktop Modem Card
6. Desktop Ethernet Card
7. Various MP3 Players
8. Tamper Tape on Computer
9. Keyghost Logger
10. Inside Computer Case
11. Hard Drives, 30 to 60 GB.
12. External USB Drives
13. Flash Drives
14. Memory Cards
15. Wireless Router
16. WiFi Detection Devices
17. Knoppix 5.1 Desktop View
18. Initial Konqueror Hard Drive View
19. Making Device Writable
20. Konqueror Results for JPG Images
21. Field Search Operation
22. D.E.F.T. Start-Up Menu
23. FTK Imager
24. WinAudit Selections
25. WinAudit Report
26. USBDeview Results
27. D.E.F.T. Log File

28. ProDiscover® Preview
29. Webcase® Control Panel

Tables

1. Cases by Circuit Supporting Technology Conditions
2. Cases by Circuit Limiting Technology Conditions
3. Cybercrime Typology Groups
4. Need for Computer Monitoring in Sex Offense Cases
5. Employer Questions
6. Some Specific File Extensions of Interest
7. Some Folders of Interest
8. Consumer Monitoring Packages

THE CYBERCRIME HANDBOOK
FOR
COMMUNITY CORRECTIONS

Chapter 1

DOES COMMUNITY CORRECTIONS
COVER CYBERSPACE?

They have computers, and they may have other weapons of
mass destruction.
–Janet Reno, Former U.S. Attorney General

Pretrial officers are responsible for insuring defendants' court appearances, while protecting the community and making rehabilitative efforts. Probation and parole officers likewise are responsible for rehabilitation, reintegration, and community protection. Their combined efforts will hopefully reduce recidivism and provide long-term community protection. Maximizing their effectiveness requires continually addressing risk wherever it may present itself. It is therefore imperative that community correction officers (CCO)[1] effectively manage their caseload's risk, including cyberspace.[2]

---

1. Pretrial service officers deal with defendants who have not been convicted and are presumed innocence. They therefore have a slightly different perspective than other supervision officers who deal with offenders after guilt has been established. The term community corrections officers (CCO) in this book will be used to collectively describe pretrial service, probation, parole, and community sanction officers. This text describes concepts and techniques that should be helpful for all officers involved in supervision of defendants and/or offenders. When needed the text will differentiate issues that apply to pretrial service officers as opposed to officers involved in supervision after conviction.

2. Cyberspace in this text describes not only actions taking place online but also any computer activity regardless of whether it has an online aspect.

CYBERCRIME OVERVIEW

Criminal behavior began intersecting with the digital age almost immediately. Early "phreaker,"[3] John Draper, aka Captain Crunch, discovered in 1971 that he could obtain free telephone service by blowing a plastic cereal box whistle into a pay phone receiver (Hafner & Markoff, 1991). During the Internet's infancy, Robert Morris released a worm, a self-replicating program, which shut down thousands of computers (Hafner & Markoff, 1991). Later, the hacker exploits of Kevin Poulsen, aka Dark Dante; Kevin Mitnick, aka Condor; and infamous groups such as the Legion of Doom and the Masters of Deception, influenced the public's cybercrime perception (Progsystem, 2009). These offenders were generally considered technically sophisticated. The correctional response was incapacitation, namely prohibiting or severely limiting their computer access. This was how community risk was managed.

Unfortunately, corrections has been slow to realize that criminal computer use is no longer limited to the so-called technically sophisticated. Since 2007, MySpace® has reportedly removed 90,000 sex offenders from its social networking site (Wortham, 2009). Youth are now finding ways to commit criminal offenses with computers that in the past only adult offenders could accomplish (Bowker, 1999, 2000). However, computers are not only being misused by sex offenders and wayward youth. Some street gangs are also committing high-tech crimes, such as movie and game piracy. Los Angles Police Department Senior Lead Officer Randy McCain noted, "They're making more money selling pirated CDs and DVDs than they would selling narcotics. They make a lot of money and they make the money faster" (Ono, 2010). Parole officers in Multnomah County, Oregon have found parolees with saved electronic data regarding bomb-making instructions, specific plans for a burglary, and how to target elderly for identify theft (Korn, 2011). Additionally, one parole officer found through a mobile phone examination and checking a social networking site that a violent offender was participating in a gang called M.O.B. (Money Over Bitches), which involved individual pimps trad-

---

3. This is a slang combination of the words phone and freak, denoting someone with an extensive understanding of how telephones function.

ing prostitutes on the West Coast (Korn, 2011). The *2009 National Gang Threat Assessment* reflects:

> Gang members often use cell phones and the Internet to communicate and promote their illicit activities. Street gangs typically use the voice and text messaging capabilities of cell phones to conduct drug transactions and prearrange meetings with customers. Members of street gangs use multiple cell phones that they frequently discard while conducting their drug trafficking operations. For example, the leader of an African American street gang operating on the northside of Milwaukee used more than 20 cell phones to coordinate drug-related activities of the gang; most were prepaid phones that the leader routinely discarded and replaced. Internet-based methods such as social networking sites, encrypted e-mail, Internet telephony, and instant messaging are commonly used by gang members to communicate with one another and with drug customers. Gang members use social networking Internet sites such as MySpace®, YouTube®, and Facebook® as well as personal web pages to communicate and boast about their gang membership and related activities. (p. 10)

In 2003, Jennifer Granick, Stanford Center for Internet and Society Director, observed "Without a computer in this day and age, you can't work, you can't communicate, you can't function as people normally do in modern society" (Richtel, 2003). Since 2003, computer and Internet access have only increased as an integral part of law abiding society. According to Nielsen Online, 220 million Americans have Internet access at home and/or work and 73 percent, or 162 million went online in May of 2008 (Nielsen Online, 2008). A 2008 Gallup poll reflected that 31 percent of Americans rely on the Internet for daily news (Morales, 2008). Online banking and shopping are realities. Many community services are located or accessed via the Internet. Taxes and licenses renewals are now done online. Quality Internet educational opportunities are increasing. Online employment searches and posting electronic resumes are also common practice. Additionally, the connectivity between mobile phones and the Internet cannot be ignored. A 2010 Pew Research study noted 75% of teens and 93% of adults ages 18-29 have mobile phones. The study found 58% of 12-year-olds own mobile phones. Additionally, the study noted that 81% of adults between the ages of 18 and 29 are wireless Internet users.

Society has clearly embraced the digital age. Managing risk, while at the same time pursuing rehabilitative and reintegration efforts, has become more complicated than just a blanket prohibition against computer and/or Internet access.

Traditional Practices

Prior to the digital age, CCO efforts in risk management were focused on the brick and mortar world. The offender's[4] residence, employment, education, or lack thereof, were all significant. Home visits were central to rehabilitation. John Augustus, the father of probation, considered them "as a necessary part of the strategy to reform people" (Panzarella, p. 39). Equally important were the offender's associations. Specifically, were they law abiding citizens or criminals? Again, Augustus considered separating offenders from criminal associates a requirement (Panzarella, p. 40). Other high-risk factors included substance use, mental health issues, and treatment compliance. Correctional efforts in addressing these risk areas focused on investigation and maintaining contact with offenders, their families, employers, schools, treatment providers, etc. These practices have rightfully continued to the present. Unfortunately, their historical relevance has blinded many in corrections to other methods that need to be explored in the digital age.

Digital Age's Advent

Correction's initial experience with computer offenders centered on those convicted of telecommunications fraud, hacking into computer systems, system manipulation for financial gain (embezzlement), or computer services theft. Conly (1989) commented that the typical computer offender was viewed as: 15–45 years of age; usually male; bright/motivated; experienced technician to minimally experienced professional; and with usually no previous experience with law enforcement. Additionally, these offenders also appeared to deviate little from accepted social norms. In short, the offenders were either young hackers or insiders who had misused their positions to steal. The of-

---

4. Offender in this text will be used to describe any individual under community supervision, including defendants, probationers, parolees, etc.

fenses committed centered on financial gain or hacking. Therefore the correctional method to manage risk was to limit computer access or positions where offenders had access to systems. Some, however, started to realize that computer crimes were changing. Conly (1989) observed, "Recent law enforcement reports suggest that just as legitimate businesses have found computers indispensable in conducting business—organized criminals, drug dealers, and even child pornographers increasingly depend on computerized transactions" (p. 5).

New offender behaviors have always been closely tied to technological developments. One only has to think of how automobiles and telephones were used for criminal purposes to realize this observation's accuracy. Computers and the Internet are no different. The first mass-marketed personal computer was the Apple® II in 1978, followed by IBM's personal computer with the Microsoft's Disk Operating System® (DOS) in 1981 (Branigan, 2005). These events no doubt increased computer use, including among offenders. However, the face of criminal behavior and computers really started to explode in the mid-1980s with the advent of graphical user interface (GIU). This was the first time users were not required to have computer command line knowledge to successfully utilize a computer. Apple and Windows® operating systems made computer use as easy as clicking a mouse. While computer operating systems became more user friendly, the Internet, whose foundations had been laid in 1969, was growing (Branigan, 2005). From 1984 to 1987, the Internet grew from 1,000 to 10,000 nodes or connections (Branigan, 2005). One early Internet component was the Usenet, which was "the world's biggest electronic discussion form" (Gralla, 1996). Individuals could post and respond to comments and upload and download files. There was communication, but it was not yet generally friendly to nontechies. In 1989, America Online® (AOL) service was launched, which was followed in 1993 by the release of the first Web browser, Mosaic (Branigan, 2005). These events, coupled with faster Internet connections, made computer and Internet use much easier.

Along with computers and the Internet, several other technological developments were simultaneously occurring. These developments included digital cameras, high-speed printers/copiers, and scanners. The first real consumer digital camera was introduced in 1990 and by 1994, Apple had developed its first camera (Marples, 2008). Now individuals could take pictures of anything, including children engaged in sex acts, without worrying about how they were going to get the film developed. In May of 1997, Hewlett-Packard® released its Photo Smart® scanner and printer, which made it "possible for amateurs to achieve near-professional results" (Wildstrom, 1997). Now the general public has access to quality equipment to counterfeit money, checks, identification documents, etc. These events (a user friendly computer/Internet and specialized imaging equipment) from mid-1980s to late 1990s fueled a new offender behavior evolution, namely, traditional offenders using high technology to commit crimes. Although the evolution was minimized or overlooked by many in corrections, it was not lost on law enforcement, particularly as it related to sex offenders.

Cyber-sex Crimes

By the mid-1980s, child pornography had almost been completely eradicated in the United States. Producing and distributing these images had become difficult and expensive. Purchasing and trading was extremely risky. Unfortunately, the above developments, namely the Internet and specialized imaging equipment, turned the tables and child pornography began to explode. In the late 1980s, Congress expanded federal children pornography statutes to specifically include computers (Harvard Law Review Association, 2009). By 1996, Congress passed major legislation to protect children from online sexual predators (U.S. Department of Justice, Child Exploitation and Obscenity Section (CEOS), 2009). Additionally, funding was provided to create Internet Crimes Against Children (ICAC) Task Forces, whose purpose was to help "state and local law enforcement agencies develop an effective response to cyber enticement and child pornography cases" (U.S. Department of Justice, Office Juvenile Justice and Delinquency Prevention (OJJDP), 2009). By 1998, ICAC Task Forces began popping up all over the United States (OJJDP, 2009). Increased law enforcement activity and the evolution of offender behavior began placing more cyberoffenders at correction's doorstep.

Current Practices

Since the digital age's beginning, many in corrections have been stuck in the mindset of merely prohibiting computer and/or Internet access for cyberoffenders. This view has increasingly had legislative support, particularly when dealing with sex offenders. Many states have legislation that restricts computer or Internet access for sex offenders on probation or parole (National Conference of State Legislatures, 2009). However, this approach has flaws for all but the most hardcore cases. Despite the legislative mandate to restrict computer use, many of the enacted statutes have provisions which provide that CCO can authorize computer use for legitimate purposes. Additionally, many federal courts have struck down total bans on computer or Internet use at the federal level as overly restrictive (Bowker & Thompson, 2001; Miller, Maulupe, Nikiund, & Shetty, 2006; Blaiadell, 2009). As a result, a total ban on all computer and Internet use for each and every offender, including sex offenders, will be harder and harder to support. This is particularly the case when life in modern society is increasingly dependent upon computer and Internet access.

Another misconception is that banning computer and Internet access is the best practice as CCO either do not have or cannot obtain the technical ability to otherwise monitor computer use. This belief holds that monitoring computer use requires extreme expertise. However, no such expertise is required to recognize the existence of a desktop or laptop in a home or employment site. Only a few years ago the writer received the editorial comment from a respected corrections publication that, "Although the subject matter (cybercrime supervision) is of great interest to probation and parole, such a program as described would require MIS/IT expertise that is generally beyond the area of probation and parole." Unfortunately, this ironic view is shared by too many corrections leaders. The irony quickly becomes apparent when we consider the general public, including offenders, are capable of embracing technology for such things as social networking, online banking, education, etc. However, CCO are somehow incapable of the same technological prowess. Additionally, this view fails to consider that CCO are already using technology in the workplace. This includes such areas as report writing, record keeping, data analysis, online records checks, location monitoring/global positioning, etc. Obviously, CCO can learn and develop the skills necessary to monitor computer use because they already are using technology for other purposes.

Current community correction supervision is also influenced by the view that computers and the Internet are just not a problem. After all, offenders don't or won't use computers or the Internet. Recently, an official working with one of the country's largest correctional populations made a remarkable comment. He noted only ten offenders in his state's entire supervised sex offender population reported access to computers and the Internet. Therefore, he concluded computer monitoring was not an issue. Again, reality dictates otherwise. As previously stated, MySpace has removed 90,000 sex offenders from their site. Computers and the Internet access are literally everywhere. Obviously, the above comment pertained only to sex offenders. Despite what has already been noted thus far, many have similar views of nonsex offenders' technical inclinations. Is it realistic to believe that offenders will not use a computer or the Internet to violate their supervision conditions? There are already numerous examples of offenders doing just that, either by being online without authorization and/or documenting their violation behavior via social networking sites (Brown, 2009; Hawley, 2006; Schrade, 2006). Clearly, this misconception is ill-advised.

Another troubling view is that what happens in cyberspace is somehow not germane to the real world and therefore it is unworthy of correction's focus. This misconception is contradicted by the number of predators caught using the Internet to arrange real world meetings with children. Thus, the online world and the real world do often intersect in sex offender cases. Consider gang members using social networking sites to maintain contact with one another. Recall that some street gangs are also involved in software piracy. Additionally, some offenders have indicated they have a gambling problem and that was the reason they committed their offense. The presence of gambling sites is probably only second to pornography on the Internet. Cyber-stalking and cyber-bullying oftentimes end up having real world consequences for the victim. One also has to realize defendants may portray a Court persona but have another online one. Notable examples are of DWI defendants whose social networking profiles flaunt their drinking behaviors, which courts rightfully considered as evidence of little remorse or insight into their illegal behavior (Tucker, 2008). An online persona can be a window into a person's personality. Sentencing officials and supervision officers should therefore not refuse to open that window if they hope to truly fashion appropriate sentences and rehabilitative strategies.

Thankfully, there are some notable examples of progressive CCO not holding these misguided supervision views. For instance, Orange County created an operational plan for a Special Enforcement Unit/ Computer Crime Lab within the probation department (Harrison, 2001). Multnomah County Department of Community Justice, Oregon also has a computer lab specifically for parole officers concerned about their offenders' computer use (Korn, 2011). Other CCO have also discovered there are approaches beyond blanket prohibitions against computer and Internet use, such as computer monitoring and conducting computer searches (Bowker & Thompson, 2001; Kelly, 2001; Newille, 2001; Bowker & Gray, 2004). Recently, a Kentucky probation officer realized that making "virtual home visits" of offender's social networking sites can provide important information about what they are doing and their associations (Blalock, 2007). In a real sense, this is applying Augustus' previously noted concepts to the digital age. The cyber-risk's importance to CCO may be best summed up by the American Probation and Parole Association (APPA) Technology Committee (2011):

> Probation and parole officers must expand their role as monitoring agents to include cyberspace. It is ill-advised to simply ignore offenders' online activities in our technology-dependent society. Too frequently what occurs in cyberspace has real world consequences. Only by adopting good computer management skills can we hope to address the cyber-risk posed by the increasing offender population using computers for criminal activities and/or other violation behavior. (p. 10)

CONCLUSION

Community corrections can and should consider cyberspace in all supervision cases. It will require reexamining old ideas and trying new strategies. However, these are not impossible tasks. They just require a willingness to learn and adapt. These approaches and more will be addressed in greater detail in the following chapters. To paraphrase a great old science fiction classic (*Star Trek*), Let us boldly go where corrections has not gone before!

REFERENCES

American Probation and Parole Association (APPA). (2011). *Managing the risks posed by offender computer use.* Lexington. APPA.

Attorney General's Address, Conference on Critical Infrastructure Protection, February 27, 1998, Retrieved from http://www.usdoj.gov/criminal/cybercrime/ag_nipc.html).

Blalock, S. (2007). *Virtual home visits: A guide to using social networking sites to assist with offender supervision and fugitive apprehension.* District 1, Division of Probation and Parole Kentucky Department of Corrections.

Blasidell, K. (2009). Protecting the playgrounds of the twenty-first century: Analyzing computer and Internet restrictions for internet sex offenders. *Valparaiso University Law Review,* Spring, 2009.

Bowker, A. (1999). Juveniles and computers: should we be concerned?" *Federal Probation,* December, 1999.

Bowker, A. (2000). Advent of the computer delinquent. *FBI Law Enforcement Bulletin,* December, 2000.

Bowker, A., & Gray, M. (2004). An introduction to the supervision of the cybersex offender. *Federal Probation,* December, 2004.

Bowker, A., & Thompson, G. (2001). Computer crime in the 21st century– Its effect on the probation officer. *Federal Probation,* September, 2001.

Branigan, S. (2005). *High-tech crimes revealed: Cyberwar stories from the digital front.*

Brown, E. (2009) Drinkin' photos on MySpace send man to prison. *Internet Cases: Covering Law and the Internet Since 2005.* Retrieved from http://blog.internetcases.com/2009/08/03/drinkin-photos-on-myspace-send-man-to-prison/.

Conly, C. (1989). *Organizing for computer crime investigation and prosecution.* U.S. Department of Justice, Office of Justice Programs, National Institute of Justice.

Gralla, P. (1996). *How the Internet works.* Emeryville: Macmillian, p. 55.

Hafner, K., & Markoff, J. (1991). *Cyberpunk: Outlaws and hackers on the computer frontier.*

Harrison, E. (2001). *Operational plan: Special enforcement unit computer crime lab.* Orange County Probation Department, Los Angeles, CA.

Harvard Law Review Association. (2009). Child pornography, the Internet, and the challenge of updating statutory terms. *Harvard Law Review,* June, 2009.

Hawley, K. (2006, October 12). MySpace reveals probation violation: Fatal brawl participant shown drinking beer. *Chicago Tribune.* Retrieved from http://archives.chicagotribune.com/2006/oct/12/news/chi-0610120145 oct12.

Kelly, B. (2001). Supervising the cyber criminal. *Federal Probation,* September, 2001.

Korn, P. (2011, July 7). County lab keeps cyber-eye on parolees technicians scour electronic devices for evidence of violations. *Portland Tribune.* Retrieved from http://portlandtribune.com/news/story.php?story_id=1309 98904988341200.

Lenhart, A., Purcell, K., Smith, A., & Zickuhr, K. (2010). Social media and young adults. Pew Internet & American Life Project. Retrieved from http://pewinternet.org/Reports/2010/Social-Media-and-Young-Adults .aspx.

Marples, G. (2008). The history of figital vameras—A short but bright picture. Retrieved from http://www.thehistoryof.net/the-history-of-digital-cameras.html.

Miller, D., Maulupe, S., Nikikund, A., & Shetty, S. (2006). Conditions of supervision that limit an offender's access to computers and Internet services: Recent cases and emerging technology. *Criminal Law Bulletin,* July-August, 2006.

Morales, L. (2008, December 15). Cable, Internet news sources growing in popularity. *Gallup.* Retrieved from http://www.gallup.com/poll/113314 /cable-internet-news-sources-growing-popularity.aspx.

National Gang Intelligence Center. (2009). *National Gang Threat Assessment.*

National Conference of State Legislatures. (2009). *Sex offender computer restriction & registration related statutes, updated February 2009.*

National Conference of State Legislatures. (2009). *SORNA related state laws, June 2009.*

Newville, L. (2001). Cybercrime and the court: Investigating and supervising the information age offender. *Federal Probation,* September, 2001.

Nielsen Online. (2008, July 8). *Nielsen reports TV, Internet and mobile usage among Americans.* Retrieved from http://blog.nielsen.com/nielsenwire/wp -content/uploads/2009/06/3_screen_report_5-08_fnl.pdf.

Ono, D. (2010, June 10). Counterfeit goods fund violent gang activity. Retrieved from http://www.streetgangs.com/news/061110_counterfeit _goods_fund.

Panzarella, R. (2002). Theory and practice of probation on bail in the report of John Augustus. *Federal Probation,* December, 2002.

Progsystem. (2009). *Greatest hackers in the world.* Retrieved from http://prog system.free.fr/greatesthackers.htm#main.

Richtel, M. (2003, January 21). Monitoring criminals' Internet use is a matter of law. *New York Times.* Retrieved from http://www.nytimes.com/2003 /01/21/technology/21MONI.html?pagewanted=all.

Schrade, B. (2006, April 12). Teacher in student-sex case arrested on probation violation, officials say. Tennessean.com. Retrieved from http://www.tennessean.com/apps/pbcs.dll/article?AID=/20060412/news03/60412003.

Tucker, E. (2008, July 16). Facebook used as character evidence, lands some in jail. *USA Today*. Retrieved from http://www.usatoday.com/tech/webguide/internetlife/2008-07-19-facebook-trials_N.htm.

U.S. Department of Justice, Child Exploitation and Obscenity Section (CEOS). (2009). Retrieved August 10, 2009 from http://www.usdoj.gov/criminal/ceos/childporn.html.

U.S. Department of Justice, Office Juvenile Justice and Delinquency Prevention (OJJDP). (2009). Retrieved from http://ojjdp.ncjrs.org/programs/ProgSummary.asp?pi=3.

Wildstrom, S. (1997, April 28). Digital photos just got smarter. *Business Week*. Retrieved from http://www.businessweek.com/archives/1997c/b3524075.arc.htm.

Wortham, J. (2009, February 3). MySpace turns over 90,000 names of registered sex offenders. *New York Times*. Retrieved from http://www.nytimes.com/2009/02/04/technology/internet/04myspace.html.

Chapter 2

UNDERSTANDING THE OPTIONS

Never tell people how to do things. Tell them what to do
and they will surprise you with their ingenuity.
—George S. Patton, U.S. General, 1885–1945

Judges are frequently faced with complex sentencing and release decisions. Should they release a defendant pending the final outcome of a criminal proceeding? If so, should the person be supervised with special prerelease conditions? After a guilty finding, do they place an individual on probation or should they sentence him or her to prison and for how long? What special conditions should be imposed while the offender is on probation or after his or her release from custody? Parole authorities frequently confront the same challenging release decisions and consideration of special supervision conditions. The options can be even more complex when technological conditions[1] (computer[2] and/or Internet monitoring/restrictions) are warranted to

---

1. Technological conditions encompasses rules that involve any restriction or monitoring of computers or Internet use. It includes conditions that prohibit access, use and/or possession of specific electronic devices. The term also encompasses conditions that require disclosure of access or possession of such devices. Finally, conditions that authorize the search and/or seizure of electronic devices are included as well.

2. In this text the term computer has the same meaning as 18 U.S.C. §1030 (e) (1), which is very similar to many state statues, and encompasses not only desktop and laptop computers, but gaming devices, cell phones, I-Phones, and similar devices yet to be invented. Specifically, ". . . 'computer' means an electronic, magnetic, optical, electrochemical, or other high-speed data processing device performing logical, arithmetic, or storage functions, and includes any data storage facility or communications facility directly related to or operating in conjunction with such device, but such term does not include an automated typewriter or typesetter, a portable hand held calculator, or other similar device."

15

manage risk. What impact will the conditions have on the individuals and/or their families? How effective can these conditions be enforced and what will the agency impact be on those charged with insuring their compliance? What are the technological challenges associated with these special conditions? What are the pros and cons associated with each technique for managing cyber-risk? Finally, will the imposition of special conditions withstand legal scrutiny? Understanding all of these issues will help mitigate possible legal challenges to the imposition of technological conditions.

RESTRICTIONS

Many supervision conditions are merely obligations to follow while under supervision. Common examples include regular reporting, filing periodic written reports, maintaining employment, reporting all contact with law enforcement, or meeting all financial obligations. However, other supervision conditions are more restrictive in nature. For instance, it has been a long-standing practice that individuals under correctional supervision may not associate with felons or leave the jurisdiction without permission. Following a curfew, refraining from alcohol and/or substance use or places where substances are illegally used are other examples of restrictive conditions. Technological conditions follow a progressive continuum, which includes functional, access, and total computer ban restrictions.

Functional Restrictions

Functional restrictions are those conditions that must be imposed or at least implied for the remaining conditions to be effective. Consider for a moment a case when a court does not order any restrictions on an individual's computer or Internet usage but does order computer monitoring. To be effective, the individual must be restricted to a monitored computer. Likewise, they can't be permitted to use a device, such as a gaming console, which can't accommodate monitoring software or hardware. Allowing such access provides a ready outlet to circumvent the rules without placing themselves in legal jeopardy.

Likewise, if they are subject to a condition requiring periodic computer searches, they must also be restricted to only use devices that have been disclosed. Otherwise, they will provide one laptop for the computer search and keep another concealed. Additionally, monitoring and search conditions will also be ineffective if supervised individuals are not prohibited from using software that can defeat the process, such as anti-spyware[3] and data destruction[4] and concealment programs.[5] Once the decision is made to manage computer risk, either via monitoring or periodic computer searches, there must be some functional restrictions imposed to make managing cyber-risk more effective.

Access Restrictions

The next level in the continuum is access restriction conditions, These are directly related to addressing an identified cyber-risk. For instance, a condition that prohibits access to materials for a sex offender, such as pornography, is an example of an access restriction. Other examples of access restrictions are prohibitions against visiting certain websites, social networking sites, chat rooms, or sites that allow minors to join. Some access restrictions may prohibit use of specific software or hardware. For instance, an individual who traded child pornography or sent obscene images to minors might be prohibited from using peer-to-peer file sharing programs[6] or webcams. Individuals convicted of check fraud or counterfeiting schemes may receive prohibitions against possessing scanners or special high quality printers. More severe access restrictions may prohibit Internet access beyond education or vocational purposes or during certain times of the day or week.

---

3. Spyware is a term frequently used to describe programs that collect user information surreptitiously and report back to the entity that deployed it. Spyware, although very similar to monitoring software, has a different, usually nefarious purpose. However, many anti-spyware programs will also detect monitoring software and therefore pose a unique challenge. CCOs should never refer to monitoring software as spyware as it is never installed without the owner's knowledge.
4. Data destruction programs refers to software that securely deletes data maintained on electronic media. A common example is a wiping program which overwrites data a specific number of times so it cannot be recovered with traditional forensic tools. In this text it also includes programs that delete information maintained in various locations about user activities on the computer, such as Internet browsing history, Internet searches, recently accessed files or any other user activity.
5. Concealment programs refer to encryption software that encrypts data so it can not be read or interpreted unless unencrypted or steganography software, which hides data's existence, usually within another nondescriptive file or electronic media. Oftentimes both encryption and steganography software are used in conjunction with one another.
6. Peer-to-peer file sharing programs allow users to upload and download files with others using the program, which allows them to network together without a central server. These programs are commonly used to trade and obtain pornography and pirated movies, music, games, and software.

The most restrictive of these access conditions would be a total Internet ban.

The lines between functional and access restrictions sometimes overlap. Some access restrictions may also be very functional for monitoring or other compliance efforts. A special condition that prohibits access to software or hardware that can defeat monitoring or searches is one such example. Other access conditions can actually make monitoring and/or searches and enforcement more challenging. For instance, a specific website restriction may be rather easy to incorporate with monitoring software that can block specific websites. However, the software will have to be continually updated to keep current if a general ban on particular websites classes, such as all social networking sites, is imposed. Prohibiting certain material can also be a problematic if it is only enforced via software that prevents access to certain materials (filtering or blocking software[7]).

Filtering software which relies solely on a list of prohibited or "blacklisted" websites, such as pornography sites, has to be continually updated due to the fluid and often changing nature of the Internet. Additionally, some filtering software will restrict too much material, including legitimate information and some will not restrict enough material. One law enforcement agency deployed "intelligent" software which prohibited employees from accessing any websites in which the word "sex" appeared beyond a predetermined level. This appears great at first glance. Unfortunately, the software also prohibited access to a police department website which contained extensive scholarly material on investigating and preventing sex crimes. Another government agency deployed blocking software that prevented employee access to pornographic websites but could not prohibit access to image

---

7. Filtering or blocking software prevents access to material and/or websites through predetermined criteria, such as specific terms or websites. Often times the software also allows the modification of the criteria. Some newer operating systems have parental controls that can be turned on that prevent access to categories of material or themes, such as pornography, drugs, and violence. However, these controls usually are only specific to a particular browser, such as Internet Explorer®. If another browser is used, such as Firefox®, a user can bypass the controls. Some Internet Service Providers (ISP), such as Yahoo!® also provide parental controls that will block access to material through a specific user's account. Filtering or blocking software usually only blocks access to material from the Internet. It does not preclude the user from accessing material that is stored on CDs, DVDs, or other electronic media. Some monitoring software also has features that allow the blocking and filtering of websites, use of certain programs, and/or some or all Internet use. These functions, in additional to being able to record all activity, create a big advantage over the use of just filtering or blocking software.

previews generated by common search engines such as Google® and Yahoo!

A complete Internet ban can also adversely effect monitoring. Some monitoring software depends upon an Internet connection to either forward information and/or problem alerts. If the supervised individual is not allowed Internet access a different monitoring software may have to be considered. Software that allows an agency's examiner to access and search an individual's computer over the Internet (remote searching) will likewise run into issues if the supervised person is prohibited from the Internet.

Sometimes the restriction imposed will require the supervised person not to possess any device that can access Internet. In the past, that was rather simple to remove a modem or even modem card from the computer. However, we now have mobile phones, which are getting harder and harder to find that don't access the Internet. Gaming consoles also now can easily access the Internet, which provides another reason beyond functional concerns that they may be restricted. There are now cars that access the Internet so drivers and passengers can be in continuous contact with their social networking sites.

Total Computer Ban

At the extreme end of the continuum is a total computer ban. This sounds like an ideal condition to many. But how is it enforced? Obviously, field visits may discourage computer possession or may detect they have been obtained. Accessing financial records may detect computer purchases, rentals, or Internet Service Provider (ISP) charges, which are a dead giveaway that somewhere there is a computer.

Periodically checking the Internet for online activity or similar online investigations, may disclose the supervised person has obtained a computer and used it to access the Internet. But, if they don't access the Internet or are good at concealing their activities, what then? Periodic general searches could be conducted, but how frequently should they be done? If a computer is found, what then? It is subject to seizure, but what about a search? What is the authority for searching a seized unauthorized computer?

We also must confront the mobile phone issue. A mobile or cell phone clearly meets the federal computer definition (18 U.S.C. § 1030

(e) (1)) which is also mirrored in many state statutes. Prohibiting a desktop computer may seem okay, but how likely will a ban on accessing any mobile phone survive legal challenges? Remember, these devices may be needed for emergencies, employment, staying in contact with a CCO, etc. and as a result may be much harder to justify prohibiting completely. Increasingly all manner of electronic devices and even cars have computers in them. Many of these computers are also connecting to the Internet. Previously, total computer bans have withstood legal scrutiny. In Kevin Mitnick's 1998 hacking case, he attempted to argue that a blanket computer ban was too vague. After all, computers could be found in ATM machines and in some cars of the time. How could he determine what constituted a computer to remain in compliance? The Ninth Circuit rejected this argument in *U.S. v. Mitnick* (1998) noting that he was being given fair notice what was prohibited. Painter (2001) articulates the reasoning further by noting:

> [F]air warning is not to be confused with the fullest or most pertinacious, warning imaginable. Conditions of probation do not have to be cased in letters six feet high, or to describe every possible permutation, or spell out every last self-evident detail [they] may afford fair warning even if not precise to the point of pedantry. In short, conditions of probation can be written—and must be read in a common sense way. *U.S. v. Gallo,* 20 F.3d7, 11 (1st Cir. 1994) (internal citations omitted) (p. 48)

Mitnick's case is over a decade old. The Internet's accessibility is now literally woven into cars, mobile devices, gaming devices, and even household appliances. With every facet of life being touched by computers and the Internet, can a total ban still be supported? Consider for a moment that even prisoners are being granted computer access, e-mail, and in some states limited Internet access (Bowker, 2010). Today's reality is that some inmates may be allowed to use computers and access the Internet while in custody, but when released to community supervision, they are prohibited from such use. It is anyone's guess how long this apparent contradiction will withstand legal challenges.

IMPACT

All conditions will have some kind of impact on supervised individuals. Standard conditions have historically been upheld as supporting a positive lifestyle and are considered a good impact. Technological conditions strive to have a similar positive outcome, promoting law abiding behavior in the supervised individual. However, make no mistake, they do have an impact which may not be considered by all to be completely positive. Technological conditions, unlike many other conditions, can also impact a supervised person's family and significant others. Additionally, condition enforcement also has an agency impact. Only by understanding these impacts can we hope to impose legally supported conditions that effectively manage cyber-risk in the least restrictive and technically feasible manner.

Supervised Person

It is rather easy to see the impact when extreme restrictions, such as on accessing the Internet or a computer are imposed. However, even with the imposition of minimum technological conditions, such as monitoring, there is going to be impact. Depending upon officers' skills, the software, and the activities completed, the installation process may take anywhere from 30 minutes to several hours. Monitoring will also require the supervised person only access equipment which can be monitored. No more gaming consoles or devices that can't be monitored. More than likely they will also have to pay the expense of computer monitoring. These can include the cost of software, hardware, and/or a monthly fee. Regular maintenance of deployed monitoring software can also involve additional time the supervised person has to be at home and/or not allowed to use his or her computer. If monitoring is dependent upon the Internet, they will likewise also have to insure they maintain Internet service. The same would hold true if they are subject to remote searches. Additionally, they may have to insure that their computer can be searched remotely, possibly ceasing their activities while the process is occurring.

Random searches also will impact the supervised person. They will take time to complete on-site. If the hard drive is imaged,[8] the process

---

8. Imaging a hard drive is a process that makes an exact copy, bit for bit, of all information on the drive, including deleted information. It is sometimes also referred to as "mirroring."

will take additional time. Computer use downtime is going to be even longer if it has to be removed to be searched. This total downtime will increase with frequency of random searches. If the search includes a general search of the premise, the time will also increase. There also will need to be more staff present to insure safety and to make sure the process can be done as effectively as possible. Even searches conducted solely on the basis of reasonable suspicion are likely to be very time consuming and disruptive when they do occur.

Family/Significant Others

Family and significant others are impacted by technological conditions, particularly if they are living with the supervised person. A total computer ban may place a family in the position of removing their computer from the home or providing adequate safeguards up to including monitoring software installation. Refusal to do so may mean that a supervised loved one can't reside in the residence. Monitoring and even computer searches opens up both supervised and unsupervised persons' lives immensely. Depending upon the monitoring software deployed, a supervised person's loved ones may no longer have any privacy expectation if they use a monitored computer. Obviously, computer and general searches, whether on a random basis or based upon reasonable suspicion, will likewise diminish their privacy.

Monitoring software on offender's computers have more than once revealed drug use and viewing of pornography by others in the home. Offender's teenagers have made arrangements to purchase marijuana during chats and have surfed pornographic sites on monitored computers. Grades of offender's minor children as well as family health concerns have been captured. Infidelity among partners of supervised individuals has also been captured by monitoring software. Searches and monitoring have also revealed naked images of supervised individuals' spouses and significant others.

Some monitoring software features allow it to only be activated with certain users. However, this raises the possibility that a supervised person will use a nonsupervised person's user account to bypass monitoring. Software developed by Internet Probation and Parole Control, Inc. (IPPC) can be deployed with a biometric device that identifies which person is using a monitored computer. Some privacy impact can also be mitigated with adequate notices to all in the home if they use the monitored computer or one subject to a search, they have no expectation of privacy.

Time taken for monitoring software installation, remote or on-site searches, or computer removal from the home will also effect non-supervised persons in the residence. They also can't use the computer or access the Internet during these activities. Restrictions on only having equipment in the home that can be monitored will also impact them. Monitoring costs, although minor and reasonable, will also impact a supervised person's family if their finances are marginal.

Significant others need not be present in the home to be impacted. For instance, if a supervised individual is prohibited from a social networking site, they may not be able to share information with loved one's in distant geographic locations. A loved one in the military may not be able to communicate via the Internet with an offender, which is a growing trend among the enlisted and their families.

Monitoring software has also captured webcam images forwarded of supervised individuals' adult friends exposing themselves as well as very intimate details of their relationships. One can only wonder whether these significant others would be so willing to share this private information if they knew that correctional personnel were also viewing it. Mandatory disclosure by offenders that the system they use is monitored may alleviate this information being shared. However, what if the individual using the monitored system is another person in the home who chooses for themselves to ignore the warning about no expectation of privacy? They are free to communicate with others, without warning them that images or their communication is being monitored by someone beyond the intended recipient.

The simple act of exchanging e-mails with loved ones, business associates, doctors, and even legal counsel, can be captured. The details of these exchanges can be very intimate in deed. Monitoring will capture this information as it occurs and searches may detect it months or even years afterwards. In short, computer monitoring or searches have impact that can extend well beyond just the supervised person's life.

Agency

A supervising agency's impact will be directly related to how receptive they are to managing cyber-risk. In many ways, it comes down to either accepting their role in protecting the community or ignoring it and hoping for the best. Some agencies may choose to ignore cyber-risk and not attempt to take on more aggressive supervision techniques such as computer monitoring or searches. However, completely ignoring the risk, such as disregarding computers in sex offenders' homes and not periodically checking the Internet can't be justified. How will these same agencies look when these offenders are found easily online by a child and later by the media after a terrible crime has been committed? Can they really argue we can't check the Internet for our supervised sex offenders presence when most children have mastered basic Internet skills? Can they likewise ignore a computer and webcam's presence in a repeat sex offender's residence without taking some action, such as seeking law enforcement's assistance? Once a court or parole authority has created a technological condition, the costs of simply ignoring it will subject the community correction agency and the officer to a civil liability if things go south with the supervision process.

Probably, the first impact for community corrections agencies will be expending resources for initial training on how computers are used to commit crimes and techniques for managing the risk. Additionally, agencies must understand that staff will have to continue to receive training to keep up to date. Technology development does not stop and neither does how it may be used for illegal purposes. Kurzweli (2001) notes in part:

> An analysis of the history of technology shows that technological change is exponential, contrary to the common-sense 'intuitive linear' view. So we won't experience 100 years of progress in the 21st century—it will be more like 20,000 years of progress (at today's rate). The 'returns,' such as chip speed and cost-effectiveness, also increase exponentially. There's even exponential growth in the rate of exponential growth.

The next impact will be equipment (hardware/software). There will have to be some equipment allocation for monitoring and/or search purposes. Even the simple act of Internet searching should be limited to a specific computer to avoid potential risks to an agency's own computer infrastructure. As with training, equipment will have to be updated as well. Yesterday's monitoring or search software may not work with today's operating systems. Monitoring software has to be purchased, if not by the supervised individual, then by the agency. Even when the offender pays for the cost, there can be an agency fee for accessing the monitoring results. Forensic software and hardware likewise must be periodically updated to keep pace with newer operating systems and equipment. If imaging or forensic examinations are necessary, there will also be a need for storage media, such as hard drives.

Agencies must also understand that those charged with managing cyber-risk are going to need time to do their jobs. Properly installing monitoring software takes longer than a typical field contact. Additionally, monitoring software can generate a lot of data, not all of it related to noncompliance. Staff need to be able to review this information to detect noncompliance. The reviews can take a few minutes to several hours, depending upon the alert criteria and the amount of data generated, both of which are related to the user's activity. Likewise, even a basic computer preview search can take an hour or two. Imaging a computer, depending upon its size, will also take a significant amount of time. A true forensic examination can also take days and even weeks, depending upon the amount of data involved.

Any agency handing off imaging and forensic examinations to law enforcement or local computer crime labs may have to accept significant delays in the processing of their electronic evidence. Agencies that opt to contract with the private sector will have to find the financial resources to pay for their services. Such services are typically billed by the hour and it is not unheard of to see billing at $250.00 an hour or more. As was noted previously, forensic examinations can take days or even weeks to complete. This can result in a significant agency cost if they choose to seek private sector assistance.

Agencies venturing into this area, particularly with monitoring and searches, will have to implement procedures for evidence storage, which will require a secure location, with limited access. The area must allow for storage of seized computers or other electronic evidence for its later use in a violation hearing or possible criminal proceeding. Even monitoring results should be maintained in a secure manner to counter any claims the results were altered prior to the proceeding. Special care must be exercised, much like occurs with seized drugs, when the evidence involves child pornography. However, unlike drugs, child pornography can be duplicated without degrading the originals. Evidence containing child pornography must be adequately secured as well as any investigating material that may contain images of it, such as duplicated drives or reports.

There also can be an impact on agency staff involved in managing cyber-risk, particularly when dealing with sex offenders. Staff involved in computer monitoring and searches will be exposed to still and movie images that can be quite disturbing, particularly when the material meets child pornography definitions. Some of these images show very young children, even toddlers and babies, being brutally victimized. Staff may also be exposed to images involving bestiality, sadomasochism, and other acts of depravity. Increasingly, there is a concern that law enforcement exposed to such images may be negatively affected and even traumatized (Russell, 2010). Monitoring and/or searching convicted sex offender's computers unfortunately exposes community correction staff to these same mental health challenges.

MONITORING, SEARCHING, AND OTHER TECHNIQUES

Thus far the discussion has centered on restrictions that accompany technological conditions and their impact on the offender, their significant others, and the community corrections agency. The discussion now must turn to the specific strategies for enforcing these technological conditions. What are the differences between monitoring and computer searches? Which is more effective and how difficult can they be to implement? What techniques can be used to make them more effective? This section will briefly highlight the least restrictive and technically feasible strategies for managing cyber-risk.

Monitoring

Installing monitoring software has the distinct advantage that it can record whatever activity the user does on the monitored system. This can include not only actual noncompliance behavior but also attempts to conceal or destroy evidence of this activity. Depending upon the software, noncompliance can be reported within minutes of its occurrence. Additionally, many times evidence is forwarded to a remote location, out of the offender's control. Disabling monitoring software itself can occur. However, such tampers without detection are usually difficult to achieve.

Software installation can usually be accomplished in less than a half hour, unless there are difficulties, which can extend the time to several hours. The time spent actually reviewing monitoring results is dependent upon number of alerts received and overall user activity. These reviews can be a few minutes to several hours per case. Depending upon the software, the reviews can occur over the Internet. However, some software requires direct access to the data maintained on the target computer. Little training and equipment is required to install and use monitoring software.

Monitoring software will not open and search files/directories. It is entirely dependent upon the user's activity, which it will, of course, record. Monitoring software is primarily limited to Windows and Apple operating systems. There are hardware devices which can be used for other operating systems. Some moblie phones can now be monitored with software. However, there is no monitoring software or hardware for gaming devices, I-Pods, cameras, and other devices. The easy and most often used method to overcome monitoring is simply to use a nonmonitored computer. Monitoring software can obviously not reveal what was done on a nonmonitored computer. Only a search can accomplish that objective.

Computer Searches

Computer searches can detect evidence months or even years after it was created. It can be used to examine all operating systems and any device with permanent memory, including all computers, cell phones, I-Pods, MP3 Players, gaming devices, GPS devices, cameras, printers, USB drives, memory sticks, etc. Although a search can be impeded with use of data destruction/concealment programs, it may also detect the presence of such programs. A search can be used to determine if monitoring software has been defeated. Obviously, searches can also be used to examine computers which were used in lieu of a monitored computer.

Searches may take up to an hour, days, or even weeks, depending upon whether the examination is just a preview or a full forensic examination. Traditionally computer searches required direct access to a device. However, there is some forensic software that allows a remote search of a system. As such, an officer installs a software agent on the system that allows an officer to view via the Internet what is on the offender's system. The more in depth the search, the greater the need for equipment, software, and training.

Officer safety also becomes a greater concern during a computer search completed in the residence. More than one suspected sex offender has attempted suicide during such a law enforcement search. The time required to do an on-site computer search can increase the opportunity for danger from the offender and/or one of his or her loved ones, particularly if he or she knows noncompliance discovery is only a few mouse clicks away. Only the ability to conduct a remote search or use of monitoring software can mitigate this issue.

One additional disadvantage to only conducting computer searches is the possible delay in noncompliance detection. Periodic computer searches done even on a weekly basis allow the offender up to seven days to engage in violation behavior and attempt to destroy the evidence, prior to its possible discovery. A lot can occur in seven days, from trading a significant quantity of child pornography up to arranging a meeting with an unsuspecting minor. However, some monitoring software allows for an alert of noncompliance within minutes of its occurrence.

General Searches

The ability to conduct general searches greatly enhances cyber-risk management both as a deterrent and as an investigative tool to locate unauthorized electronic devices or other contraband, such as hard copy child pornographic images. To be effective, they must also be somewhat of a surprise to the offender. They obviously can detect actual electronic devices and storage media. Additionally, they can detect evidence that may point to noncompliance with computer Internet restrictions, such as hard copy website printouts or images; notebooks or documents containing e-mail addresses, or websites; unexplained power cords, such as to laptops; and peripheral electronic devices that are useless without a computer (printers, scanners, routers, etc.). Obviously, a general search can also detect contraband, such as guns or drugs.

General searches can be very time consuming, particularly in light of the small size of many electronic devices that may need to be discovered. One such example is flash drive, which can be as small as a quarter and contain a gigabyte (GB)[9] or more of data. Equally problematic with these devices is that they may look like anything but a flash drive, such as a wrist watch (Figure 1), a pen (Figure 2), a pocket knife, even a child's Lego® block.

Officer safety is obviously also a concern. CCO may be more at risk as a general search extends beyond a computer to include shared space with nonsupervised persons in the residence. Finally, a general search will detect nonapproved electronic devices and storage media but not how they were used or what evidence they contain. Only a computer search can answer these questions.

Online Investigations

Unlike computer monitoring and computer searches, online investigations do not require special supervision conditions. Officers can search for online information, regardless of whether the supervised individual is a sex offender, gang member, or white-collar offender. If it is posted on a social networking site or website, there usually is no expectation of privacy and it is fair game for discovery by a supervision officer. Such investigations can and do disclose incidents where individuals have gained access to nonmonitored computers. Sometimes, the evidence is not even being posted by the supervised individual. There have been incidents where friends or family have posted information, such as photos, reflecting an offender is in noncompliance. Examples include pictures of offenders out of the jurisdiction without permission or images of them at parties drinking or in the possession of firearms. Again, this information is fair game for discovery even it is posted by a nonsupervised person. However, online data, like other forms of electronic evidence, is very fragile and can be destroyed or altered very easily. As a result, these investigations require knowledge of proper online data collection techniques to insure the evidence found can be maintained and used in a violation or criminal proceedings. Equally important is the use of a designated computer, with appropriate software for collecting web evidence, and its own Internet

---

9. A GB is equal to 1,024 megabytes (MB) or about 1,000 copies of *War and Peace*. A GB contains 1 to 1.5 million pages of information. Put another way way, 1GB worth of information would fit on the paper filling up a pickup truck.

Figure 1. Wrist Watch Containing 2 GB USB Flash Drive.

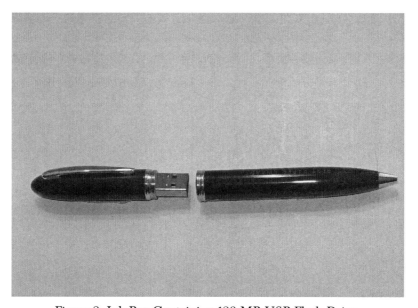

Figure 2. Ink Pen Containing 128 MB USB Flash Drive.

connection. This helps safeguard against a virus infection or attack against an agency's entire computer system.

Polygraph

Polygraph examinations have become a mainstay of sex offender treatment and management. They can be very useful in detecting sex offender noncompliance as it relates to computer or Internet use. Sex offenders have disclosed access to the Internet, computers, and pornography websites during examinations. CCO must promptly interview sex offenders after the exam to solidify what was disclosed during the examination and to identify additional areas for further investigation. One downside is sex offenders are aware that they have failed a polygraph or truthfully disclosed noncompliance immediately after the examination is completed. Without quick CCO action, electronic evidence of their noncompliance may be destroyed or altered. Such evidence may be needed to clarify the problem behavior circumstances, such as access to adult pornography vs. child pornography. Additionally, polygraph examinations' effectiveness is somewhat diminished if completed too frequently. Like random searches, this can give ample time for offenders to engage in noncompliant behavior and destroy or alter electronic evidence. Finally, polygraphs routinely ordered in sex offender cases for treatment purposes may not be easily justified for other cases, such as hackers and counterfeiters.

Home Confinement/Location Monitoring

Restricting offenders with electronic monitoring devices to locations where no computer or Internet is available can be helpful. Global positioning (GPS) devices can also trace offenders' movements outside the residence, further restricting their access from locations with free Internet access. However, these efforts do not in themselves establish that no computer or Internet access is present in the residence prior to their implementation. Additionally, they are not a guarantee that a computer will not find its way into the residence. Only frequent home visits and possibly a general search will uncover computer or Internet access. Again, without computer search capabilities, the actual use of such unauthorized devices will remain open to conjecture. Finally, they cannot be used to monitor authorized devices to insure offenders have not engaged in problematic behavior. A prime example would be a stalker being restricted to home confinement with GPS, without any Internet restrictions. The stalker can remain in the residence using the Internet for victim research or to engage in cyberharrassment against his or her victim. There maybe no indication he or she is in noncompliance until the electronic monitoring device is off his or her ankle.

Field and Collateral Contacts

Traditional field visits at residences, employment, etc. and regular contact with family and significant others are important components to managing cyber-risk. Surprise home visits may uncover an unauthorized computer. Contact with family may reveal frequent visits by the offender to a friend's home and follow-up at that location may reveal regular unauthorized Internet use by the offender. Employment contacts may reveal unknown computer risks, such as open Internet access in an employee lounge. However, as valuable as these efforts are, they frequently cannot overcome an offender's claim that their computer and Internet access was completely benign. Although a thorough investigation with appropriate third parties may counteract these claims, the only real proof may be access to the unauthorized device in question and the capability to search it.

Interviewing and Records Examination

CCO need good interviewing skills and the ability to mandate records to manage cyber-risk. These skills, tempered with knowledge of how computers are used in criminal behavior, can assist greatly in supervision of these cases. Initial interviews can establish a baseline of the offender's computer use and problem behaviors. Information about how long they typically are online and mandating disclosure of all e-mails and Internet identifiers can shed important information that will assist in managing the case. The disclosure of e-mail accounts on monthly supervision reports can be the key in locating social networking profiles used by offenders under assumed names. Questioning about the use of specific profiles can be equally important. For instance, one male defendant was questioned during a presentence investigation why one of his screen names was Kitty14. He replied that he used the screen name to facilitate the receipt of child pornography from others and to role play and masturbate online. Another offender questioned about his screen name, "Pyro1," revealed an interest in starting fires. Without this kind of questioning, such problematic conduct would not have come to light until possible noncompliance or a new law violation had occurred. Regular review of bank and credit statements can also disclose questionable charges such as purchases for computer components or services and even charges for adult sex chat lines. Some supervised individuals will make admissions and even confessions under questioning. Unfortunately, others will not without evidence of their noncompliance. This frequently can only be obtained by computer monitoring or the ability to conduct a computer search.

CONCLUSION

It should be quite clear that managing cyber-risk does not involve a one size approach. Each restriction has its own impact on offenders, their families, and the agency charged with insuring compliance. Each supervision technique has its advantages and disadvantages. Agencies must look to these techniques and decide how best to incorporate them in cyber-risk management in their jurisdiction. They would be well served to consider Tanner's (2007) following comments:

> Computer management is like everything else we do in community supervision. We set reasonable conditions and monitor them routinely and randomly. Can an offender get away with taking one drink and us not catching them? Of course. Can an offender get away with being late on curfew and we not notice? Of course. Can an offender visit one or two pornographic websites and we not catch it? Of course. But if they engage in any illicit activity long enough or often enough, we will find evidence of this and take action. Our goal with computer management is to set responsible conditions of probation/parole and to routinely monitor compliance with these conditions. (p. 6)

The next chapter will address the current legal standing of restrictions and these techniques. Later chapters will explore the mechanics of making these supervision techniques effective as possible.

REFERENCES

Bowker, A. (2010). Inmates and computer access: Good or bad. Retrieved from http://www.corrections.com/cybercrime/?p=65.

Kurzweli, R. (2001). The law of accelerating returns. Retrieved from http://www.kurzweilai.net/the-law-of-accelerating-returns.

Painter, C. (March 2001). Supervised release and probation restrictions in hacker cases. *United States Attorney's Bulletin,* March, 2001, Vol. 49, No. 2.

Patton, G. (n.d.). Retried from http://www.brainyquote.com/quotes/quotes /g/georgespa106027.html.

Russell, A. (2010). Vicarious trauma in child sexual abuse prosecutors. *Center Piece*. National Child Protection Training Center. Retrieved from http://www.ncptc.org/vertical/Sites/%7B8634A6E1-FAD2-4381-9C0D-5DC7E93C9410%7D/uploads/%7B9D34399E-F962-4B86-9C3F-4B2979A8AFA3%7D.PDF.

Tanner, J. (2007). *Beyond prosecution: Improving computer management of convicted sex offenders.* Boulder, CO: KBSolutions. Retrieved from http://www.kbsolutions.com/beyond.pdf.

United States of America v. Kevin Mitnick, 145 F.3d 1342, 1998, WL 255343 (9th Cir.(Cal.).

Chapter 3

CONDITION LEGALITY

> Nothing is more destructive of respect for the government
> and the law of the land than passing laws which cannot be
> enforced.
> —Albert Einstein, scientist, 1879 to 1955

CCO, like other criminal justice professionals, are concerned about legal scrutiny of their actions. These concerns generally fall into two broad categories, condition and operational legality. Condition legality refers to whether a special restriction recommended or imposed is lawful. For example, under what circumstances, if any, can an offender be barred from the Internet? Operational legality pertains to whether procedures to manage compliance are lawful. For instance, how can computer monitoring be conducted in a lawful manner? Despite rapid technology changes, there are core legal principles that can be applied to insure CCO recommendations and actions are above legal reproach. Clear, Cole, and Reisig (2011) provide a useful conceptional framework for this purpose which includes examining correctional law through (1) federal/state constitutions; (2) statutes; (3) case law; and (4) regulations. This chapter will use these four foundations to examine condition legality. The following chapter will do a similar analysis of operational legality.

It is of paramount importance that only lawful conditions are recommended or imposed. The recommendation of a questionable condition deteriorates confidence in the sentencing process and expertise level of the recommending officer. Likewise the imposition of such a condition creates offender confusion about what is required for compliance as well as officer trepidation about managing its compliance. It is therefore imperative that CCO are aware of what can and cannot be imposed in their respective jurisdictions.

FEDERAL/STATE CONSTITUTIONS

The *U.S. Constitution,* specifically the *Bill of Rights,* contains provisions that protect basic liberties of all citizens. State constitutions likewise provide basic guarantees to their respective citizens and in some ways can provide greater protections than are contained in the *Bill of Rights.* Individuals under correctional supervisions can have some of these liberties restricted when it is related to legitimate correctional purposes and there is no least restrictive method for addressing those objectives. With regard to technological conditions, CCO need to be cognizant specifically of the First, Fourth, Fifth, Sixth, Eighth, and Fourteenth Amendments contained in the *Bill of Rights* as well as provisions of their respective state constitutions.[1]

First Amendment (U.S. Const. Amend. I)

Technological conditions which prohibit the access to the Internet or specific areas thereof can directly impact freedom of speech and association. Individuals barred from the Internet cannot communicate via e-mail, chats, instant messages and cannot associate with others on social networking sites or in chat rooms. Other First Amendment rights might also be impacted if such restrictions prohibit online access to the press or even religious services.

Fourth Amendment (U.S. Const. Amend. IV)

The imposition for a search condition obliviously impacts this right directly. Monitoring conditions, however, may have a more profound impact than traditional search conditions. Specifically, computer mon-

---

1. The discussion under this section is not intended to imply all of the raised issues are serious constitutional challenges to the imposition of technological conditions. They are merely pointed out to insure CCO fully understand the possible implications and so they can minimize their impact wherever possible.

itoring is usually a continuous process and is not conducted only upon probable cause or reasonable suspicion. Additionally, as was noted in the previous chapter, computer monitoring can impact the privacy interests of individuals not on supervision or not even in the supervised person's home.

Fifth Amendment (U.S. Const. Amend. V)

One technological condition that may have Fifth Amendment implications (self incrimination) is a requirement that a supervised person provide all passwords, Internet accounts, and computer system information to his or her officer. A password to an encrypted drive could unlock it for law enforcement to find evidence of child pornography possession. Likewise, required disclosure of a previously hidden drive that has contraband could also have Fifth Amendment implications. Finally, there have been Fifth Amendment arguments made against polygraph requirements, common in cyber-sex offense cases (Vance, 2011).

Sixth Amendment (U.S. Const. Amend. VI)

Although not a common accordance, some defendants and even some offenders act as their own attorney in disputing matters pertaining to either their guilt and/or the sentence imposed. A condition that prohibits access to the Internet or use of computer could impact the ability of the person to do legal research online or otherwise access case law maintained in computer databases. Additionally, computer monitoring that takes place prior to a conviction may capture attorney-client communication exchanged via e-mail.

Eighth Amendment (U.S. Const. Amend. VIII)

The Eighth Amendment prohibits cruel and unusual punishments. In at least one case, *U.S. v. Fields,* 324 F. 3d 1025 (8th Cir, 2003), a defendant attempted unsuccessfully to appeal computer restrictions based upon the premise they amounted to cruel and unusual punishment. The Eighth Circuit denied this argument, noting in part the defendant could cite no other precedence for such a claim.

Fourteenth Amendment (U.S. Const. Amend. XIV)

The Fourteenth Amendment brings all the previously discussed rights into play by making it clear that states cannot impose laws that abridge freedoms provided for any U.S. Citizen. The Fourteenth Amendment also requires due process of law if any person is going to be deprived of liberty or property. Technological conditions that prohibit not only access to the Internet but also possession of specific devices could therefore have implications if they are not weighed carefully.

State Constitutions

Each state likewise has its own constitution. The Fourteenth Amendment makes it clear that states cannot abridge freedoms provided to any U.S. citizen. However, there is no prohibition against a state guaranteeing more freedoms than are contained in the ***U.S. Constitution***. There are ten states (AK, AZ, CA, FL, HA, IL, LA, MN, SC, and WA) that have state constitutions that recognize a right to privacy (National Conference of State Legislatures, 2010). Some state constitutions clarify and expand on privacy issues, something that has been noted can be greatly impacted by the use of computer monitoring and/or searches. CCO should therefore be familiar with those provisions of their state constitutions that are similar to the ***Bill of Rights*** as well as areas such as privacy that can impact conditions being recommended or imposed.

STATUTES

Federal Law

Federal statutes 18 U.S.C. §§ 3563 and 3583 authorize federal courts to impose specific restrictions, including technological conditions tailored to the specific offense and offender. However, any such condition must be "reasonably related" to the factors set forth in 18 U.S.C. § 3553(a). Those factors include: "(1) the nature and circumstances of the offense and the history and characteristics of the defendant; (2) the need for the sentence imposed; (B) to afford adequate deterrence to criminal conduct; (C) to protect the public from further crimes of the defendant; and (D) to provide the defendant with need-ed educational or vocational training, medical care, or other correc-tional treatment in the most effective manner" (18 U.S.C. § 3553(a)). Additionally, such conditions must impose "no greater deprivation of liberty than is reasonably necessary" to deter future criminal conduct, protect the public, and rehabilitate the defendant (18 U.S.C. § 3583-(d)(2)). The 2010 Federal Sentencing Guidelines Manual (§§5B1.3-(d)(7)(B) and 5D1.3.(d)(7)(B)) also clearly delineates such conditions should be considered in sex offender cases.

State Law

At least 16 states (CA, FL, GA, IL, IN, KY, LA, MD, MN, NC, NY, NJ, ND, NV, OK, and TX) have statutes authorizing computer and Internet prohibitions and/or restrictions (Council of State Governments, 2010; LaMagna & Berejka, 2009; Maryland Division of Probation and Parole, 2010; National Conference of State Legislatures, 2009). Several states are very specific with regard to their technologi-cal conditions. For instance, Minnesota provides very specific tech-nology conditions which may be imposed by its commissioner based upon cyber-risk (LaMagna & Berejka, 2009; Minnesota Office of the Revisor of Statutes, 2010). Likewise, Georgia provides specific statuto-ry authorization for conditions requiring computer monitoring and searches and that they may be "conducted by a probation officer, law enforcement officer, or computer information technology specialist working under the supervision of a probation officer or law enforce-ment agency" (LaMagna & Berejka, 2009, p. 27). Most statutes provide these conditions be imposed as part of a probation sentence. Many parole agencies also have the ability to impose special conditions. The vast majority of states authorize these conditions specifically as the result of a sex offense conviction.

Interstate Compact

In 1937, the agreement, now known as the Interstate Compact Adult Offender Supervision, was created. It was eventually signed by all 50 states and the District of Columbia, Puerto Rico, and the U.S. Virgin Islands. The agreement provides the "sole statutory authority for regulating the transfer of adult parole and probation supervision across state boundaries" (Interstate Commission for Adult Supervision, 2011). In present day, this agreement continues to govern transfers, including offenders to and from states with and without computer restrictions.

The Second Circuit held in *M.F. v. State of New York Executive Department of Parole,* Case No. 10-2074-CV, (2011) that a sex offender authorized to have a computer and Internet access for work purposes in one state, could not sue for an alleged violation under the Interstate Compact for Adult Offender Supervision. In this case, the offender wished to relocate to a state that would only accept his supervision on grounds his computer use would be monitored at home and at work and that he would have to notify his employer of his conviction and lifetime supervision. The Second Circuit upheld the District Court decision that the Compact creates no express or implied private right of action.

CASE LAW

Currently, there is a split between federal circuits pertaining to technology conditions imposed in federal cases. As of this publication, no less than nineteen federal cases support technology conditions and thirteen cases restrict their imposition in some fashion. Fourteen of the nineteen dealt with child pornography offenses (possession, receipt, selling, production, or transporting). Two cases dealt with enticement via a computer. Of the offenses involving child pornography or enticement, seven involved real victim(s) or a similar aggravating circumstance. Three of the cases dealt solely with fraud offenses (see Table 1).

Of the thirteen cases limiting technology conditions, eight dealt with child pornography offenses (five receipt and three possession). One case dealt with enticement, which was an undercover sting operation. Two cases involved fraud offenses, with a prior sex offense. One case involved counterfeiting (see Table 2).

The Eighth Circuit has been the most active in dealing with technology conditions with seven cases, five supporting their use and two narrowing their scope. The Eleventh circuit has had four cases all supporting technology conditions. The Second Circuit has three limiting

Table 1.
CASES BY CIRCUIT SUPPORTING TECHNOLOGY CONDTIONS

	Conviction
U.S. v. Love, 593 F. 3d 1 (DC Cir. 2010)	TCP
U.S. v. Balon, 384 F. 3d 38 (2nd Cir. 2004)	TCP
U.S. v. Johnson, 446 F. 3d 272 (2nd Cir. 2006)	Enticement
U.S. v. Crandon, 173 F. 3d 122 (3rd Cir. 1999)	RCP
U.S. v. Keller, 366 Fed. Appx. 362 (3d Cir. 2010)	Mail Fraud
U.S. v. Paul, 274 F.3d 155 (5th Cir. 2001)	CP
U.S. v. Suggs, 50 Fed. Appx. 208 (6th Cir. 2002)	Fraud
U.S. v. Ristine, 335 F. 3d 692 (8th Cir. 2003)	RCP
U.S. v. Fields, 324 F. 3d 1025 (8th Cir. 2003)	SCP
U. S. v. Boston, 494 F. 3d 660 (8th Cir. 2007)	PCP
U.S. v. Alvarez, 478 F. 3d 864 (8th Cir. 2007)	RCP
U.S. v. Demers, Court of Appeals, (8th Cir. 2011)	CP
U.S. v. Mitnick, 145 F.3d 1342 (9th Cir. 1998)	Access Devices
U.S. v. Rearden, 349 F. 3d 608 (9th Cir. 2003)	SHCP
U.S. v. Walser, 275 F. 3d 981 (10th Cir. 2001)	CP
U.S. v. Riggs, 967 F. 2d 561 (11th Cir. 1992)	Access Device/Fraud
U.S. v. Zinn, 321 F.3d 1084 (11th Cir. 2003)	CP
U.S. v. Taylor, 338 F. 3d 1280 (11th Cir. 2003)	Enticement/Firearm
U.S. v. Tome, 611 F. 3d 1371 (11th Cir. 2010)	CP/TSR Violation

KEY: TCP=Transporting Child Porn; RCP=Receiving CP; CP=CP Possession; PCP=Producing CP; SCP=Selling CP; and SHCP=Shipping CP

Table 2.
CASES BY CIRCUIT LIMITING TECHNOLOGY CONDTIONS

	Conviction
U.S. v. Ginyard, 215 F. 3d 83 (DC Cir. 2000)	RCP/Fraud
U.S. v. Russell, (DC Cir. 2010)	Enticement
U.S. v. Peterson, 248 F. 3d 79 (2nd Cir. 2001)	Bank Larceny
U.S. v. Sofsky, 287 F. 3d 122 (2nd Cir. 2002)	RCP
U.S. v. Lifshitz, 369 F.3d 173, 175, 190-92 (2nd Cir.2004)	RCP
U.S. v. Freeman, 316 F. 3d 386 (3rd Cir. 2003)	RCP/CP
U.S. v. Voelker, 489 F.3d 139, 154 (3d Cir.2007)	CP
U.S. v. Holm, 326 F. 3d 872 (7th Cir. 2003)	CP
U.S. v. Scott, 316 F. 3d 733 (7th Cir. 2003)	Fraud
U.S. v. Crume, 422 F. 3d 728 (8th Cir. 2005)	CP
U.S. v. Wiedower, (8th Cir. 2011)	CP
U.S. v. Sales, 476 F.3d 732 (9th Cir. 2007)	Counterfeiting
U.S. v. White, 244 F. 3d 1199 (10th Cir. 2001)	RCP

KEY: RCP=Receiving CP and CP=CP Possession

technology conditions and two supporting their use in some manner. The Third Circuit has two cases limiting technology condition and one supporting their imposition. In all circuits these decisions frequently rely on the specific fact patterns, most notably, the offense of conviction and the individual's criminal background. In one case, *U.S. v. Scott,* 316 F. 3d 733 (7th Cir. 2003), a technology condition was remanded for reconsideration as there had been no advance notice given that it was going to be imposed. As noted above, some circuits have upheld technology conditions in one case but rejected their use in another. States' courts are also grappling with these issues.

The discussion that follows includes seven federal and three state cases, all dealing with computer restrictions in some manner. Eight cases deal solely with sex offenses, one involves a sex crime and criminal threats, and one is purely a property offense. Most deal with special conditions imposed at the time of sentencing. However, there is one case that involves restrictions imposed at a revocation hearing. Another case involves conditions imposed by a probation officer after sentencing. There is also a case that involves the imposition of a special parole restriction and finally a case where computer restrictions were imposed in a juvenile case. It is hoped that this broad sampling of cases will prove helpful in understanding the legal issues involved in recommending and imposing such technological conditions.

U.S. v. Paul, 274 F.3d 155 (5th Cir. 2001)

Ronald Scott Paul, a part-time photographer, had taken his computer in for repair. The technician found child pornography images and alerted the FBI. A background check revealed Paul had a previous child pornography conviction. After he retrieved his computer from the repair shop, the FBI executed a search warrant at his residence. His computer was found to contain approximately 1,200 child pornography images, many downloaded from the Internet. Additionally, the search found photographs of naked neighborhood children, as well as assorted children photographs, a magazine with nude photographs of children and adults, books with pictures of nude prepubescent boys, videotapes of random children filmed in public settings, a large bag of children's clothes, and several children's swimsuits covered with sand. Additionally, the agents also seized a medical bag containing basic medical supplies and flyers reflecting Paul was advertising lice removal for children, which included a physical examination of each child. Further review of the computer revealed electronic mail (e-mail) discussing sources of child pornography, including websites, and chat rooms. In one of Paul's e-mails, he discussed how easy it was to find "young friends," by scouting single, dysfunctional parents through Alcoholics Anonymous or local welfare offices and winning their friendship, thereby securing access to their young sons.

Paul pleaded guilty to possession of child pornography and was sentenced to five years imprisonment followed by three years supervised release. He received several special conditions including that he "not have, possess or have access to computers, the Internet, photographic equipment, audio/video equipment, or any item capable of producing a visual image" (p. 160).

Paul appealed the blanket prohibition on computer or Internet use as being excessively broad, which could not be justified based solely on the fact his offense involved these technologies. Additionally, he noted that computers and Internet had "become indispensable communication tools in the modern world and that the restriction imposed by the district court would prohibit him from accessing computers and the Internet for legitimate purposes, such as word processing and research" (p. 168). The Fifth Circuit rejected his arguments and noted that such a supervised release condition can be acceptable if it is reasonably necessary to serve the statutory goals outlined in 18 U.S.C. § 3583(d).

U.S. v. Lifshitz, 369 F.3d 173, 175, 190-92 (2d Cir.2004)

Brandon Michael Lifshitz was convicted of receiving child pornography and was sentenced to three years probation rather than a prison term. A special supervision condition was ordered which provided that he would consent to having software/hardware installed on his computer. Lifshitz's defense counsel objected to this condition, contending it violated *Griffin v. Wisconsin,* 483 U.S. 868 (1987), which counsel believed established a threshold of reasonable suspicion for probationary searches. The Second Circuit reasoned, after considering not only *Griffin* but *U.S. v. Knights,* 534 U.S. 112 (2001) that:

. . . the Fourth Amendment offers protection against searches of home computers, the "special needs" of the probation system are sufficient to justify conditioning Lifshitz's probation upon his agreement to submit to computer monitoring. The scope of the computer monitoring condition as it stands may, however, be overbroad. (p. 36)

The Second Circuit's concern over the installation of monitoring revolved around its ability to capture "non-criminal information". The opinion suggested that the sentencing court:

. . . might wish—through a hearing or other appropriate procedures—to evaluate the scope and efficacy of the methods of computer monitoring that the probation office intends to employ. If it appears that filtering is no less effective than monitoring, the court might decide to revise the condition to eliminate the first sentence and instead permit filtering rather than monitoring. If, on the other hand, there are demonstrable advantages to monitoring, the court might instead prefer to ensure that a narrower but still effective condition is imposed, if one is reasonably available. For example, two ways in which the condition might be more narrowly tailored would be by limiting it to Internet-related activity and e-mail and by implementing monitoring software that searches for particular suspect words and phrases rather than recording all varieties of computer-related activity. It appears from our brief review of available software that the kind of monitoring described would be technologically feasible. Furthermore, if at some point in the future the defendant presents clear evidence that less intrusive, but still effective, methods of controlling his computer use have become technologically available, nothing we decide here precludes the district court from modifying its order. The district court is, however, in a better position than we are to assess the range of available alternatives. (pp. 35–36)

U.S v. Zinn, 321 F.3d 1084 (11th Cir. 2003)

Karl Zinn contacted an undercover United States Customs Service website and expressed an interest in purchasing two pornographic videotapes depicting girls between the ages of 6 and 13 years old. He subsequently received an order form, which he completed and mailed to the website operators along with a check for $85. On April 3, 2001, child pornographic videotapes arrived at his home as part of a controlled delivery. Hours later, a search warrant was executed which recovered compact discs and computer diskettes containing in excess of 4,000 child pornographic images. Zinn later acknowledged downloading the images from the Internet. He was sentenced to 33 months custody followed by three years supervised release. One of his conditions of supervised release was:

> You shall not possess or use a computer with access to any online service at any location, including employment, without written approval from the probation officer. This includes access through any Internet service provider, bulletin board system, or any public or private computer network system. (p. 1087)

Zinn asserted the Internet usage restriction was improper under 18 U.S.C. § 3583(d) because it is not reasonably related to legitimate sentencing considerations and overly burdened his First Amendment rights. The Eleventh Circuit disagreed noting in part:

> . . . the facts of this case highlight the concomitant dangers of the Internet and the need to protect both the public and sex offenders themselves from its potential abuses. We are also satisfied that the restriction in this case is not overly broad in that Appellant may still use the Internet for valid purposes by obtaining his probation officer's prior permission. (p. 1093)

U.S. v. Sales, 476 F.3d 732 (9th Cir. 2007)

Thomas Sales was convicted of counterfeiting $20.00 federal reserve notes. He and his friend Dan Flynn had used a scanner and printer to make the counterfeit currency. Sales had no prior criminal record but Flynn did have a criminal record, including for forgery. Sales was sentenced to eight months imprisonment followed by four years supervised release. He also received a special supervision condition that required in part that he obtain approval from his probation officer for use of all Internet capable devices, as well as gaming devices.

The Government contended the above conditions were necessary to deter further criminal behavior since a computer was used in the offense and Sales had extensive computer expertise. However, the

Ninth Circuit found the technology conditions imposed to be excessive, noting they included the Internet and the offense did not involve same. Additionally, Sales had no prior criminal record. The Ninth Circuit concluded that computer monitoring condition in some form was reasonable. However, "to comply with the Fourth Amendment, it must be narrowly tailored-producing no greater deprivation of liberty than is reasonably necessary" (p.738).

U.S. v. Voelker, 489 F.3d 139, 154 (3d Cir.2007)

During an FBI investigation into the online activity of Wyndell Williams, agents monitored a computer "chat" between Williams and Daniel Voelker. During this online communication Voelker briefly exposed his three-year-old daughter's buttocks over a webcam connected to his computer. The FBI subsequently confronted Voelker and he acknowledged downloading child pornography onto his computer. He also admitted to partially exposing his daughter over his webcam, but he insisted he was only "role-playing." The FBI subsequently searched Voelker's home and seized computer files containing child pornography. He was sentenced to 71 months in prison followed by a lifetime term of supervised release after he pleaded guilty to possessing child pornography. As a specific condition, he was

> prohibited from accessing any computer equipment or any "online" computer service at any location, including employment or education. This includes, but is not limited to, any Internet service provider, bulletin board system, or any other public or private computer network. (p. 143)

Voelker appealed this condition, noting that an absolute lifetime ban on computer and the Internet involved a greater deprivation of liberty than is reasonably necessary. The Third Circuit agreed with him and remanded the case for resentencing, noting in part,

> The District Court could clearly have imposed some limitations on Voelker's access to computers and the Internet. However, it is equally clear that any such restriction had to be narrowly tailored and consistent with the sentencing factors set forth in 18 U.S.C. § 3553(a). (p. 146)

U.S. v. Love, 593 F. 3d 1 (DC Cir. 2010)

Allen Love, was in an incest chat room on the Internet when he began chatting with an individual named "James." During the ensuing months, Love communicated online his desire to have sex with James's daughter and asked for nude pictures of her. Love also suggested that James bring his daughter to Chicago, so he could engage in sexual relations with her at a local hotel. In addition, Love sent James four photographs and two video clips of child pornography, including one clip in which a child was forcibly raped and a photograph of an adult male's genitals. It turned out that James was in fact an undercover police officer working with the FBI. A later search of Love's computers discovered over 600 images of child pornography. Love also confessed to the FBI that he regularly traded child pornography with people he met online. He later pleaded guilty to transporting or shipping material involving child pornography. He was sentenced to 188 months imprisonment, followed by supervised release for life. Love challenged his sentence as well as numerous supervision conditions imposed. One of these conditions which he appealed was: "The defendant shall not possess or use a computer that has access to any 'online computer service' at any location, including his place of employment, without the prior written approval of the Probation Office" (p. 12).

Love argued that this condition was too broad, noting the Internet's necessity in modern society. He further argued that the conditions could be tailored to only ban electronic communication involving prohibited sexual material or that his Internet use be remotely monitored by the probation office. The D.C. Circuit disagreed, noting that the condition was reasonable based upon Love's conduct, which included soliciting sex with a minor. The D.C. Circuit also concluded:

> . . . the continuing development of the Internet makes it reasonable for the district court to give the Probation Office broad authority to determine the scope of Love's permissible Internet use. Love's term of supervised release will not begin any time soon. Sentencing courts can predict neither the new ways in which child pornography will then be available nor the new technologies the government may use to police its availability. An Internet restriction that today imposes 'no greater deprivation of liberty than is reasonably necessary' to

deter illegal conduct may, by the time Love is released, be either wholly inadequate or entirely too burdensome. A broad Internet prohibition, which the Probation Office will tailor to the technology in use at the time of Love's release, is an appropriate way to deal with that uncertainty. We assume the Probation Office will reasonably exercise its discretion by permitting Love to use the Internet when, and to the extent, the prohibition no longer serves the purposes of his supervised release. The Internet restriction therefore imposes no greater deprivation of liberty than is reasonably necessary to serve the purposes of supervised release. (p. 13)

U.S. v. Tome, 611 F. 3d 1371 (11th Cir. 2010)

Joseph Tome initially pleaded guilty to one count of possessing child pornography. His offense involved possession of several computer disks containing over 100,000 child pornography images, all of which were downloaded from the Internet and many depicting prepubescent minors or minors under the age of 12. He was sentenced to 27 months imprisonment, followed by 3 years supervised release. He was allowed Internet use for authorized employment purposes, but he had to maintain a daily Internet log, including use for personal reasons. Tome was eventually released on supervision, but during his second year of supervised release he was arrested for violating his conditions.

At his revocation hearing, he admitted to multiple violations, which included: (1) sending to an inmate a graphic letter describing Tome having sex with at least seven children; (2) failing to register as a sex offender in violation of Florida law; (3) sending e-mails and letters to other felons, some of whom were convicted of sex-related crimes involving minors or child pornography; (4) failing to maintain a daily log of Internet addresses accessed via any personal computer; and (5) lying on monthly supervision reports and to his supervision officer about the above, including that he only used the Internet and computers for employment purposes.

At his violation hearing, his term of supervised release was revoked and he was sentenced to 24 months imprisonment followed by one year of supervised release, with a special condition prohibiting Internet use. Tome appealed his sentence and the one-year Internet ban. The Eleventh Circuit upheld the Internet ban condition, noting in part:

We also reject Tome's contention that his Internet ban is a greater deprivation of liberty than reasonably necessary. Tome was convicted of child sex offenses involving the Internet and then violated his initial supervised release conditions by using the Internet to contact other sex offenders. Tome's case involved his first being put on supervised release that allowed him limited access to the Internet for employment-related reasons and required him to disclose to his probation officer all non-employment-related Internet use. Tome promptly violated those conditions multiple times. He not only failed to disclose that he accessed the Internet for personal reasons, but also used the Internet to contact by e-mail six sex offenders, several of whom also had child pornography convictions. Tome has shown his unwillingness to conform his behavior to more-lenient restrictions. (p. 1377)

In Re Hudson (49 Cal. Rptr. 3d 74 - Cal: Court of Appeals 1st Appellate Dist., 1st Div. 20, 2006)

Davey Hudson was convicted by plea of lewd conduct with an 11-year-old boy whom he had coached. Hudson was arrested after the victim had reported that he had unbuttoned the boy's pants and fondled the victim's genitals on three to six occasions. Police conducted a search of his vehicle and found paperwork that had been downloaded from the Internet. The paperwork included an article concerning false child abuse allegations and a list of instructions on what to do if one is accused of child molestation. Hudson was sentenced to one year in county jail and five years of formal probation.

While under supervision, his probation officer noticed that he quickly logged off a computer when he entered a room during a probation search. During another probation search, several questionable items were found, including a paper publication of "obvious" child pornography; newspaper articles about children and about child molesters being arrested; and various thank you letters Hudson had received from children's organizations. Hudson's computer was seized but could not be examined as it was encrypted. Hudson refused to provide the password. During another search, officers seized hundreds of children's photographs, a desktop computer with an attached web-camera and Internet access, and a laptop computer.

Hudson was later convicted of two misdemeanor counts of annoying or molesting a child under the age of 18. This conviction was the result of a police investigation that found he had taken photographs of two neighborhood young boys and had displayed these photographs on his computer. He had also placed his hands on the boys' shoulders while they played games on the computer.

Following the conviction, his officer recommended his probation be revoked. It was revoked and he was sentenced to six years imprisonment. Near release on parole, Hudson filed a habeas corpus petition with a superior court regarding a condition restricting his computer and Internet access and his access to camera equipment noting it was unreasonable and over broad. He prevailed at the superior court level.

As a result, the California Department of Corrections and Rehabilitation appealed the superior court order which had invalidated the special parole condition. The appellate court was immediately troubled by Hudson's encryption and withholding his password while on probation. The appellate court also concluded that the proposed condition was related to his offense and was reasonably related to deterring future crimes. Additionally, they noted the special condition was not a blanket prohibition. He would be allowed computer and Internet access if he first obtained permission. The appellate court also observed that the condition language was similar to that referenced in several federal cases, notably *U.S. v. Rearden* (9th Cir.2003) 349 F.3d 608, 621 and *U.S. v. Zinn* (11th Cir.2003) 321 F.3d 1084, 1093.) The appellate court reversed the superior court decision and remanded with direction to deny Hudson's petition.

State of New Hampshire vs. Steven Merrill, Case No. 2009-811

On December 7, 2007, Steven Merrill pleaded guilty in the Nadeau Superior Court to two counts of child pornography possession. He was sentenced to Rockingham County House of Corrections and three years probation "upon the usual terms of probation and any special terms of probation determined by the Probation/Parole Officer."

Following his release from custody, Merrill met with a probation officer, and reviewed and signed Terms and Conditions of Adult Probation. In addition to the specific conditions of probation imposed at the time of sentencing, the probation officer added a condition that Merrill have "no computer access," except for work purposes. Apparently, the probation officer added this condition based upon the police's investigation that Merrill had stated he wanted to view child pornography only after viewing adult pornography on his computer.

In December 2008, two probation officers conducted a random visit and inspection of the Merrill's home and found a computer, which they seized. After a preliminary forensic examination of the computer detected child pornography, Merrill was arrested. A specific violation of probation was filed against Merrill, alleging several violations of his supervision conditions, including having access to a computer. Merrill moved for a finding of not chargeable on the violation of the computer access condition, contending that probation officers do not have the authority "to impose additional terms of probation." The trail court granted his request and the state moved to appeal the decision.

The Supreme Court of New Hampshire ruled that both statutory language and court rules allow probation officers to set special conditions. Additionally, the sentencing court placed Merrill on probation upon "any special terms of probation determined by the Probation/Parole officer," thus his due process rights were not violated by the probation officer imposed computer restriction. The Supreme Court reversed the trial court's decision and remanded the case.

People v. TR (Cal: Court of Appeals, 4th Appellate Dist., 1st Div. 2010)

TR was adjudged a delinquent for sexual battery and criminal threat incidents involving his girlfriend and her family. TR had made threats against his girlfriend's father and continued to maintain contact with her through MySpace®. TR used MySpace® several times to communicate with the victim's daughter, including in coded messages pertaining to them running away together. He was placed on probation with the following conditions:

> The minor is prohibited from participating in chat rooms, using instant messaging such as ICQ®, MySpace®, Facebook®, or other similar communication programs; (2) Minor is not to use a computer unless supervised by a responsible adult over the age of 21 who is aware that the minor is on probation and of his charges; and (3) The minor is not to use a computer for any purpose other than school

related assignments. The minor is to be supervised when using a computer in the common area of his/her residence or in a school setting.

TR objected to these conditions, noting his computer had nothing to do with his crimes. He contested the conditions as being not reasonably related to his offenses or future criminality and being unconstitutionally over broad restrictions on his First Amendment rights. The appellate court upheld the first two conditions, concluding they were addressing conduct leading to his criminal behavior and were therefore related to his offense. Additionally, TR was free to exercise his First Amendment rights through "less sophisticated means, such as a landline phone, the mail, or in person contact." They also further reasoned the condition would aid in his rehabilitation, a legitimate state interest.

However, the appellate court concluded that blanket restriction on his computer use for only school-related assignments was not narrowly tailored and reasonably related to the compelling state interest. They noted such a restriction would prohibit him:

> . . . from using a "stand-alone" computer to write letters and other documents or to use computer software to learn foreign languages, create art, or learn new skills or information (except as required for a specific school-related assignment). Furthermore, the probation condition, as currently worded, precludes TR from using a computer connected to the Internet to learn about current local, national, and international news, medical information, and other legitimate information wholly unrelated to his instant criminal threat conduct, his future criminality, and his rehabilitation.

The Appellate Court modified the condition as follows: "The minor is not to use a computer for any purpose other than school-related assignments, except as his probation officer may from time to time reasonably permit for legitimate work or personal purposes by a written notice delivered to the minor, his parents, and other adults supervising his computer use. The minor is to be supervised when using a computer in the common area of his residence or in a school setting."

REGULATIONS

Many states grant their community corrections agencies the authority to craft their own regulations on special technology conditions. For instance, Oregon has no specific computer restriction statute but does grant authority to craft special conditions to its Board of Parole and Post-Prison Supervision. For sex offense cases directly related to the use of a computer or an electronic device, the Oregon Board of Parole and Post-Prison Supervision will impose Special Condition 10, which reflects:

> No access to a computer, the Internet, digital storage devices or other computer-related devices and peripheral computer equipment without the prior written approval of the supervising officer and, where applicable, the sex-offender treatment provider, and only under conditions set by them. Conditions shall include random or unannounced examinations by the supervising officer or designee of any and all computers or other electronic devices to which the offender has access, as well as the installation or use of software capable of determining whether or not sexually explicit materials have been accessed, exchanged or stored.

Minnesota provides statutory authority for specific conditions to be imposed but provides the authority to the Corrections Commissioner to pick and choose which conditions to impose based upon cyber-risk (Minnesota Office of the Revisor of Statutes, 2010).

CONCLUSION

It obviously is not an easy task to recommend technological conditions, particularly as courts are moving to more narrowly tailor such restrictions based upon the factors of each individual case. Nevertheless, this added judicial scrutiny does not reflect that it is improper to recommend such conditions. Krause and Pazicy (2008) specifically provide the following advice to Assistant U.S. Attorneys to consider in cybercrime cases:

. . . ask a sentencing court to require the defendant to abide by any of the following conditions:

- Participate in a computer and Internet monitoring program conducted by the United States Probation Department;
- Identify every computer which he or she has access and permit random inspections of them;
- Install monitoring software and hardware at the defendant's expense;
- Install Internet filters on every computer to which the defendant has access, to block access to objectionable webs sites;
- Periodically provide all credit card and banking statements, as these would likely offer insight into the defendant's Internet use. (p. 204)

The path for CCO is clear if they want to have valued input in crafting supervision conditions in these cases. They must educate themselves on the legal issues as well as the factors present in each case, not to mention the available technology. The following eight steps should be common practice for CCO recommending technology conditions:

1. Know constitutional rights, jurisdictional case law, statutes, and/-or regulations pertaining to technology conditions.
2. Understand the technology available, both to supervise the case and that can be used by the offender to defeat the supervision objectives.
3. Fully understand the current offense and how technology was used in its commission.
4. Fully understand the individual's prior criminal background and how technology was used on prior offenses and/or in violation behavior.
5. Know the individual's technological ability to circumvent computer management efforts. Particularly take note of occasions where he/she has circumvented or disregarded a previously imposed technology conditions.
6. Identify a risk for potential new criminal conduct based upon Items 3-5.

7. Evaluate and access the need for computer/Internet access for schooling, employment, or other legitimate purposes.
8. Based upon the above steps, only recommend conditions that are the least restrictive and technically feasible to manage risk.

REFERENCES

Clear, Todd, Cole, George, & Reisig. (2011). *American corrections* (9th ed.). Belmont, CA: Wadsworth.

Einstein, Albert (n.d.). Retrieved from http://www.brainyquote.com /quotes/quotes/a/alberteins136890.html.

In re Hudson, 49 Cal. Rptr. 3d 74 - Cal: Court of Appeals, 1st Appellate Dist., 1st Div. 20, 2006.

Interstate Commission for Adult Supervision. (2011). Retrieved from http: //www.interstatecompact.org/About/History.aspx.

Krause, C., & Pazicy, L. (2008). An un-standard condition: Restricting Internet use as a condition of supervised release. Vera Institute of Justice, *Federal Sentencing Reporter,* Vol. 20, No. 3, February 2008. pp. 201–205.

Maryland Division of Probation and Parole. *The management of sexual offenders by the Maryland Division of Parole and Probation.* Retrieved from http: //www.dpscs.state.md.us/publicinfo/features/DPP_Workshop_Mng_Sex _Offenders.shtml.

M.F. v. State of New York Executive Department of Parole, Case No. 10-2074-CV, (2011).

Minnesota Office of the Revisor of Statutes. (2010). 243.055 Computer Restrictions, Retrieved from https://www.revisor.mn.gov/statutes/?id= 243.055.

National Conference of State Legislatures. (2009). Sex offender computer restriction & registration related statutes. Updated February 2009. Denver, CO: author.

National Conference of State Legislatures. (2009). *State Legislation relating to Internet social networking sites.* Updated April 2009. Denver, CO: author.

People v. TR, Cal: Court of Appeals, 4th Appellate Dist., 1st Div. 2010.

State of New Hampshire vs. Steven Merrill, Case No. 2009-811. http://www.courts.state.nh.us/supreme/opinions/2010/2010069merri.pdf.

U.S. v. Lifshitz, 369 F.3d 173, 175, 190-92 (2d Cir.2004).

U.S. v. Love, 593 F. 3d 1 (DC Cir. 2010).

U.S. v. Paul, 274 F.3d 155 (5th Cir. 2001).

U.S. v. Sales, 476 F.3d 732 (9th Cir. 2007).

U.S. v. Tome, 611 F. 3d 1371 (11th Cir. 2010).

U.S. v. Voelker, 489 F.3d 139, 154 (3d Cir.2007).

U.S. v. Zinn, 321 F.3d 1084 (11th Cir. 2003).

Vance, S. (2011). Looking at the law: An updated look at the privilege against self-incrimination in post-conviction supervision. *Federal Probation,* June, 2011.

Chapter 4

OPERATIONAL LEGALITY

> Avoid lawsuits beyond all things; they pervert your con-
> science, impair your health, and dissipate your property.
> –Jean de la Bruyere, French Philosopher, 1645–1696

Once a lawful supervision condition has been imposed compliance enforcement falls to the CCO. The Supreme Court held in *Pennsylvania Bd. of Probation and Parole v. Scott,* 524 U.S. 357 (1998) that the exclusionary rule does not apply to evidence used in a violation hearing. It would seem at first blush that this is then a straightforward task, particularly if one is only concerned about getting evidence into a violation hearing. However, in many cases, simply getting a violation hearing resolved pales in comparison to the possible penalty that comes with new criminal charges. Few would argue that justice is well served if a supervised sex offender found to have molested a new child victim gets a few more months custody on a violation, compared to new criminal charges filed. As such, CCO should insure that evidence collected is done in a manner that can get it admitted regardless of the legal venue. One also has to consider there are legal minefields that must be avoided when dealing with advanced technologies. These minefields are not limited to just making sure discovered evidence is admitted into a violation hearing or even a new criminal case. There can also be civil and even criminal repercussions involved if inappropriate enforcement actions are taken. This chapter will focus on the perimeters of operational legality in enforcing technological conditions from a nonattorney's perspective.

SEARCH CASE LAW

The Fourth Amendment provides that searches are generally prohibited unless based on a warrant issued upon probable cause. However, the Supreme Court has ruled that probationers and parolees can be searched without a warrant under certain circumstances. Harrold (2007) notes that the Supreme Court evaluates warrantless searches in probation/parole cases based upon: (1) consent[1]; (2) a special needs exception to the Fourth Amendment; and (3) a general "reasonableness" under a totality of circumstances analysis. He notes that three approaches are put forth in *Griffin v. Wisconsin,* 483 U.S 868 (1987); *U.S. v. Knights,* 534 U.S. 112 (2001); and *Samson v. California,* 547 US 843, (2006).

Well before the prevalence of computers, the Supreme Court decided in a 5-4 decision in *Griffin v. Wisconsin,* 483 U.S 868 (1987) that probation searches without a warrant were totally acceptable under a special needs exception. The special needs identified in this case was the rehabilitation of the probationer. In *U.S. v. Knights,* 534 U.S. 112 (2001), in a 9-0 decision, the Supreme Court ruled that a probation search based upon a condition authorizing same and reasonable suspicion of wrongdoing was totally acceptable.

In 2006, the Supreme Court again addressed community correction searches, this time in connection with a parole. In *Samson v. California,* 547 US 843, (2006), a 5-4 decision, the Supreme Court concluded that a parolee search by law enforcement, authorized by a state law, was "reasonable" based upon totality of circumstances.

None of these cases dealt specifically with computer searches or monitoring, which frequently involves issues beyond those encountered in a general search. Oftentimes, either by the condition's language, or by its operation, computer searches are completed on a random basis as opposed to a reasonable suspicion justification. This is particularly the case for agencies which do not use computer monitoring

---

1. Consent in this context is slightly different than consenting to a search that is about to take place. Individuals placed on probation or parole oftentimes agree or consent to conditions, including searches in exchange for their release on supervision. The wording of many search conditions reflects that a refusal to allow a search is a violation in and of itself. Some argue that even without a search condition, a probationer or parolee can never really give a completely voluntary consent to a search because of their special status. However, few if any courts have adopted this expanded reasoning.

software. Computer monitoring, depending upon its deployment acts somewhat akin to a continuous search.[2] Harrold (2005) contrasts computer monitoring and searches in community supervision as:

> Probationary computer monitoring is part of an overall goal of containment. As such, it is distinguishable from traditional computer forensics. The primary distinction is that computer forensics looks backwards in time to collect evidence to convict an individual of a particular offense, while computer management, including monitoring, looks forward to determine the manner in which an individual is living while on probation and whether this manner is consistent with the terms of probation. (p. 341)

At present, there are less than a handful of federal circuit cases that discuss computer searches in probation or parole settings and only one which touches on monitoring. All of them involve offenders who are on supervision for crimes involving child pornography and/or sexual exploitation. They are discussed below.

U.S. v. Tucker, 305 F. 3d 1193, (10th Cir. 2002)

Jeffrey Tucker's 1990 Utah conviction was for sexually abusing a child. He was paroled by the Utah Department of Corrections in 1996. His parole agreement included provisions that he would permit Adult Probation and Parole Agents to conduct searches of his person, residence, vehicle or any other property under his control upon reasonable suspicion to ensure his compliance with his parole conditions. Additionally, he agreed not to view or have in his possession any material exploiting children or depicting nonconsensual sex acts or acts involving force or violence; that he was to have no contact with persons under the age of 18 without appropriate adult supervision; and was to obey all laws.

The Salt Lake City Police Department received reliable information that Tucker had child pornography on his computer and had contacted a child. After checking his criminal history, police discovered Tucker was on parole and contacted his supervision officer regarding

---

2. As will be discussed later in this chapter, there is some concern that computer monitoring is more akin to a wiretap.

the tip. His supervision officer discussed the information with his supervisor who concluded there was reasonable suspicion that Tucker had violated his parole agreement. The search was planned for the next day with the assistance of the Salt Lake City Police Department.

Parole agents and several police officers proceed to Tucker's residence the night of June 11, 1998. Parole agents approached the apartment from the front. The apartment's screen door was closed, but the main door was open. Before entering, a parole officer observed Tucker near a computer. Upon entry, a parole officer ordered Tucker away from the computer. Immediately, a police officer with expertise in computer crimes, approached the computer. Before taking control of the computer, he noticed that it was connected to the Internet and that Tucker had been visiting a newsgroup labeled "alt.sex.preteen." The police officer ran software on Tucker's computer designed to prevent alteration of the hard drive. He then discovered that a large number of files had been recently deleted from Tucker's hard drive. The police officer ran another program that allowed him to view deleted files, but none of the deleted files he viewed contained pornography. However, in his investigation of Tucker's Web browser history, he noticed that Tucker had visited other newsgroups whose names suggested they contained child pornography. The officer informed Tucker that technology existed to recover the deleted files. Tucker's parole officer then asked him "What are we going to find?" Tucker responded, "There's some stuff on there that's going to cause me problems." The parole officer then ordered the computer seized and Tucker was placed in administrative custody.

After receiving Miranda warnings and waiving his rights, Tucker told investigators that his computer contained over 5,000 images of children between the ages of ten and twelve engaged in sexual acts and poses. He also acknowledged that he had spoken with a seven-year-old girl on two occasions, as had been alleged. Following this interview, Tucker was placed in Utah Department of Corrections' custody pending a determination whether his parole should be revoked.

The police then obtained a search warrant. Pursuant to the warrant a computer forensic examination was completed on July 28, 1998, which discovered some 27,000 images stored on Tucker's computer, most of which were child pornography. Some of those images were very small, called "thumbnail"[3] images, but many were larger images. Files containing child pornography were recovered from different parts of the hard drive. Some were located in the Web browsers' cache[4] files. Others were located in the computer's recycle bin and in "unallocated" hard drive space.[5] The police officer who completed the forensic examination found that Tucker had accessed the cache files and manually deleted images in the files by dragging them to the computer's recycle bin. The officer also rejected the suggestion that Tucker had accidentally run across these images online, citing Web browser history files which showed he repeatedly visited the same sites. Additionally found was an email from Tucker to a website operator asking to be given access to pictures of "naked young girls." The evidence found led to Tucker being charged federally with possession of child pornography.

Before trial, Tucker moved to suppress the evidence taken in the search at his apartment and the later search of his computer. He argued that the search of his apartment was not supported by reasonable suspicion as required for a parole search. He also argued that the parole search was not conducted to further the purposes of the parole system but was a subterfuge for a law enforcement investigatory search.[6] The district court rejected both arguments, concluding the parole offi-

---

3. A thumbnail image is miniature version of an image. It is frequently created independent of the user's actions and facilitates quick browsing through multiple images. In a Windows operating system, these thumbnail images can be left behind after the larger, original image has been deleted.

4. Computers save images to a cache, independent of the user's action, as a way to make Internet browsing more efficient. After a user goes to a website, the computer will first attempt to retrieve many of the images from the cache for viewing. This alleviates the need to have to download from the Internet all the images each time a person visits a website. This also makes viewing a website much faster as some of the images are being viewed from the computer directly as opposed to over the Internet.

5. In a Windows operating system, once a file is deleted, it can be temporally recovered from the Recycle Bin. The Recycle Bin does not really contain the file. It just contains the file name and a pointer to location of the data previously making up the file. After a time or if the Recycle Bin is emptied, the location maintaining the file's data will be released to "unallocated" space by the computer. Unallocated space is the part of the hard drive the computer can use or reuse to save new data. Until data in unallocated space is overwritten it can be recovered. Saved files and folders are maintained in allocated space.

6. This was once known as police using probation or parole officers as a "stalking horse" to conduct a search as opposed to getting a search warrant based upon probable cause. In *U.S. v. Reyes,* 283 F. 3d 446, 2nd Cir. (2002) the term "stalking horse" was referred to as "a decoy." Additionally, the Second Circuit noted the term was a technique by the hunter to hide behind a stalking horse to conceal themselves from game in order to get close for the kill. Regardless, this argument no longer has much weight since the *Knight* case was decided.

cers had reasonable suspicion and the search was advanced for a parole purpose because the initial tip contained information indicating Tucker had violated the terms of his parole.

The district court also rejected Tucker's argument that his parole agreement did not authorize seizure of his computer. Although the parole agreement did not mention seizures, the district court concluded that seizure of contraband or evidence found from a valid parole search is clearly implicit in any parole agreement.

Tucker's final Fourth Amendment argument was that the later forensic examination of his computer was not a valid parole search because he was already in custody and the search could not therefore have any parole purpose. The district court rejected the argument, reasoning that Tucker's parole was not yet revoked when the forensic examination was conducted and therefore officers had an incentive to compile evidence for a parole revocation hearing. Tucker was convicted and sentenced to 60 months imprisonment. He appealed the district court's decisions on the denied motions as well as his conviction.

The Tenth Circuit upheld the district court's decision on the denied motions and Tucker's conviction. Relying in part on the *Knight* case, the appellate court noted that even if the search was a subterfuge for a law enforcement investigation, it was permissible under general Fourth Amendment principles as it was based upon reasonable suspicion that contraband was located at Tucker's residence or that a crime had taken place.

Tucker also attempted to claim that a search of his home was permissible but not a search of his computer. The Tenth Circuit surmised that Tucker was apparently misreading another circuit case, *U.S. v. Carey,* 172 F.3d 1268 (10th Cir.1999) and his parole agreement. The Tenth Circuit rejected his reasoning noting unlike the other case, which was consent to search for drugs and not child pornography, Tucker's parole conditions expressly allowed officers to search for any evidence that he had violated his parole by possessing or viewing child pornography.

Tucker also argued that his parole agreement did not authorize the seizure of his computer at the conclusion of the June 11 search. He again stressed that his parole agreement did not mention seizures and therefore the officers were not authorized to seize the computer. The

Tenth Circuit rejected this argument noting that the seizure was valid under a plain view doctrine. In this case, the officers had not violated the Fourth Amendment in arriving at the location where the evidence could be plainly viewed, the item observed in plain view was immediately recognized as contraband and the officers had a lawful right to access the computer.

Tucker's final Fourth Amendment argument was that the forensic examination of his computer on July 28, 1998 was unconstitutional as the justification for a parole search ended after he was taken into custody. The Tenth Circuit concluded they did not need to address this argument because the police officers had obtained a valid warrant to search his computer.

U.S. v. Lifshitz, 369 F. 3d. 173, 175, 190-92 (2nd Cir. 2004)

This case was introduced in the last chapter and wrestled with computer searches and monitoring in light of the *Griffin* and *Knight* cases. The Second Circuit found that a computer search conducted based upon reasonable suspicion fell nicely in the special needs exception. However, the court concluded the computer monitoring condition as written was too broad. They reasoned that computer monitoring had the ability to capture "noncriminal information." As a result, the Second Circuit ordered the sentencing court to narrow the monitoring condition and made suggestions based upon available technology that it capture only activity that was related to possible noncompliance, such as Internet and e-mail activity. They also suggested that monitoring software might be targeted for particular suspect words or phrases as opposed to capturing all activity. However, in the end, the Second Circuit reasoned that the district court was in a better position to ascertain the best solution for using monitoring and/or filtering software, consistent with their finding that as written the condition was too broad.

U.S. v. Yuknavich, 419 F. 3d 1302, (11th Cir. 2005)

In the fall of 1998, Timothy Yuknavich was discovered printing out pictures of child pornography at work and using his work computer to access pornographic images involving children. On March 18, 1999, he pleaded guilty in the Superior Court of Cobb County,

Georgia to four counts of child exploitation and one count of distributing obscene material. He was sentenced to seven years probation.

According to his probation terms, he could "not use the Internet at any time unless work related during work hours." Because of the nature of his offense, he was also subject to a list of special conditions for sex offenders, including treatment and prohibiting contact with minors. However, his probation conditions did not expressly require him to submit to searches of his home or person upon the behest of probation or law enforcement officers.

A few months after Yuknavich's probation began he put a bid in on house and was reminded by his officer that he was not to live near a school or day care center. Additionally, it was suggested that he select an area containing few young children. Despite this direction, Yukavich moved to an area where small children were everywhere. Shortly afterward he was urged to move by his officer.

In January of 2000, a parent in the neighborhood informed Yuknavich's probation officer that he had set up an e-mail account at the local library. When questioned about it, Yuknavich told his officer it was for job searching. However, the officer pointed out that Yuknavich already had a job and had not been looking for a new one at the time. The following month, Yuknavich revealed to his officer that he had recently helped set up equipment for a rock concert for teenagers at his church, then stayed for the show. Yuknavich was told that was inappropriate and, if he wanted to be in those types of situations, he would need to be monitored by someone trained to supervise him.

On March 21, 2000, Yuknavich sought permission to go on a church retreat involving kid activities. His officer suggested he talk to his therapist about his desire to go and the possibility of increasing his medication. In response, Yuknavich revealed he had not been taking his medication and that he had masturbated on three occasions to a fantasy of the young boy he previously assaulted. He also told his officer on several occasions, he was not "invested" in his therapy. Given the reaction to his living in that neighborhood and his recent behavior, his officer strongly encouraged him to move to a new area, which he eventually did later that year.

In February of 2001, after he moved, Yuknavich's therapist told his probation officer that Yuknavich had gotten into trouble at his church. The pastor had agreed to help him with job resumés on the church's computer, but subsequently learned Yuknavich had been using the computer by himself and had even signed up with an Internet Service Provider (ISP). Yuknavich eventually terminated the account.

During a subsequent home visit, his officer and another officer saw that Yuknavich had a twelve-pack of beer in his kitchen. When confronted, he claimed he did not know having beer was against the terms of his probation. During this same visit, Yuknavich admitted he had obtained a computer. He said he bought it for his son, but then discovered his ex-wife had already bought him one, so he kept it. The officers checked to see if the computer had a modem, but it did not. The probation office would occasionally check, with Yuknavich's permission, to see what was on the computer.

On January 30, 2002, Yuknavich's probation officer called him to see if he was working and where, so they could set up a meeting. He informed her he was at home for the day because he had a phone interview at 2:00 p.m. Yuknavich's officer and another probation officer arrived at his house between 10:30 and 11:00 a.m. They were wearing street clothes, did not have weapons of any kind, and did not have handcuffs. It took Yuknavich ten minutes to open the door and, when he did, he was shirtless. He explained he was shirtless because he was about to take a shower.

One of the probation officers felt Yuknavich was acting "very nervous." After sitting down in the living room and talking briefly, the three of them moved into another area of the house. As they moved through the house, the officers observed several computers and other computer equipment in a spare bedroom, including one with an external modem connected to a phone line. The officers were unaware Yuknavich's computer had a modem.

One of the probation officers asked Yuknavich to sit down at the computer and click on "Start" and then "Documents." When Yuknavich moved the mouse, the screen saver disappeared and it became apparent that the computer was connected to the Internet and files were being downloaded. The Documents folder contained several JPEG[7] files. The officer then asked Yuknavich to open one of the JPEG files that had been recently viewed. Yuknavich complied. The

---

7. JPEG stands for Joint Photographic Experts Group and is a common type of digital image. Files of this type usually have file name ending in .jpg.

file Yuknavich opened contained a picture of a nude young boy with an erection. At this point, Yuknavich admitted he had been downloading child pornography for the past month and a half and asked for a second chance. Yuknavich's probation officer told him to stop talking and the other officer told him to step away from the computer. He was not read his Miranda rights and was not placed under arrest.

Yuknavich's probation officer phoned a fellow probation officer and requested a search warrant be obtained for his computers. In the meantime, his officer was advised by a local police department sergeant to obtain Yuknavich's consent to seize his computers. His officer then wrote out a short consent form which read, "I hereby agree that Probation Officers M. Goldstein and Don Spencer may take my computers and related media to be analyzed by the Cobb County Police Department." Yuknavich signed the consent form. A later computer search pursuant to a warrant revealed 535 child pornography images. Based upon this evidence, he was federally charged with five counts of receiving child pornography.

Yuknavich filed a motion to suppress, arguing that although the probation officers had a right to visit him at his home as a part of his probation, they could not conduct a search without a warrant, probable cause, an expectation to the warrant requirement, or his consent, none of which they had. A magistrate judge recommended the motion be denied because Yuknavich's expectation of privacy in his residence, especially in his computer use and Internet access, was greatly reduced if not eliminated. Thus, according to the magistrate judge, the probation officers needed reasonable suspicion, and not a warrant based on probable cause, before searching his computer. The magistrate judge found the officers had reasonable suspicion to search his computer based upon Yuknavich's two previous improper acquisitions of an e-mail account; his moving into a neighborhood populated with young children; his participating in events involving minors at his church; his fantasies about his prior victim; and on the day in question, his delay in opening the door, shirtlessness, his nervousness, and his possession of a modem and multiple computers. Additionally, the magistrate judge concluded:

> Once the probation officers observed the illicit material on the computer, not only did they have a reasonable suspicion of a probation

violation, there was probable cause justifying seizure of the computers and the related media materials. In this case, the pornographic and sexually explicit materials constituted contraband just like drugs or firearms and should have been, as they were, seized. (p. 1308)

The district court adopted the magistrate judge's report and recommendation, denying the motion to suppress, except for the magistrate judge's conclusion that Yuknavich failed to consent to the search. After his motion to suppress was denied, Yuknavich entered a conditional plea of guilty to all five counts of receiving child pornography, pending the outcome of his appeal to the Eleventh Circuit appeal. He was sentenced to 41 months.

The Eleventh Circuit concluded that the search of Yuknavich's computer was reasonable under the balancing test set out in the *Knight* case. They discussed how the Supreme Court had concluded in part that "inherent in the very nature of probation is that probationers do not enjoy the absolute liberty to which every citizen is entitled." However, the Eleventh Circuit was mindful that unlike the *Knights* case, Yuknavich had no search condition imposed in his case. As such they set to consider whether "the lack of a search condition upset the *Knights* balancing test so as to require more than reasonable suspicion to justify a search of Yuknavich's computer" (p. 1310).

They first considered his expectation of privacy in his computer and computer-related activities, i.e., accessing the Internet. They concluded his expectation of privacy in this regard was reduced by a restriction limiting his Internet use to "work related purposes" during "work hours." As such, they reasoned he would have to always be prepared for three questions: "Do you have a computer? If yes, can you access the Internet? If yes, what are you doing online?" Not only should he have been prepared to answer those questions, but he also should have been prepared for the officers to conduct their own investigation to find the answers. The Eleventh Circuit also found Yuknavich's history of repeated inappropriate conduct and noncompliance as justifying closer monitoring and a greater infringement on his privacy. The Eleventh Circuit upheld the district court's denial of Yuknavich's motion, concluding:

Despite the absence of a state regulation or search condition requiring Yuknavich to submit to warrantless searches, he had a greatly reduced expectation of privacy in his computer. Under the *Knights* balancing test, the probation officers needed no more than reasonable suspicion of a probation violation to conduct a search of his computer. Because the search was supported by reasonable suspicion, Yuknavich's motion to suppress was properly denied. (p. 1311)

U.S. v. Herndon, 501 F. 3d 683 (6th Cir. 2007)

Jeffrey Herndon was on Tennessee supervision for multiple counts of sexual explication of a minor. A specific condition of his release was that he was not to have Internet access on his computer unless given written permission and he was to consent to his officer checking the computer at anytime for Internet capability or activity. Additionally, Herndon was required to participate in a sex offender treatment program.

Herndon was later unsuccessfully terminated from the sex offender treatment program. His counselor also noted that he was a "high risk" to the community. During a later meeting with his supervision officer Herndon disclosed that he had been on the Internet seeking employment. Based upon Herndon's termination from treatment, the nature of his offense, and his admission that he had been on the Internet, his supervision officer sought and received administrative approval for a computer inspection.

His supervision officer along with another officer later arrived at Herndon's home. Herndon retrieved a laptop computer from under a pillow on his bed. His supervision officer proceeded to check the computer's Internet history, where he found a number of file names with female names but was unable to access any of them as the necessary drive was missing. His officer did a further search of the computer and found thumbnail images, which appeared pornographic. However, he could not ascertain whether they involved adults or children. While he was searching the laptop, the other officer alerted him to the presence of an external hard drive placed at the foot of Herndon's bed. This drive was plugged into the wall but not to the computer. A search of this device revealed multiple thumbnail images of child pornography. The supervision officer contacted his supervisor who in turn contacted local law enforcement. Upon their arrival, Herndon was placed under arrest. A detective who arrived later on the scene observed 12 images of child pornography displayed on Herndon's computer. The laptop and several hard drives were seized as evidence. Police later obtained a search warrant to examine the computers and drives and found approximately 58,000 images and 3,000 videos of child pornography.

Herndon was charged federally with receipt and possession of child pornography. Herndon initially filed a motion to suppress on the grounds the probation search was a violation of his Fourth Amendment rights, which was denied. He then filed a second motion asserting that the scope of consent provided to his supervision officer extended no further than the activities of his probation officer and that police seizure of his computer was therefore unlawful. The district court likewise denied this second motion citing a plain view exception to the Fourth Amendment's requirements.

The Sixth Circuit upheld the district court's rulings denying Herndon's suppression motions. It noted, using a *Knight* reasoning, that there was reasonable suspicion for the probation officer to conduct a search. Additionally, the Sixth Circuit concluded that law enforcement called to the scene after the discovery of child pornography, observed contraband images in plain view upon their arrival. As they were authorized to be on the scene and the images were in plain view, law enforcement had the authority to seize the computers.

Discussion

These cases mention several key points that need to be stressed. First is the concept of reasonable suspicion, which was articulated in *Maryland v. Buie,* 494 U.S. 325 (1990). In this case, reasonable suspicion was discussed as a "belief based on specific and articulable facts which, taken together with the rational inferences from those facts, reasonably warranted' the officer in believing" a particular fact pattern existed (p. 329).

Since the *Knight* case, reasonable suspicion that an offender is violating either the terms of supervision or committing a new law violation have consistently been viewed as a compelling factor in deciding the legality of a probation or parole computer search. The next key factor is the concept that an offender has a reduced expectation of privacy because of their status as well as the conditions imposed in a case. As was noted in the *Yuknavich,* his reduced expectation of privacy, coupled with the presence of reasonable suspicion, validated a search conducted without a specific statute or condition authorizing same.

Reasonable expectation of privacy and ownership often comes into play with computer searches involving solely consent. An offender using a computer owned by another party frequently has no reasonable expectation of privacy and the owner's consent will suffice to search the computer, even without a search condition or statute. Theoretically, the search would stand even without reasonable suspicion as one is not searching the offender's property. Realistically no one would search a computer without some suspicion of wrongdoing. After all, the offender is using another person's property and that person could view what was done on it at any time.

However, there can be exceptions. For instance, an employee can maintain an expectation of privacy in using an employer's computer, unless the employer has a policy and/or uses banners that expressly inform employees they have no privacy in using a company-owned computer. As such, officers would be well advised to ascertain not only who owned the computer but what the employer's policy was before seeking consent and conducting a search. The same may be true for computers issued by schools to their students.

Oftentimes an issue will come up with searching a family computer owned by someone other than the offender, for instance a parent. The offender would not seem to have a reasonable expectation of privacy in this situation. But if the computer has separate user accounts, requiring a password, the offender may have some privacy interest and mere owner's consent may not suffice. Equally problematic is a computer owned by an offender and spouse. The spouse may give consent unless the offender objects to the search.

One case, not involving a computer search deserves mentioning, particularly as it may be useful in supervising offenders convicted of check fraud or similar crimes. These offenses by their nature may involve hard copy drafts of counterfeit identification, checks, or information pertaining to victims (stolen bank or credit card statements). Offenders must dispose of these items and may conclude that just putting it out for trash collection is a safe method. The Supreme Court held in *California v. Greenwood*, 486 U.S. 35 (1988) that a warrant was not needed to search or seize trash put out outside a home's "curtilage" for collection. As such a CCO does not need a condition to collect an offender's trash from the curb for noncompliance evidence. This truly is a turnaround on the old hacker technique of "dumpster diving."[8] A note of caution is in order if such activity is undertaken. Be aware that trash may also contain items that may be hazardous, such as discarded needles. Appropriate protections should be utilized.

Regarding the issue of consent, the Eleventh Circuit did not address the issue of whether Yuknavich's consent was in fact valid as their decision rested on the conclusion the search was justified based upon reasonable suspicion and his lack of a reasonable expectation of privacy. Some might argue that an offender's consent is always questionable as they may be merely acquiescing to their supervision officer's requests. As such, officers would be well advised to also have reasonable suspicion of a violation before they make a consent request to search from an offender. Otherwise, they will have to justify that the consent was given willingly and knowingly by the offender, without fear of a possible sanction for refusal.

Another area that must be addressed is the idea of seizing a computer, which is different than searching a computer. In both the *Tucker* and *Herndon* cases, different circuits found seizing a computer that contained contraband was proper. In the *Tucker* case, the Tenth Circuit concluded that a computer could be seized by a parole officer after a search using a plain view doctrine. Specifically, the officers were not violating the Fourth Amendment as they were legally allowed in the home and observed evidence in plain view reflecting the computer contained contraband, and they had a lawful purpose in accessing the computer. This same plain view rational would justify seizure of a computer if during a home visit an officer observed child pornography on the monitor or counterfeit currency being printed. Likewise in *Herndon,* police officers were justified in seizing a computer that was displaying child pornography (albeit after discovery by a probation officer), which police observed in plain view upon their arrival on the scene. One final comment on plain view seizures. If an offender was not permitted to have a computer, a found computer itself would be contraband and could be seized. However, searching the computer, absent a search condition, consent, or some judicial approval, might be problematic. Law enforcement also might be unwilling to examine

---

8. Hackers would sometimes dig through trash, particularly at businesses, looking for passwords, directories, technical manuals, or anything that could be used to hack into a businesses network. This term was used to describe such activity.

the computer without a search condition or a search warrant. Once the computer is safeguarded, take the additional steps to legally justify that it should be searched as well. Justifications for a computer search in such cases are to show that it is in fact the offender's property, it was used by him or her and to show that it was not stolen. A search could also establish that the computer was not only contraband but that it was used for some purpose contrary to the conditions and/or the law. Ask questions and find out why the computer was in the offender's possession and use the answers to place the matter on firm legal ground.

In *Litshitz,* the court did not find monitoring software a per se violation of only conducting searches based upon reasonable suspicion. However, they did place possible obstacles in the unfettered use of monitoring software. In light of this case, it is not inconceivable that deploying monitoring software without some kind of rationale of what to monitor and what to alert is very risky. Doing so would appear to open the door for someone to argue foul, contending such activity amounts to conducting suspicionless searches. Officers deploying monitoring software would be well advised, beyond just practical considerations, to carefully craft the perimeters of what they are capturing. Don't use a one size fits all approach. For instance, key phrase alerts that are appropriate for sex crimes involving minors are not going to fly for cyber-stalking cases where the victim was an adult. Likewise, alerting on websites containing adult pornography when supervising someone convicted of Internet fraud is going beyond what will probably withstand legal scrutiny. Tailor the key phrases and monitoring to the needs of the case.

STATUTES

Depending upon circumstances, CCO may need to obtain records maintained by an ISP, such as posting on an offender's social networking profile. CCO may also need to install monitoring software, which has been considered by some courts to be a wiretap. Officers may also be confronted with seizing material on a computer that either the offender or his or her family is contemplating publishing. There are federal and, in some cases, state statutes that impact these areas. Violation of these statutes can have civil and even criminal penalties.

In some cases, evidence obtained in violation of legal requirements can also be suppressed in new criminal prosecutions. As such CCO must become familiar with three statutes: the Stored Communications Act, 18 U.S.C. §§ 2701-2712 (SCA); the Wiretap Act, 18 U.S.C. §§ 2510-2522 (Title III); and the Privacy Protection Act (PPA), 42 U.S.C. § 2000aa. The following is a brief discussion of these statutes in a community corrections context based upon information contained in the U.S. Department of Justice's *Searching & Seizing Computers and Obtaining Electronic Evidence in Criminal Investigations,* Third Edition, September 2009.

The Stored Communications Act, 18 U.S.C. §§ 2701-2712 (SCA)

The SCA was passed by Congress to provide statutory privacy rights for customers and subscribers of computer network service providers. SCA does not apply to information maintained on a user's own computer that may be recovered during a computer search. It only applies to information maintained by a public provider. Common examples of service providers include traditional Internet Service Providers (ISP) such America Online (AOL) as well as social networking sites, such as Facebook. An employer who provides e-mail solely to its employees, is considered a nonpublic provider and would not be covered by the SCA (the Fourth Amendment would apply then). Likewise, opened e-mail information that might be saved to an employee's work station would covered by the Fourth Amendment and not the SCA.

SCA classifies information into three different types: (1) Contents (such as e-mail); (2) Basic subscriber/session information (name address, length of service, etc.); and (3) Noncontent records (such as e-mail address of other individuals with whom the account holder corresponded). The SCA also provides legal restrictions on how this information can be disclosed to the government. Depending upon the information sought, a subpoena, court order, or a warrant is required, each of which requires a different standard of proof to justify it being issued.

SCA provides some limited exceptions to these legal requirements, such as subscriber consent. However, very few, if any, of the remaining exceptions apply to CCO's normal activities. SCA (18 U.S.C. § 2703(f)) also provides a mechanism for officers to request providers preserve existing records pending the issuance of the proper legal mechanism.

CCO sometimes require information maintained by an ISP to ascertain if an offender is noncompliant. For instance, an officer suspects an offender is associating with other felons or making threats via a social networking site or e-mail. In such cases, the officer may request the offender sign a release authorizing the ISP to disclose information in the account to the officer. However, not all ISPs will honor the consent or provide the information needed. Additionally, some require their specific own consent form be utilized.

Officers could also simply direct the offender to provide access to the account in their presence to determine what is going on relative to the account. If the offender refuses to consent or to provide supervised access, the only way to get at the information is to follow SCA requirements. Additionally, logging in this manner also doesn't reflect from where the account was opened or accessed after being created. This information is only available from the ISP.[9]

Unfortunately there are occasions where a offender may be using the account in some manner in which one can't establish it is clearly theirs. For instance, an offender can have a social networking profile that has very specific information, but not his or her real name or picture. The officer could ask the offender to access the account, but he or she is just as likely to deny it is his or her account at all. Again, the only way to get access to the account is to follow SCA requirements.

CCOs may also receive information from a potential witness or a victim that an offender has communicated to them via e-mail. For instance, a victim receives a threatening communication from an offender. These individuals can provide the message to the CCO as they are a party to the communication. SCA does not prohibit such disclosures.

One of the major pitfalls for seeking consent access is it that may give the offender the ability to delete information, or even the account, before officers get access. As such, depending upon the needs of the case, CCO would be well advised to seek preservation under 18 U.S.C. § 2703(f)) with the provider before requesting consent access. A note of caution is in order. Some ISP will "freeze" the account, not prohibiting the user access after such a request is made. If a new law

---

9. One might want to know where an account was created or logged in from to locate a computer that was used by the offender for possible searching.

violation is suspected it may be best that the CCO obtain assistance from law enforcement to obtain information consistent with SCA requirements.

Thus far the discussion has pertained to instances where CCO might want to gain information pertaining to e-mail and social networking profiles. However, SCA would also apply to situations where an offender is storing information, like that occurring with "cloud computing." Take Google for an example. Google is an ISP. It provides e-mail accounts and chat functions to the public. However, it also allows account holders to create documents and maintain them on Google's servers. Access to these documents would likewise require compliance with SCA requirements.

Suppression is not a remedy for nonconstitutional SCA violations. However, the SCA does under certain circumstances create a cause of action for civil damages.

Some officers may obtain password and account information from offenders during the supervision process. Oftentimes this information is initially requested by supervision officers in case it is needed later. For instance, such information can prove helpful to establish who used an account or to assist in certain computer forensic processes. During the monitoring operations, officers may also come to learn passwords and account log-ins of not only the offender but all individuals who use the monitored system. Additionally, passwords can be recovered by searching a computer. Again, this information can be beneficial if needed later. One thing that cannot be done with this information is for the officer to use it to access the respective account on their own. The SCA (18 U.S.C.§ 2701) prohibits unlawful access to certain stored communications and anyone who obtains, alters, or prevents authorized access to those communications is subject to criminal penalties.

The Wiretap Statute (Title III) 18 U.S.C. §§ 2510-2522

This statute prohibits the inception of private wire, oral, or electronic communications between the parties unless one of several statutory exceptions applies. Kerr writes:

The basic structure of the Wiretap Act is surprising simple. The statute envisions that an individual is exchanging communication with another person or machine. The statute makes it a crime for someone who is not a party to the communication to use an interrupting device to intentionally access the private communication in 'real time.' (p. 451)

Many in community corrections may believe that there would be few reasons for a wiretap to be used, thinking it pertains only to intercepting telephone conversations. However, in *O'Brien v. O'Brien,* Case No. 5D03-3484 (2005), a Florida appellate court ruled that computer monitoring by a spouse was governed by the state's wiretap statute, which was patterned after the federal law. In this case the spouse used software to capture chats, instant messages, and web browsing by her husband, without his knowledge. The software eventually captured the husband's communication with his girlfriend, who also was unaware of the monitoring. The appellate court ruled in part that "spy-ware installed by the wife intercepted the electronic communication contemporaneously with transmission, copied it, and routed the copy to a file in the computer's hard drive, the electronic communications were intercepted in violation of the Florida Act" (p. 8).

Similar monitoring software is used by many CCO and would therefore also seem to be governed by Title III. The installation is usually through a supervision condition authority and the specific consent of the computer owner, usually the offender. Many agencies also place electronic consent banners at the start up of the operating system and place hard copy warning stickers. The purpose of these banners and stickers is to insure anyone using the computer understands that it is being monitored and they have no expectation of privacy during their use.

Federal law provides a minimum level of privacy protection with the wiretap statute. Some states have greater protections. Title III and states with similar laws provide for some exceptions to a wiretap, several of which are germane here. The first is commonly known as consent. There are two kinds of consent. The first is one party consent, which is contained in the federal law and 38 state statutes.

Under one-party consent, if one person knows about the inception (monitoring) and agrees, the monitoring can occur. In a correctional setting, the offender knows as well as all who use the system, that the computer is being monitored. This is established by the use of the banner and/or hard copy notices. Additionally, under federal law, there is also an exception for a person acting under "color of law" to intercept a wire, oral, or electronic communication with consent of one party to the communication. Federal CCO would be covered by this exception. State CCO would also be covered by this kind of exception if it is contained in their state law.

The other type of consent is called two-party. This means that both parties to the communication have to consent to the monitoring. There are 12 states that have two-party consent (CA, CN, FL, IL, MD, MA, MI, MO, NV, NH, PA, and WA) (Reporters Committee for Free Press). Some two-party states, such as Florida, allow an exception to law enforcement with one party consent, when "the purpose of such interception is to obtain evidence of a criminal act" (FL 934.03 (1)(c)). The purpose of correctional computer monitoring is to insure compliance not necessarily to obtain evidence of a criminal act. For instance, monitoring may be used to insure a sex offender is not viewing adult pornography, which would be a treatment issue and not a criminal act.

CCO operating in two-party consent states must therefore understand that this can be an issue for them in computer monitoring. The offender and his or her household's consent means little when they communicate via the computer with someone who is not aware the monitoring is taking place. The third-party person they may communicate with can't see the warning banner or the stickers. To illustrate this, lets consider Tom, a sex offender under supervision in a two-party state. Tom lives with his mother, Jane, who also owns the computer he uses. Jane consents to monitoring software installed on her computer. Both Tom and Jane understand all of their computer activity is being captured.

Sometime after the installation, Jane gets online and enters a chat room where a discussion on breast cancer is taking place. There are five others in the chat room. Jane posts in the chat room as well as communicates via instant messaging with the other participants. Additionally, she sends and receives e-mails from all of them after exiting the chat room. All of this activity is being recorded by the monitoring software. Jane knows about the monitoring software, but the five individuals she communicated with do not. They therefore can't consent to something they know nothing about.

Some monitoring software alleviates this problem by limiting monitoring to only the offender's usage. One company, Internet Probation and Parole Control (IPPC), actually uses a biometric device to ensure only the offender is being monitored. But the offender's communications are still obviously being monitored. It is hard to imagine why a sex offender would be allowed in a chat room, but use of e-mail is another matter. The offender's exchange of e-mail with someone else could also create the same consent issues to monitoring in a two-party state.

Now the second exception to wiretaps is the issuance of a court order. Under federal law, there are specific time constraints and judicial oversight of the entire process. Additionally, there are specific requirements to get a wiretap order issued. They include a finding that the following exists:

> a) there is probable cause that an individual is committing or about to commit a specific crime[10]; there is the belief that particular communications concerning that offense will be obtained through such interception; and c) normal investigative procedures have been tried and have failed or reasonably appear to be unlikely to succeed if tried or to be too dangerous. (18 U.S.C. § 2518 (3))

Even a supervision condition for monitoring software, ordered by a court, is hard to imagine being the same. There is no probable cause to believe the offender is committing or about to commit a new crime. Additionally, a periodic computer search can be used to find the evidence so a normal investigative procedure could be used. Finally, computer monitoring on an offender can literally be on the entire term of supervision, which is often years in duration as opposed to days or months common in wiretap orders.

Some states, such as Georgia (Section 5. Code Section 42-8-35 A), have a specific statute in place that authorizes the use of monitoring software by corrections or law enforcement. However, Georgia is also a one-party state, and would likely fall under the consent exceptions noted above. Currently, there is no case law on this issue. It may be that a court or legislature carves out some kind of exception for com-

---

10. These crimes are specified under 18 U.S.C. § 2516, which does not include violations of terms probation, parole or supervised release.

puter monitoring for probation/paroles because they have an reduced expectation of privacy. However, such action would be disregarding the privacy interests of others inside and outside of the offender's home who may be involved in communications with the offender's monitored computer.

There is a downside to breaking a wiretap law. There can be criminal (18 U.S.C. § 2511(4)) and civil penalties imposed for violations. There is no statutory suppression remedy under federal law for inception of electronic communication. All CCOs using monitoring software should thoroughly understand what it captures and its limitations. Some important considerations are:

- Is an electronic consent "banner"[11] part of the program?
- Can it be configured to only capture the offender's activities?
- Can it be set to prevent incoming communication from non-supervised person's from being captured?
- Can it block programs that might create two-party consent issues, such a chat or Instant message programs?
- Can it filter data to monitor or alert to only that which is germane to the conviction or problem conduct?
- Can it be set to capture only outgoing communication from the offender?

With a working knowledge of the software discuss the situation with a Title III legal expert in the jurisdiction to insure that if monitoring can be deployed that it is done only in a manner consistent with state and federal law.

The Privacy Protection Act (PPA), 42 U.S.C. § 2000aa

The PPA provides additional legal protection for materials related to the "freedom of expression" and the distribution of those materials

---

11. A banner is a notice that pops up at the start of the operating system which advises the party that the computer is being monitored. Some monitoring software has this banner built into their product with boilerplate language and some allow the user to modified the banner. Some banners will also periodically pop up after start up to insure if a new user is using the system they are aware it is being monitored. This differs from a log on banners that some companies use that require the person to see the banner before being granted access to the system. Many Windows operating systems allow such warning banners to be created by making changes to Registry. This is not something recommended for a CCO working on an offender's computer.

to the public. It makes it unlawful for a government officer to search for or seize materials with a warrant when the materials are some used or intended "in anticipation of communicating such material to the public" (42 U.S.C. § 2000aa-7(b)(1)). For instance, an individual is writing a newsletter which they intend to distribute to the public. When the PPA was passed, it was not envisioned that with the computer age, anyone could literally be a publisher. Today, numerous individuals are composing materials digitally and with a click of the mouse they can be posted online. It does not seem that PPA would normally impact CCO actions as they usually don't opt for a search warrant, relaying on a condition or statute authority. However, they sometimes are involved in getting a search warrant. It is also conceivable that someone would make a PPA issue regarding a CCO search, regardless of a search warrant being issued.

There are exceptions to PPA-protected material. For instance, it does not apply to "contraband or the fruits of a crime or things otherwise criminally possessed, or property designed or intended for use, or which is or has been used as, the means of committing a criminal offense" (42 U.S.C. § 2000aa-7(a), (b)). It also does not apply if "there is probable cause to believe that the person possessing such materials has committed or is committing the criminal offense to which the materials relate" (42 U.S.C. § 2000aa(a)(1)). The statute sets forth a further exception in certain circumstances where the offense "consists of the receipt, possession, communication, or withholding" of the targeted materials (42 U.S.C. § 22000aa(b)(1)). So a sex offender claiming he or she is working on a graphic story concerning incest or rape of a minor would have difficulty claiming that it was PPA-protected material as it may violate obscenity laws and/or the terms of supervision. However, if his or her spouse or a family member was working on a legitimate story intended for publication that material would likely be covered under PPA.

PPA violations are civil in nature. Additionally, a PPA violation does not bring with it any suppression remedies for evidence obtained along with the material. That said, one cannot just simply ignore PPA material that was inadvertently seized during a computer seizure. In *Steve Jackson Games, Inc. v. Secret Service,* 816 F. Supp. 432 (W.D. Tex. 1993), aff'd on other grounds, 36 F.3d 457 (5th Cir. 1994), the Secret Service was found in violation of PPA and ordered to pay $300,000 in attorney fees and $50,000 in damages. In this case the Secret Service was not aware until the day after the seizure that the computers they had taken contained publishing material. However, they did not return the computer until months later. State officers or employees under certain circumstances may be liable for PPA violations, subject to a reasonable good faith defense.

To protect against lawsuits, determine at the outset if any PPA digital or even print material is a possibility. A good supervision practice in cases involving computer management is to ascertain if the offender or the family is involved in any activity, such as writing or publishing, before one ever needs to seize a computer. Additionally, when a seizure is required, determine if PPA material might be present by making the appropriate inquiries. PPA material does not have to be removed from the computer immediately prior to the seizure as that raises chain of custody issues. However, after the computer has been imaged, make a copy of legitimate PPA material and return it as appropriate and as soon as possible. If someone raises a PPA issue later, check it out and follow through with their concerns. In short, be reasonable and professional.

OTHER LEGAL CONCERNS

There are issues that come up that CCO have never had to confront before, particularly if they have not been involved in conducting searches or investigations. The following issues are raised to alert CCO of potential problems that might be encountered in digital evidence cases.

Fifth Amendment Issues

It is a frequently a standard condition that offenders under supervision are required to truthfully answer all inquires of their supervision officer. In *Minnesota v. Murphy*, 465 U.S. 420 (1984), the Supreme Court ruled that such disclosures could be used in a future criminal prosecution. The Fifth Amendment privilege only applies to situations where an offender's answers would lead to a new criminal prosecution. They can not simply refuse to answer any and all questions if it might lead to a revocation of their supervision. Additionally, supervision officers do not have to provide *Miranda* style wordings prior to questioning an offender. Fifth Amendment issue oftentimes come up with polygraph examinations, common in sex offender cases, which frequently also involve computer restrictions. The Third Circuit held in In *U.S. v. Lee,* 315 F. 3d 206, 3rd. Cir. (2003) that:

> The Fifth Amendment, therefore, is not infringed upon when a person on supervised release is asked during the polygraph examination about his compliance with a release condition, if violation of that condition could not serve as the basis for a future criminal prosecution. For example, the examiner may ask Lee whether he had unsupervised contact with minors or had used the internet, without running afoul of the Fifth Amendment. Such an inquiry relates to Lee's compliance with release conditions and does not involve conduct that by itself would be criminal. Thus, appellant's Fifth Amendment right is not implicated with respect to questions that do not pose a threat of future criminal prosecution. (p. 213)

There are other cases out there relative to the use of polygraph, such as *U.S. v. Antelope,* 395 F. 3d 1128, 9th Cir. (2005) and *U.S. v. Stoterau,* 524 F. 3d 988, 9th Cir. (2008), which recognize that compelling offenders to answer questions on a polygraph, which may lead to new criminal prosecutions, is covered by the Fifth Amendment protections. Maiano (2006) discusses some solutions to these issues, such as the government foregoing use of any information disclosed during treatment and a polygraph or providing clear warnings during supervision that an offender may refrain from answering questions that may lead to new criminal prosecution. For most jurisdictions, questions regarding accessing the Internet or a computer will not impact a Fifth Amendment privilege as doing so is not new criminal act. However, there are some jurisdictions where such questions can lead to new criminal charges. For instance, North Carolina General Statutes § 14-202.5 provide criminal penalties for certain sex offenders who access social networking sites which minors may access. So, in North Carolina, a sex offender asked if he or she had a profile on a social networking site, such as Facebook®, would have a legitimate Fifth Amendment concern. There are ways to work around these situations, particularly as they relate to polygraph questions. For instance, if it is only illegal for the offender to have a profile on a social networking site, the question might be asked, has the offender been online. Offenders would probably have difficulty refusing to answer this question based upon the rationale that their answer would lead to Fifth Amendment concern. Even if they answer yes, they can still refuse to answer any follow-up question that might incriminate them in new criminal charges. The point is, CCO need to understand when an inquiry into computer or Internet issues may go beyond noncompliance to new criminal charges. Be aware that offenders may wish to invoke a legitimate Fifth Amendment privilege. This does not mean one has to advise them of this privilege or suggest they invoke it. Just be aware that it may be invoked and be prepared accordingly.

Cyberspace Investigations

There is no law that prohibits conducting cyberspace investigations, namely searching websites or social networking sites for information posted in public areas. Likewise, it not illegal per se to use a covert e-mail account or a social networking profile to conduct investigations. For instance, it is legal to set up a covert[12] profile to gain access to a social networking site so you can search for an offender's activities in public areas. Many of these sites will grant access to anyone without question; all that is required is that one creates a profile. The key to accessing these sites in this manner is not to exceed the limits of access that have been freely granted. In other words, don't use software or other techniques to break into areas that are restricted.

Some may raise the issue of entrapment with using covert online identifies. Specifically, some mistakenly believe merely verifying an offender has violated an Internet restriction through use of a covert online identity is unlawful. Entrapment in cyberspace hinges on two interrelated questions, did the Government induce an individual to commit a crime and is the individual predisposed to commit a crime (*U.S. v. Poehlman*, 217 F.3d. 692 (9th Circuit, 2000)). An offender online, against the law or a condition, has already engaged in prohibited conduct. Hence, in this scenario, a covert online identity cannot be an inducing factor in violation conduct that has already occurred.

---

12. Some social networking site user agreements prohibit creation of bogus profiles but this is not a violation of a criminal law. The penalty is they will simply delete the account. Some sites will allow law enforcement agencies to set up accounts provided they are notified.

CCO can use a covert identity to access a site to gain information that is there, such as on a social networking site. A prime example would be creating a profile to get on a social networking site to view a profile believed to be an offender. Additionally, a covert profile could be used by a CCO to establish the offender's online presence against a condition or law. For instance, sending an e-mail from covert account to an e-mail believed to be that of the offender to see if they response and interact to a point that their identify might be further established. This is one technique that can be used when a profile is suspected to be that of an offender.

CCO, unlike police, have a wealth of information available on the offender's background, as well as their psychological make up. It is contained in presentence reports and in mental health evaluations. Taking advantage of that information and using it to play on an offender's weakness via a covert identity to get them to violate a condition or law is at minimum not ethical. Aggressive techniques, i.e., purporting to be a minor online to a sex offender authorized on the Internet, are clearly problematic and not consistent with a CCO's role in corrections. These are more law enforcement techniques. Probation or parole officers do not pose as drug dealers to try to test offenders who are substance abusers. They should likewise not undertake such actions in cyberspace. Creating a covert identify to gain access as a "friend" on offender's profile also seems to be troublesome. It could be argued that it was like hiding in an offender's home waiting for trouble. However, some might argue it was similar to conducting surveillance. CCO should therefore seek legal advice before contemplating such aggressive online techniques.

Collecting evidence in cyberspace, such as a troubling profile, needs to also be done in a legally defensive manner (Shipley & Silbert, W., 2008; Shipley, 2007). Covert accounts must not be real individuals' names or identifiers, such as impersonating a codefendant or known felon. They should be made up entirely. Additionally, profile pictures or images should not just be pulled off the Internet. Those pictures are of real individuals who might find it highly objectionable that a CCO is pretending to be them to investigate an offender's noncompliance.

Privileged Materials

Doctors, lawyers, and clergy, like the rest of us, are using computers. One might think that a CCO would never have an opportunity to be concerned about these issues. However, computer monitoring, will capture an offender's communication with his or her doctor, clergy, and/or lawyer, just as easily as it captures material from other parties. CCO involved in pretrial supervision material must be particularly aware of these issues and take appropriate measures, consistent with their roles as officers of the court. As much as possible CCO should avoid capturing these materials or at a minimum safeguard these items as privileged material.

It is hard to imagine a CCO having the need to search an offender's doctor or lawyer's computer. However, it is possible an offender would use a public computer at his or her doctor's office or even a church to bypass restrictions or monitoring efforts. It is important to note that public computers in a health care facility could conceivably involve health care information, which is protected by *Health Insurance Portability and Accountability Act* (HIPAA). These are obviously novel situations and CCO should accordingly seek legal advice in their jurisdiction to ensure they act appropriately.

Use of WiFi Detectors

Anyone who uses a newer laptop realizes that it will quickly ascertain if there are wireless networks present and will identify them. There are also hand-held devices that will do the same activity. There are more sensitive devices which use directional antennas that can locate wireless devices. For this discussion, these devices will simply be referred to collectively as WiFi detectors.

It is not unheard of for some offenders to use a neighbor's wireless network to gain access to the Internet. As such, CCO are concerned about the presence of a wireless network, particularly unsecured access points that would allow the offender to gain Internet access. Additionally, there are WIFI hard drives, which can and have been concealed in walls and floor boards, to avoid detection of child porn collections. As a result, some CCOs would have no issue with using a wireless detector or even a laptop to check for wireless networks close to their offenders' domicile.

Some, however, have raised an issue with the use of the devices absent either the offender's consent or a specific condition authorizing their use. The rational is based in large part by the *Kyllo v. U.S.*, 533 U.S. 27 (2001). In this Supreme Court decision, the use of a thermal-imaging device by law enforcement to detect an indoor marijuana growing operation, without a warrant, was ruled a violation of the Fourth Amendment. In part, the 5-4 decision found that Government's use of "a device that is not in general public use, to explore details of the home that would previously have been unknowable without physical intrusion" was in fact a search (p. 41).

Kyllo, however, is not appropriate for prohibiting the use of WiFi detectors by CCOs. First, WiFi detectors are literally built into laptops and are devices that are in general use by the public. Second, and more importantly, Kyllo dealt with an imager that converts radiation into images based on relative warmth.

Wireless devices transmit radio signals that can pass through most walls and windows. These signals are broadcast under the rules of the Federal Communication Commission (FCC). In fact, there is an FCC identification associated with these devices. Individuals using wireless devices understand that they are using a device that broadcasts a signal, which, unless they take steps, will be broadcast to the community.

This is the heart of expectation of privacy. How can one expect something that broadcasts signals to the community to be "private"? WiFi detectors do not look into one's domicile, like might be implied with thermal-imaging. They passively grab the information that users are broadcasting to the rest of the world under FCC license.

The idea one needs the offender's consent to use these devices or a special condition gets a bit hazier when you consider the device might be used to detect an unsecured network that is coming from a neighbor. Under this rationale one could ask the offender to use the device to check for the presence of his or her neighbor's wireless network. Where did the neighbor's expectation of privacy go and how can the offender consent to use a device to check for the neighbor's network? Can asking consent from the neighbor then overcome the need to ask consent from the offender? It is simply illogical.

Basically, wireless devices transmit signals and no one has a reasonable expectation of privacy of their detection unless they turn them off or prevent them from transmitting signals. As such, absent a court decision, asking consent prior to using one of these devices is likely overkill.[13] Now, please be aware detecting and identifying the wireless network is not the same as gaining unauthorized access to that network or intercepting the traffic on that network, both of which are considered illegal, either as a computer intrusion or under the Title III concerns noted previously.

Use of Ultraviolet Light

It is frequently shown on television shows forensic personnel will use ultraviolet light to detect trace evidence, notably semen. Some computer forensic units will likewise use such devices to detect semen where is not normally found, such as on computer keyboards, mouses, CDs, etc. Their use of such devices is usually consistent with the execution of a warrant. It would seem that using such devices in a CCO setting, would unlike wireless devices, fall more in line with the *Kyllo* decision noted above. As such either a consent or a condition would be required before directing such a device at an offender's property. It maybe helpful to use an ultraviolet light, particularly on new computer equipment, to detect an offender masturbating to digital pornography. However, the device's use would only be reasonable in dealing with an offender under supervision for a sex offense involving a computer. There is no reason such a device would be used in a hacker or property case without some other justification. Likewise, using such a device should be limited to areas where semen should not be present, such as near keyboards, monitors, mouses, CDs, etc. For instance, it would not seem appropriate just to point the detector at a bed for curiosity sake without some other noncompliance justification. Additionally, the device's use should only be undertaken with proper training and equipment. Finally, be aware that these devices will not differentiate between traces left recently or prior to when an offender was placed under supervision.

---

13. To be prudent, one might verbally ask immediately prior to turning the detector on, "Hey you mind if I check for wireless networks?" A no response would be a green light to check. Of course, if the offender indicates yes, he or she does mind, there now is a real concern that there is one and he or she doesn't want it located. Securing the area until obtaining supervisor and/or legal direction would then follow.

CONCLUSION

This chapter has focused on the legal issues associated with many of the new techniques that are employed in computer management. These are new areas for many CCO, not only from a technological standpoint but from a legal framework. CCO have always been involved in supervising offenders, but many of these techniques, particularly computer monitoring, are more invasive than previous supervision practices. The previous chapter began with a legal framework advocated by Clear, Cole, and Reisig (2011) to discuss correctional law. It is appropriate that this chapter end with five general legal suggestions they mention from Clair Cripe, formerly the general counsel for the Federal Bureau of Prisons. They are very germane and a fitting close to this chapter. They are paraphrased in line with the information presented in this chapter:

1. Follow agency policies and supervisor instructions. Following polices ensures compliance with legal standards and helps avoid lawsuits. Specifically, don't start using one of the techniques mentioned in this chapter if it is against a policy. Discuss what you intend to accomplish with your supervisor.
2. Get more training. If this chapter reflects anything, these areas are very novel and frequently get updated. Individuals involved in this area need to keep abreast of new developments, whether they are legal or technical in nature.
3. Become familiar with the law directly affecting the job, in this case, cyber-supervision practices, searches, and monitoring.
4. Develop a good mentor. Get connected with someone in corrections or even law enforcement who deals with these issues on a regular basis.
5. Document what you do. Keeping good records of your actions, particularly when following a new process, will prove invaluable, if it later becomes an issue (pp. 127–128).

REFERENCES

Bruyere, J. Retrieved from http://www.brainyquote.com/quotes/quotes/j/jeandelabr151275.html.

California v. Greenwood, 486 U.S. 35 (1988).

Clear, Todd, Cole, George, & Reisig. (2011). *American corrections* (9th ed.). Belmont, CA: Wadsworth.

Federal Trade Commission. 16 CFR Part 318. *Health breach notification rule: Final rule.* Retrieved from http://edocket.access.gpo.gov/2009/pdf/E9-20142.pdf.

Florida Statute 934.03: Interception and disclosure of wire, oral, or electronic communications prohibited. Retrieved from http://www.leg.state.fl.us/Statutes/index.cfm?App_mode=Display_Statute&Search_String=&URL=0900-0999/0934/Sections/0934.03.html.

Griffin v. Wisconsin, 483 U.S 868 (1987).

Harrold, M. (2005). Computer searches of probation's-diminished privacies, special needs & whilst, quiet pedophiles–Plugging the Fourth Amendment into the "Virtual Home Visit." *Mississippi Law Journal,* Vol. 75, No. 273.

Harrold, M. (2007). Suspicionless searches in probation and parole in light of Samson v. California. *Perspectives,* American Probation and Parole Association, Winter 2007.

Health Insurance Portability and Accountability Act (HIPPA), Pub L. No. 104-191, 110 Stat. 1936 (1996).

Kerr, O. (2006). *Computer crime law.* St. Paul, MN: Thompson.

Kyllo v. U.S., 533 U.S. 27 (2001).

Maryland v. Buie, 494 U.S. 325 (1990).

Maiano, M.(2006). Sex offender probationers and the Fifth Amendment: Rethinking compulsion and exploring preventative measures in the face of required treatment programs. *Lewis & Clark Review,* Vol. 10:4.

Minnesota v. Murphy, 465 U.S. 420 (1984).

North Carolina General Statutes § 14-202.5. *Ban use of commercial social networking web sites by sex offenders.* Retrieved from http://www.ncga.state.nc.us/EnactedLegislation/Statutes/HTML/BySection/Chapter_14/GS_14-202.5.html.

O'Brien v. O'Brien, Case No. 5D03-3484, (2005), Retrieved from http://www.5dca.org/Opinions/Opin2005/020705/5D03-3484.pdf.

Reporters Committee for Free Press. *Can we tape?* Retrieved from http://www.rcfp.org/taping/.

Samson v. California, 547 U.S. 843, (2006).

Shipley, T. (2007). *Collecting legally defensible online evidence: Creating a standard framework for Internet forensic investigations.* Vere Software (http://www.veresoftware.com).

Shipley, T., & Silbert, W. (2008). *Online investigation best practices.* Presented at 2008 National Symposium on Cyber Crime, U.S. Pretrial Services, Southern District of California.

The Stored Communications Act, 18 U.S.C. §§ 2701-2712 ("SCA").

The Privacy Protection Act (PPA), 42 U.S.C. § 2000aa.

The Wiretap Act, 18 U.S.C. §§ 2510-2522 (Title III).

U.S. Department of Justice, Computer Crime and Intellectual Property Section. (2009). *Searching & seizing computers and obtaining electronic evidence in criminal investigations* (3rd ed.). Retrieved from http://www.cyber crime.gov/ssmanual/index.html.

U.S. v. Antelope, 395 F. 3d 1128, 9th Cir. (2005).

U.S. v. Herndon, 501 F. 3d 683 (6th Cir. 2007).

U.S. v. Knights, 534 U.S. 112 (2001).

U.S. v. Lee, 315 F. 3d 206, 3rd. Cir. (2003).

U.S. v. Lifshitz, 369 F. 3d. 173, 175, 190-92 (2nd Cir. 2004).

U.S. v. Poehlman, 217 F.3d. 692 (9th Circuit, 2000).

U.S. v. Reyes, 283 F. 3d 446, 2nd Cir. (2002).

U.S. v. Stoterau, 524 F. 3d 988, 9th Cir. (2008).

U.S. v. Tucker, 305 F. 3d 1193, (10th Cir. 2002).

U.S. v. Yuknavich, 419 F. 3d 1302, (11th Cir. 2005).

2010 Georgia Code, Title 42–Penal Institutions, Chapter 8, Probation, Article 2, § 42-8-35–Terms and conditions of probation; supervision. Retrieved from http://www1.legis.ga.gov/legis/2009_10/fulltext/hb1030 .htm.

Chapter 5

ACCESSING CYBER-RISK

Risk comes from not knowing what you're doing.
—Warren Buffett, American Businessman

Accessing offender behavior is not new to CCO. It is practiced on almost a daily basis when it comes to substance abuse and mental health concerns. Individuals involved in sex offender supervision are also well versed in identifying risky situations and behaviors. However, assessing computer risk is a bit more complex as it pertains to an activity that is normally legal. The activity, when used appropriately, can be highly productive. Computer usage is also rapidly becoming a necessity in the 21st century. How do CCO make informed decisions about what is a low- and high-risk situation in the computer age? This chapter focuses on assessing cyber-risk, a required skill set in managing an offender's computer use.

COMPUTERS AND CRIMINAL BEHAVIOR

Cybercrime definitions have been historically elusive. Initially they focused on crimes with financial loses, such as attacks on a computer or systems and/or the manipulation, destruction, or theft of data. Early definitional efforts distinguished computer abuse from computer fraud and computer crimes (Conly, 1989). Computer abuse covered a broad array of intentional acts that were based upon computer or technological knowledge. These acts involved the possible gain to the perpetrator(s) and/or loss to the victim(s). Computer fraud was computer use directly or as a vehicle to steal goods, services, or data. Finally, computer crime was considered any violation of a computer crime statute. Conly (1989, p. 6) defined computer-related crime as "any illegal act that requires the knowledge of computer technology for its perpetration, investigation, or prosecution."

Carter (1995) later wrote there are four computer crime categories: (1) the computer as a target; (2) the instrumentality of the crime; (3) incidental to other crimes; and (4) crimes associated with computer prevalence. The computer as the the target included offenses in which there was data theft or damage and/or unlawful access to systems. The computer as a crime's instrumentality involved computer use in the fraudulent transfer or theft of services. Cases in which the computer was incidental to other crimes meant the computer was related but not essential to an offense's commission. Examples included child pornography, check fraud, websites supporting unlawful activities, organized crime record keeping and bookmaking. This category encompassed any crime, even murder, where the computer was used in some manner to commit the crime. His last category were offenses where technology essentially creates new crime targets. Examples included software piracy/counterfeiting, copyright violations and theft of technological equipment.

Harris (1995) later articulated computer-related crime as consisting of three primary categories, specifically, the computer as a tool, a target, or incidental to the offense. In this later description a computer as a tool, included not only Carter's concept of instrumentality of the crime, but also offenses such as counterfeiting and check fraud, where the computer was used to complete the law violation. The other two categories however were similar to Carter's descriptions for target and incidental to the offense. Additionally Harris noted that there could be overlap where an offense falls in one or more categories.

The President's Working Group on Unlawful Conduct on the Internet (Working Group) (2000) noted computers can play three distinct roles in a criminal case. These roles were defined as computers as: targets; storage devices; and communications tools. In this description computers as targets included offenses in which the confidentiality, integrity, or availability of computer information or services were attacked. This description condenses Carter's categories of target and instrumentality into one. Computers as storage devices encompassed any offense in which data was stored as part of the crime. Such data ranged from stolen information (passwords, intellectual property, etc.), to records pertaining to illegal drug transactions, and child pornography images. This category in many respects includes Carter's two categories (computer as incidental to other crimes and crimes associated with the prevalence of computer).

The Working Group (2000) concluded that computers as communications tools should be a separate and stand-alone category. This new category included offenses in which online facilities were used as a communication method in criminal behaviors. Examples included e-mail and chat sessions for planning or to coordinate crime and online threats or extortion. Offenses in which the computer was used strictly as a tool and not communications device, such as making counterfeit checks, would fall under computers used as storage devices.

Goodman (2001) considered computer crime as any incident that attacks the confidentiality, integrity, or availability of digital information or services. These offenses involved a computer system as the direct attack target. He considered computer-mediated offenses as any criminal act in which a computer was used as a tool. Goodman (2001) noted this could include check fraud, prostitution, gambling, money laundering, child pornography, fencing operations, narcotics sales, and stalking. His last category was offenses in which a computer use was completely incidental to the crime. This category is not synonymous with Carter's group of incidental computer offenses. Goodman (2001) noted that this group is for cases where an offender might have used a computer before, during, or after the offense, but it was unrelated to the criminal activity. He provides an example where a homicide occurs and the murderer writes an e-mail afterwords which implicates himself. Goodman's position is that leaving computer evidence behind does not make the offense a cyber-homicide.

These typologies can be summarized as falling into three broad groups: Technology to Commit High-Tech Offenses; Technology to Commit Traditional Offenses; and Traditional Offenses (see Table 3). In examining these various typologies, it should quickly become apparent that there is overlap between the typologies themselves as well as between the various definitions within each typology. For instance, some hacking offenses will involve a computer as a tool to target another computer to steal electronically stored intellectual prop-

Table 3.
CYBERCRIME TYPOLOGY GROUPS

	Technology to Commit "High Tech" Offenses	Technology to Commit Traditional Offenses	Traditional Offenses
Conly (1989)	Computer-Related Crime		
Carter (1995)	Target Instrument of Crime Prevalence of Computers	Incidental Other Crimes	
Harris (1995)	Tool Target		Incidental to Other Crime
Working Group (2000)	Target	Storage Devices Communications Tools	
Goodman (2001)	Computer Crime	Computer Mediated Crimes	Committed Incidental to Other Crimes

erty. In this example, the conduct cuts across numerous definitional components of each of the typologies presented. Does an offense that cuts across several components, such as tool, target, or storage, make it more serious for risk assessment purposes? Few would argue that a simple hacking offense is more serious than a child pornography offense where the images are merely electronically stored. Additional factors are obviously needed to make informed assessment decisions.

RISK ASSESSMENT

True risk assessment requires going beyond just categorizing the behavior. One criminological theory, Routine Activities Theory (RAT), is particularly useful in understanding the cyber-risk. Using RAT, Lawrence Cohen and Marcus Felson believe that crime occurs when the following three factors converge in time and space: (1) a motivated offender; (2) a suitable target; and (3) the absence of a capable guardian (Fritsch, Holt, Taylor, & Liederback, 2011). Remove one factor and the theory holds that a crime is less likely to occur.

Motivation is the key component for CCO purposes in risk assessment. Not only must the offense be considered but the person's motivation for committing the crime. Additionally, regardless of motivation, the offender must have the means and/or ability to make the crime occur. Finally, an offender's prior record has historically been used as a gauge of their propensity to commit future offenses. Therefore, evaluating cyber-risk requires: (1) determining the offender's motivation; (2) how the computer was used in the offense; (3) the minimum technical means needed to accomplish the offense; (4) the offender's technical ability; and (5) the offender's prior history of committing criminal behavior. Additionally, this assessment is not static but an ongoing consideration. For instance, a motivated offender, who suddenly obtains the means, such as Internet access, represents a more serious cyber-risk than a motivated offender without a computer. Finally, from an organization perspective, one must be aware that supervision resources, including those for computer management, must be allocated to only those cases that represent the greatest cyber-risk.

Offender's Motivation

The offender's motivation for committing an offense can give an indication of what the risk is that he or she will commit a similar offense. A financial incentive to commit a fraud may be a short time solution to a financial difficulty or a "career" path. Some offenses, although clearly criminal, may show less mala in se than other crimes. For instance, a youth who exceeds authorization on a school network and inadvertently causes damage probably has a different motivation than a foreign (spy) hacker caught inside a defense department computer system.

Involvement in child exploitation offenses, with limited exceptions, reflects a sexual interest in minors, something that is recognized as a difficult motivation to address. Revenge against an individual in cyber-harrassment or cyber-bullying may be a short-term concern or a continuing problem. A cyber-attack against one's former employer may show the same pattern. In these cases, looking at the offense history will give some insight into whether the offender is still motivated to cause the victim harm. A prolonged and /or intensive cyber-harassment or bullying crime usually reflects more commitment than an offense that is relatively short in duration. Obviously, any case that involves emotional, sexual, or physical harm to another involves motivations that increase risk. Investigating material (police report, presentence report, etc.) and contact with the investigating officer may provide clues into the offender's motivation. Obviously, interviewing the offender can also provide insight into why he or she committed the offense.

Criminal Computer Use

An assessment is also necessary to ascertain computer usage, if any, in an offense's commission. Was the computer central to the offense's commission or was only some element of the crime committed with a computer? Obviously, offenses such as hacking require computer use. However, other offenses require further examination of police reports, charging documents, presentence reports, etc. For instance, a check fraud may or may not involve technology. Embezzlement can still occur without a computer. Theft of a computer may simply mean a laptop was stolen from an office, much like a purse or other valuable. This offense type does not normally reflect a cyber-risk, unless the true target was the data on the computer as opposed to just the device.

Identify theft often involves computer use, either to obtain the victim's identifiers or to sign up online for credit cards accounts in the victim's name. However, many identify theft cases only minimally involve a computer, such as when an offender steals a friend's or coworker's identifiers and uses them to apply online for credit.

Some offenses such as child pornography possession are getting harder to imagine without computer use involved somewhere in the process. Harder still are offenses involving receipt, distribution, and/ or production of child pornography. Contact sex crimes, such as child molestation/incest and rape obviously do not require a computer to occur. However, a computer may still have been involved in targeting or meeting the victim or reducing offense barriers, i.e., showing pornography to minors.

Stalking or bullying is another example of a crime requiring closer examination. These offenses do not require a computer but when technology is involved, the negative implications can be much more serious. Was the victim located through Internet research? Was the victim harassed via the computer? Was spyware installed by the offender on the victim's computer to track them? All of these computer activities can make the victim impact much greater than a traditional stalking case.

Offenses where the computer was merely used as communication or for record keeping may not necessitate further examination. Examples include drug trafficking, gambling, and prostitution.

However, some offenses such as those involving sexual exploitation require additional scrutiny even if a computer was not used in the conviction offense. The reason for this closer examination is the Internet provides a ready access to new victims. Remember the second factor in RAT for a crime to occur is a "suitable victim." The Internet provides the ability to research, connect, and exploit them. Any offense involving cyber-terrorism in which a computer was used in an act of terror, such as in conjunction with a coordinated attack in the real world, also demands extra scrutiny.[1] The community risk for these offenses is just too great to ignore.

Technical Means

The term technical means refers to the minimum requirements, be they software, hardware, or access, that were needed to commit a particular offense. For instance, did an offender use software that was designed by someone else[2] to commit a computer crime, such as denial-of-service attack (DoS attack) or distributed denial-of-service attack (DDoS attack)?[3] Some of these programs are very easy to use and can be obtained if one knows where to look. It is also far easier to obtain

---

1. Most of these cases would likely never be placed on community supervision. However, there may be cases involving hate, environmental movements, and/or terrorists groups that commit lesser computer-related crimes that might receive community supervision as part of a sentence.

2. Individuals that predominately use menu driven programs for hacking or other malicious activities that are designed by others are commonly referred to as "script kiddies." Their technical ability is usually far less than the person who created the program.

3. These attacks send repeated requests for information to a website, usually using numerous computers. These repeated requests for information or services either cause the website to shutdown or cause legitimate requests for information or services to go unanswered as the website is too busy responding to the illegitimate inquiries. These attacks are frequently done with Botnets, which are networks of compromised computers that are controlled by someone.

a computer virus[4] than it is to create one. Did they use over-the-counter software to produce counterfeit documents or did they obtain the documents from someone else?

Some offenses, such as counterfeiting or check fraud, require specific equipment, such as a scanner or high quality printer. Other examples include card skimmers, which are devices used to capture credit card information for fraud and laminators for creating fake identification documents. Webcams are sometimes used by sex offenders to transmit live indecent images of themselves. Other sex offenders have used gaming devices to arrange meetings with minors who are gamers. Without these devices the offender oftentimes can't commit the crime unless, of course, he or she is teamed up with someone else.

Although offenses are committed from the outside of a company (hackers), historically, many more have been committed by insiders. It is far easier to steal intellectual property or data if one works inside of a company as opposed to hacking into the system from the outside. It also may be far simpler to exceed one's authorized level of access, as opposed to stealing or breaking access controls. A bank teller is in a better position to alter records to cause a loss as opposed to a hacker trying to get into a financial institution's system from the outside. Crimes where the offender misuses his or her position of trust are much easier to commit.

Identify theft offenses are also much simpler if the offender has access to the victim's information because they know them. For instance, an offender who steals a former girlfriend's identification for a credit card application is different than someone who steals 25 complete strangers' identifiers.

In the case of a cyber-stalker, it is far easier to install spyware on the victim's computer if one has direct access to it. Many times, if were not for the access being willingly granted to the offender the crime might not have occurred. Special software, hardware, and/or access oftentimes is what makes many cybercrimes possible. However, others crimes, particularly child exploitation offenses, merely require computer and/or Internet access.

---

4. Computer viruses are malicious programs that perform unauthorized functions when executed. They differ from computer worms, which infect networks, in that they require some user action to initiate their action. Worms once executed can replicate and spread without further action by a user.

Looking at the police reports may provide answers to these questions. However, it may be necessary to speak with the investigating officer regarding an offense's technical complexity. The investigating officer also may have information pertaining to how the offender may have known the victim, thereby gaining access to him or her.

Technical Ability

The offender's technical ability can range from a novice all the way up to a computer engineer. What about when the offense shows an expertise beyond that of a normal computer user? For instance, did the offender actually create software or a technique that facilitated a DDoS attack? Maybe the offender hacked into a system from the outside. This shows an ability beyond the norm.

A sex offender who uses extensive tools, such as encryption and steganography to conceal their illicit activities, represents a technical knowledge that many do not possess. Technically sophisticated sex offenders have been known to conceal their images in other methods, such as creating a special section (partition) on a computer hard drive that only they know about and can access. Some have concealed wireless hard drives within walls or floors. Other examples are individuals who are very familiar with illegal websites, peer-to-peer networks, etc. where illegal material can be readily obtained.

In counterfeiting and check fraud offenses, the quality may be such that the bogus items could not be easily differentiated from legitimate material. Conversely, a particularly bad counterfeiting attempt shows a lack of skill. An identity theft offense can be as simple as obtaining identifiers out of trash, from the mail, or a stolen purse or wallet. It can also be technically sophisticated, such as e-mail phishing schemes[5] and website spoofing.[6]

---

5. Sending out mass e-mails with bogus information to entice users to provide personal identifiers is known as "phishing." These e-mails can contain company logos and appear very legitimate. However, the links point to websites, again very official looking, but completely bogus, that collect information which is then used to commit credit card fraud. There is also "spear phishing," a term used to target specific individuals, usually those with higher credit scores, to entice them to provide their personal identifiers.

6. Website spoofing is when the offender duplicates a legitimate website, such as for a financial institution. The user is misdirected to this bogus website and attempts to log in providing the offender information needed to steal the user's identify.

Beyond the offense's commission, what does the offender have in his or her background that represents a special computer skill? Are they self taught computer experts? Do they belong to a computer user group, which can be either prosocial or antisocial groups (hacker)? Have they taken computer courses? If they were ever in the military, did they receive computer training while in the service? Do they have a computer certification or a degree? Did their current or prior employment involve computers, particularly servicing, repairing, maintaining a network, etc.? How much time do they normally spend using a computer or online? All of these questions help assess the offender's computer expertise. Some of the questions can be answered by looking at the investigation material. Interviewing the offender during a presentence report investigation and/or during the initial supervision intake regarding their computer expertise should also be considered. Obtaining educational and/or employment records can also provide answers to these questions. Depending on the case, interviewing third parties (family, significant others, employers, etc.) can also provide information on the offender's technical sophistication.

Prior Criminal Behavior

CCO are accustomed to gathering prior criminal record information. In this regard, review the record for offenses that are similar in nature as well as those that involved a computer and/or Internet use. In check fraud cases, look to see if the offender was involved in the creation of bogus material or as a leader in previous fraudulent schemes. The same goes for credit card and identify theft schemes. A sex offender with a prior sex crime is obviously a very high-risk situation. Prior instances where computer restrictions were imposed are important, particularly where cyber-management efforts, such as computer monitoring, were circumvented or defeated.

Oftentimes, a presentence report may only contain very basic information. This particularly happens due to time constraints on their completion. Prior offenses may not reflect the conduct involved. For some offenses, particularly in which the current offense involved a computer, further inquiry might be warranted on prior offenses of a similar nature.

Sometimes the prior offense alone necessitates digging deeper, particularly when it is a sex crime. Take the case of an offender on supervision for robbery who was also a registered sex offender. The prior sex offense was not very detailed in the presentence report. The offender moves into a situation and begins using his landlord's computer to access pornography sites. The supervision officer requests information from the institution which reflects a sex offender evaluation was completed revealing that the prior sex offense involved extensive Internet and computer use. The bottom line is, if the record is unclear, seek additional information from other sources. Finally, don't be afraid to ask the offender details about their prior offense conduct.

Evaluating Risk

Once information is obtained on the above areas, it now becomes necessary to collectively evaluate the information to answer the question, does this offender have the motivation, the means, and/or ability to commit this offense or similar crime again? The more factors present, the greater the potential they will intersect into new criminal conduct. Figure 3 provides a graphic representation of these factors, with their intersection representing the greatest cyber-risk.

Along with this evaluation, it must be clear that not every case involving a computer should necessitate computer monitoring. Agencies do not have the resources to monitor all offenders' computers.

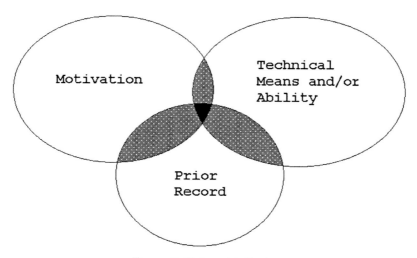

Figure 3. Cyber-risk Factors.

Only the cases which represent the highest risk should be considered for computer restrictions.

For instance, if the offender used their access to their employer's computer to commit a theft and he or she is no longer employed in such a position, can he or she realistically commit the same offense again? In such cases, it may only be necessary to insure the offenders do not get into positions where they have access to other computer systems or the offenders' prior conduct is disclosed to any potential employer.

Other cases, such as a hacking offense, may reflect the offender has the ability to carry out additional offenses regardless of where he or she is employed. But does he or she have the motivation? If motivated for continued criminal behavior, it may be necessary to place a special conditions either restricting computer/Internet use, requiring monitoring software, and/or the ability to conduct a computer search.

Cases involving check, credit, and identify fraud may warrant special measures to manage cyber-risk. The extent of these measures though has to be tempered based upon the evaluation. It is easy to just suggest computer monitoring on all cases just because they involved a computer. However, one must realize that such measures are very time and resource intensive. Outside of time and cost of installing monitoring software, it is very difficult to develop key words and phrases that will not trigger hundreds of false alerts. Installing monitoring software on a first-time offender who stole someone's identity and applied for credit online can result in extra supervision activity that is being diverted from more serious offenders. It may be appropriate in such cases to merely have a computer search condition, which serves not only as possible deterrent but can be conducted based upon reasonable suspicion of a violation.

Some offenses such as cyber-bullying and cyber-stalking may require computer management because of the potential for further harm to the victim. The same holds for any offense in which a potential for violence existed. Sex offenders, also because of the offense nature, warrant serious consideration of computer management because of the easy Internet access to minors as well as pornography. The next section provides further details on evaluating risk when dealing with cyber-sex offenders.

CYBER-SEX OFFENSES

Sex offenders use computers to view, store, produce, receive, and/ or distribute child and other forms of pornography; to communicate, groom, and entice children and others for victimization; and to validate and communicate with other sex offenders. The U.S. Department of Justice (2000) identified the following three general cyber-sex offenders: (1) the dabbler; (2) the preferential offender; and (3) the miscellaneous offender. Dabblers were described as curious adults with a newly found access to pornography or offenders who are profit-motivated to deal in child pornography. A dabbler could also be the typical adolescent searching for pornography who downloads child pornography. The preferential offender is the sexually indiscriminate individual with a wide variety of deviant sexual interests or a pedophile with a definite preference for children. Lastly, miscellaneous offenders are pranksters or misguided individuals conducting private investigations or exposés who have been found in possession of child pornography.

Beyond the cyber-risk evaluation, CCO need to explore the the following areas: (1) files found in the offender's possession; (2) the offender's equipment and Internet Service Provider(s) (ISP); (3) the offender's online activities; and (4) other activities of the offender. Looking at these areas collectively will help assess the offender's commitment to sexual deviance. This knowledge is also helpful for dealing with treatment obstacles, such as denial and rationalization.

Files Found

Knowledge of the files found in the offender's possession is very important. Obviously, sheer quantity reflects the offender's commitment level. Other areas to be aware of are types of files found. Specifically, were they still images, such as those with a file extension of .jpg, .bmp; .gif, etc., or were they moving images, such as those with a file extension of .avi or .mpg? Having a collection of moving images reflects a different aspect of offender behavior than just having still images. Additionally, it usually takes longer to download moving images than it does to download still images. An individual with a large collection of moving images shows an advanced degree of commitment or motivation to getting them because of the time involved in amassing them over the Internet. Finally, moving images take more electronic space to store than still images. What were file names of the images? Were the names descriptive? This is important because it can counter the offender's claim not to know that the images were of child pornography. Were the pornographic files found in the temporary Internet folders or did the offender save them in specific folders of his choosing? Files saved to specific locations reflects direct offender action as opposed to images saved by the computer to make the user's Internet browsing more efficient.[7] Did the offender's pornography reflect a specific theme and how were the images organized? Was there a particular age group or possible sadistic or masochistic (S & M) images? These issues provide important information on the offender's areas of interest or deviancy.

Image organization is also significant because it takes active offender participation. It takes commitment (motivation) to organize and sort hundreds or thousands of images. How many pornographic files were saved on the offender's computer? How many such files did the offender forward to others or did the offender receive images from others? Were the images downloaded from locations that clearly signify they were illegal? This information provides insight into the offender's involvement with the community of deviancy. Additionally, did the offender forward any child porn images to juveniles? Remember, this can be one of the initial online activities to entice children into sexual acts. In all of the above incidences—i.e., possession, receipt, and distribution—what were the percentages of child porn to adult porn? Specifically, let's suppose an offender has 1,000 pornographic images on his or her computer. Of that 1,000, only 15 were of child porn. This offender shows a different level of commitment from the offender with 1,000 images, of which 900 were of child porn. Likewise, did the offender have a high percentage of violent pornography, such as rape and torture themes?

Are the images used to enhance the sex offender's "status" with other individuals who collect child porn, i.e., my collection is larger and better, etc.? Did he use them to barter for other forms of pornog-

---

7. *U.S. v. Tucker,* 305 F. 3d 1193 (10th Cir. 2002) is noteworthy in this regard. In this case, the parolee was repeatedly accessing the Temporary Internet Folders and revisiting images that had been saved by the computer during his Internet browsing sessions. He would then move the images from the Temporary Internet Folders to the Recyle Bin, believing they were deleted.

raphy (adult, incest, S & M, bestiality, etc.)? Was he involved in selling child pornography?

Finally, how were the images used by the offender? Did he masturbate to them? Did he use them to entice children? Does he claim he has them so that he won't abuse children? Be aware that a study of federal offenders convicted of child pornography offenses (possession, receipt, distribution) found that nearly two-thirds admitted during treatment that they had abused both prepubescent and postpubescent victims, an increase of 52 percent from what was known prior to sentencing (Bourke & Hernandez, 2009). Clearly, child pornography collectors may in fact be hands-on offenders.

Equipment and ISP

Offenders' equipment also provides insight into how committed they are to deviancy. Top-of-the-line computers, scanners, digital/video cameras, etc. may reflect an interest in producing and/or viewing "quality" images. Also, the offender may want large hard drives to store more image files, as they take more space. Better equipment also can provide faster access to images for viewing. Additionally, better equipment can facilitate the production of media containing child pornography to distribute to others.

Beware of what type of ISP offenders have or had. Dial-up services are slower for downloading image files. Cable and Digital Subscriber Line (DSL) connections provide faster Internet speeds and make it easier to download these files. At one time, cable and DSL were much more expensive than dial-up services. Again, remember to look at all factors together. For instance, two offenders, both with the same number of moving image files, may have different levels of commitment if one considers how they obtained the images. Specifically, one offender may have a dial-up service and the other may have obtained the images with a cable service. The first offender would have had to spend more time downloading the images than the second offender because of the slower speed of the dial-up Internet connection.

There also have been cases of sex offenders caught downloading child pornography on public access computers, such as libraries. This shows a strong motivation to get these images, disregarding the higher likelihood of being caught.

Online Activities

Information about offenders' online activities is equally important. How many screen names do they have and are any of the names suggestive, implying some deviant interest? For instance, the screen name K9trainer123 or Slavemaster789 may reflect that the offender has an interest in bestiality or S & M respectively. Did an offender have a screen profile and what interests did the profile mention? Was the offender's photo on the profile? Was the profile accurate? For instance, did the profile reflect the offender's true age and gender or did it claim that the offender was a child or maybe a member of the opposite sex?

How long has the offender been accessing the Internet: one year, five years, or ten years? How much time did the offender spend online and was the offender frequently online when juveniles were present, such as after school or before 9:00 p.m.? How many people communicated with the offender? How many names were in the Buddy List (for chats) or email address book? Were these names of other adults or juveniles? Were the other adults possibly interested in child porn? How many messages, with and without attachments, did the offender send or receive? What were the favorite websites? Was the offender paying for access to porn sites? Did the offender use file-sharing programs such as Gigatribe, Frostwire, Kazaa, BearShare, Shareaza, BitTorrent, Ares, Kazza, Limewire, eMule, etc. to obtain and trade porn?

In cases involving enticement over the Internet, what did the messages/chats reflect? What was the offender discussing? Were there references to S & M, incest, etc. themes? If possible, obtain copies of these messages to include in reports and for the supervision file. The text of such messages can be very useful during treatment when offenders attempt to minimize or rationalize their conduct. Equally important are the items the offender brought to any planned meeting with a juvenile or undercover officer posing as a juvenile. Possession of digital cameras, condoms, sex toys, handcuffs, whips, blindfolds, weapons, drugs (including sexual enhancement drugs), etc. sheds a spotlight on the offender's intentions during and after the encounter. One graphic example is the offender who was arrested in an undercover sting operation to which he brought a shovel, axe, gasoline, and garbage bags to meet someone he thought was a minor.

Other Activities

What were the offenders' real-world activities? Have they been employed in jobs involving juveniles? Are they or were they involved in voluntary activities where juveniles are active (Boys Club, YMCA, coach, etc.)? Do they reside near places juveniles frequent or are there juveniles in the home? An offender's history of organizing life around juveniles is an indication that the offender may be strongly drawn to minors. Does an offender have a history of extensive foreign travel (certain countries are lax in enforcing laws prohibiting sex acts with minors)? It also is extremely important to know a sex offender's technical ability. Does their prior record include sex offenses with or without computers? Does the record show a prior period of supervision in which monitoring software/hardware was circumvented? Again, past convictions for such conduct help assess possible future risks.

Risk Level and Monitoring

Brake and Tanner (2007) have developed a two-factor risk grid that is useful in determining a monitoring level for sex offenders. Their grid incorporates the offender's Internet behavior history and the offender's overall risk of acting out as based upon various sex assessment tools[8] for an overall assessment of an appropriate monitoring level. Their historical Internet behaviors are as follows:

> ***Low:*** Reactive Type of user: Incidental use, downloads small amounts of pornography when prompted, or less than 1 hour per month spent viewing pornography.
> ***Low-Moderate:*** Active User of pornography, actively seeks images via web pages, OR more than 1 hour per month but less than 10 hours a month spent viewing pornography.
> ***Moderate:*** Collector behavior: Actively seeks pornography through file sharing or catalogs material, or more than 10 hours a month but less than 30 hours a month viewing pornography.
> ***Moderate-High:*** Engager behavior: Solicits or grooms children online.

---

8. The tools they identified were Minnesota Sex Offender Screening Tool-Revised (MnSOST-R) Rapid Risk Assessment for Sex Offense Recidivism (RRASOR); STATIC-99, or STATIC-2002 and the STABLE/ACUTE.

Table 4.
NEED FOR COMPUTER MONITORING IN SEX OFFENSE CASES

B E H A V I O R					
	VERY HIGH				
	HIGH			High	
	MOD-HIGH	Mod-High		High	
	MOD	Moderate	Mod-High		
	LOW-MOD	Low-Mod	Moderate	Mod-High	
	LOW	Low	Low-Mod	Moderate	Mod-High
	LOW	Low/Mod	Moderate	Mod-High	High
		RISK OF CONTACT (From Risk Assessment Instruments: MnSoST-R, RRASOR, Static/Stable/Acute)			

Source: Brake and Tanner (2007).

> ***High:*** Abuser behavior: Engages in sex with child met online or more than 30 hours per month of viewing pornography.
> ***Very High:*** Promoter of commercial behavior: Produces or distributes child pornography. (p. 2)

Where these Internet behaviors converge with various risks of a contact offense (Low to High) as determined by a sexual assessment, there are various suggested levels of monitoring (see Table 4). Black and Tanner suggest that cases falling in the Low category on their grid may be addressed with "passive monitoring" (Field Search, use of periodic random searches, and deploying E-Blaster®, Spector®, or Cybersential®). Cases falling in higher categories are appropriate for "active" monitoring, involving programs such as Impulse Control®.[9] They further note:

> The level and type of monitoring is perhaps less important than making the decision to monitor. Offenders rated as "Moderate" or higher in the grid should have their computer activity monitored. The

---

9. Field Search, E-Blaster, Spector, Cybersential, and Impulse Control® will be discussed in the following chapters on searches and monitoring.

particular type of monitoring employed may be driven by risk but also by technical issues, accessibility and case-specific elements. (p. 1)

Juvenile Texting[10]

In 2000, when the U.S. Department of Justice suggested the previous mentioned categories for cyber-sex offenders, "juvenile sexting" and its impact were not envisioned. Are these cases truly sex offenders or wayward youth? Is some type of diversion warranted or is something much more serious needed? In assessing risk in sexting cases involving solely minors as the offenders, the following issues need to be addressed.[11] How old is the victim? Did she know about the photograph? Did the victim take it herself without the encouragement or direct participation of any other person? Did she forward the image to anyone? What is the age difference between the victim and the recipient of the image? Does she now face harassment because of her inappropriate behavior? Answers to these questions can help indicate if the image subject is a true victim in every sense of the word or an offender.

Although, perhaps, not in the image, the youth offender somehow took part in the juvenile sexting. His actions could include soliciting the picture or actively participating in creating, possessing, receiving, or distributing the image. Did he request the picture, or did someone just send it to him? Did he keep it or forward it on and why? Were they trying to embarrass or harass the victim? What is or was the relationship between the youth offender and victim? How old are they, and what is the age difference between them? It may be a mitigating factor where there is little or no disparity in age. However, if the offender is significantly older (e.g., a 15-year-old with pictures of an 8-year-old), there may very well be serious treatment issues to address. Did the offender participate in similar misconduct in the past? Consideration of these factors can assess risk in these cases which are unfortunately finding their way more and more into the juvenile and adult justice systems.[12]

---

10. Bowker and Sullivan (2011) define juvenile sexting as "youths sending or posting sexually suggestive text messages and images, including nude or seminude photographs, via cellular telephones or over the Internet."

11. While members of both sexes commit or fall victim to these types of crimes, for this discussion's purposes, examples feature male offenders and female victims.

12. Jim Tanner, of KBSolutions has also developed a "Sexting Decision Grid" which is very useful to assist law enforcement and prosecuting attorneys in charging decisions in these cases. It can be obtained at http://www.kbsolutions.com/SextingGrid.pdf.

OTHER RISKS

Cyberspace clearly places a new dimension on criminal behavior. However, it also creates new venues for problem issues that CCO have become accustom to dealing with only in the brick and mortar world. Two of these issues, substance abuse and gambling, are addictive in nature. The third is suicide. Elements of all three are now appearing online.

Substance Abuse

The National Drug Intelligence Center (NDIC) (2002) concluded that drug use facilitation appeared to be the most common drug-related activity on the Internet. NDIC (2002) categorized this facilitation as:

Use: Online information is readily available depicting the supposedly positive effects of drug use at the same time downplaying the negative effects. The sites also present on how to use readily available products, such as cold medications, in order to get "high." Additionally, the sites frequently explain drug use terminology and slang, thereby acclimating individuals to the drug culture.

Production: Some sites provide recipes for individuals to produce their own cocktails of abuse. Oftentimes the site include not only the ingredients but where to obtain them as well as the how to get the production equipment. Unfortunately, misinformation is not unusual, which can lead to serious injury/illness or death.

Sale: Individuals can easily search online for drug suppliers or as noted above drug substitutes. Sites marketing drugs with no prescription needed are not unusual.

Many of NDIC observations seem valid even today. A small 2005 study found of 12 patients (9 male, 3 female) 100 percent reported that Internet-based information had affected the ways in which they had used psychoactive substances. Additionally, eight respondents described adopting behaviors intended to minimize the risks associated with psychoactive substance use. The respondents also reported changes in the use of a wide variety of illicit substances as well as over-the-counter and prescription pharmaceuticals based upon their online research.

Leinwand (2007) also cited a study that found 10 million online messages written by teens in 2006 showed they regularly chat about drinking alcohol, smoking pot, partying, and hooking up. The Drug Enforcement Administration (DEA) also concluded in 2010 that "Social networking sites provide information from teens on their personal experiences on how to get high with prescription drugs." Lyon (2008) also observed that the Internet is also ripe with methods for users to defeat drug tests, some "downright dangerous."

Actually obtaining illegal drugs online appears a smaller portion of the overall cyber-effect on drug use. A U.S. government study noted that only .04% of persons aged 12 or older in 2008-2009 who used pain relievers nonmedically in the past 12 months obtained their drugs online. Nevertheless, a 2010 United Nations report reflected that India has "emerged as a major source for illegal drugs traded on the Internet with narcotics smuggled via the country's courier and postal services to the rest of the world." The report further noted that India firms, disguised as software companies, were allowing transactions of banned pharmaceutical preparations to be made over the Internet.

It should therefore be clear that CCO must also be aware how offenders may be using the Internet to facilitate their substance abuse issues. Although computer management techniques may not be warranted, inquiring about online habits is justified.

Gambling

Internet gambling has nearly doubled every year since 1997—in 2001 it exceed $2 billion (Center for Counseling & Health Resources, Inc.) A recent simple Google search for the term "online gambling sites" generates over 6,000,000 results. At the same time, Internet gambling is growing several studies reflect that offenders have the highest overall rate of problem gambling of any known population (Lahn & Grabosky, 2003; Williams, Royston, & Hagen, 2005).

Williams (2010) observes, "Correctional professionals should be aware of the possibilities in which gambling may develop among offenders, particularly at a time when legalized gambling opportunities are increasing." Additionally, Psychology of Addictive Behaviors (2002) and CyberPsychology & Behavior (2009) produced studies which suggest that people who gamble on the Internet are likely to have a gambling problem. Griffiths, Wardle, Orford, Sproston, and Erens (2009) noted "that the medium of the Internet may be more likely to contribute to problem gambling than gambling in offline environments."

Online gambling addictions, much like other online problem behaviors, can be easily concealed from significant others and CCO. As such, supervision officers need to be aware of their offenders' online habits, particularly if they have a history of problem gambling.

Suicide

Dobson (1999) reported that there were more than 100,000 sites about suicide on the Internet. He further noted that many of the suicide sites forbid entry to anyone offering to dissuade users from taking their own lives and some sites appear to be discouraging people from seeking psychiatric help. A more recent Google search with the term "how to commit suicide" reflected 4,290,000 hits. There were some sites that were preventative in nature or hotlines, but many more contained explicit instruction on how to commit suicide. One site had the troubling title, "What is the best way to commit suicide when you're under 13?"

Additionally, there are numerous reports of suicide victims posting their notes online. Again, CCO need to be aware that the Internet may be used by suicidal offenders for research purposes as well as to post their suicide note. Making inquiry with the offender about online habits and if necessary a check of their browser history may prevent an Internet facilitated suicide.

CONCLUSION

This chapter discussed the complex issue of assessing cyber-risk. Key to understanding risk is: (1) determining the offender's motivation; (2) how the computer was used in the offense; (3) the minimum technical means needed to accomplish the offense; (4) the offender's technical ability; and (5) the offender's prior history of committing criminal behavior. This assessment process requires review of police reports, presentence reports, mental health/sex offender evaluations or any other document that addresses the offense, the offender and his or her prior record. Obviously, interviewing the offender will also provide needed information. This process can also involve contact with significant third parties, such as family, employers, and/or schools. The time invested in this process will help insure that computer management is vested in only those cases which represent the greatest risk. This is paramount in a supervision environment that is oftentimes hampered by budgetary and resource shortfalls. Additionally, as the discussion on substance abuse, gambling, and suicide revealed, CCO must be constantly vigilant to how the Internet may be used to the determinant of their cases and the community and respond accordingly. The remaining chapters will address the nuts and bolts of computer management.

REFERENCES

Bourke, M., & Hernandez, A. (2009). The 'Butner Study' redux: A report of the incidence of hands-on child victimization by child pornography Offenders. *Journal of Family Violence,* Volume 24.

Bowker, A. Online gambling: Offenders trying to roll "7's" in a binary world. Retrieved from http://www.corrections.com/cybercrime/?p=271.

Bowker, A. The 21st century substance abuser: Cyberspace intersecting with the drug culture. Retrieved from http://www.corrections.com/cyber crime/?p=246.

Bowker, A., & Gray, M. (2004). An introduction to the supervision of the cybersex offender. *Federal Probation,* December, 2004.

Bowker, A., & Sullivan, M. (2010). Sexting: Risky actions and overreaction. *FBI Law Enforcement Bulletin,* July. Retrieved from http://www.fbi.gov /stats-services/publications/law-enforcement-bulletin/july-2010/sexting.

Boyer, E., Shannon, M., & Hibbert, P. The Internet and psychoactive substance use among innovative drug users. *Pediatrics,* 115, 302–305. Retrieved from http://www.pediatrics.org/cgi/content/full/115/2/302.

Brake, S., & Tanner, J. *Determining the need for Internet monitoring of sex offenders.* Retrieved from http://www.kbsolutions.com/MonitoringNeed.pdf.

Buffett, W. Retrieved from http://www.brainyquote.com/quotes/quotes/w /warrenbuff138173.html.

Carter, D. (1995). Computer crime categories: How techno-criminals operate. *FBI Law Enforcement Bulletin,* Volume 64, Number 7, 21–26.

Center for Counseling & Health Resources, Inc. *Gambling facts and statistics.* Retrieved from http://www.overcominggambling.com/facts.html.

Conly, C. (1989). *Organizing for computer crime investigation and prosecution.* U.S. Department of Justice, Office of Justice Programs, National Institute of Justice.

Dobson, R. (1999) Internet sites may encourage suicide. *British Medical Journal,* August 7; 319(7206): 337. Retrieved from http://www.ncbi.nlm .nih.gov/pmc/articles/PMC1126981/.

Drug Enforcement Administration (DEA). (1999). *Chemicals used in "Spice" and "K2" type products now under federal control and regulation.* Press Release Retrieved from http://www.justice.gov/dea/pubs/pressrel/pr030111 .html.

Drug Enforcement Administration (DEA). (2010). *Hidden dangers in your home.* Retrieved from http://www.getsmartaboutdrugs.com/Files/File/Current CoPPresentations_December2010/DEA_HiddenDangersSpeakerNotes_ 2010.pdf.

Drug Intelligence Center (NDIC). (2002). *Information bulletin: Drugs, youth, and the Internet.* Retrieved from http://www.justice.gov/ndic/pubs2/2161 /index.htm.

Goodman, M. (2001). Making computer crime count. *FBI Law Enforcement Bulletin,* Volume 70, Number 8, pp. 10–17.

Griffiths, M., Wardle, H, Orford, J. Sproston, K., & Erens B. (2009). Sociodemographic correlates of Internet gambling: Findings from the 2007 British gambling prevalence survey. *CyberPsychology & Behavior,* 12(2). Retrieved from http://www.ncbi.nlm.nih.gov/pubmed/19072080.

Harris, K. (1995). *Computer crime: An overview.* SEARCH'S Technology Bulletin, Issue 1.

Ladd, G., & Petry, N. (2002). Disordered gambling among university-based medical and dental patients: A focus on Internet gambling. *Psychology of Addictive Behaviors,* Vol. 16, No. 1, 76-79. Retrieved from http://www.apa .org/pubs/journals/releases/adb-16176.pdf.

Lahn, J., & Grabosky P. (2003). Gambling and clients of ACT corrections. Centre for Gambling Research. Regulatory Institutions Network. Australian National University. Retrieved from www.problemgambling.act .gov.au/Gambling%20and%20Clients%20of%20ACT%20Corrections .pdf.

Leinwand, D. (2007). Teens use Internet to share drug stories. *USA Today.* Retrieved from http://www.usatoday.com/news/nation/2007-06-18- online_N.htm.

Lindsay, L. (2008). Ways teens might cheat on drug tests and how to catch them. *US News.* Retrieved from http://health.usnews.com/health-news/articles/2008/08/06/5-ways-teens-might-cheat-on-drug-tests8212and-how-to-catch-themNational.

Reuters. (2010). Illegal drug trade via Internet on the rise in India. Retrieved from http://in.reuters.com/article/2010/02/24/idININdia-46438820100 224Reuters.

The electronic frontier: The challenge of unlawful conduct involving the use of the Internet: A report of the president's working group on unlawful conduct on the Internet, March 2000. Retrieved February 26, 2009, from http://www .usdoj.gov/criminal/cybercrime/unlawful.htm#co.

U.S. Department of Health and Human Services, Substance Abuse and Mental Health Services Administration, Office of Applied Studies. (2009). *Results from the 2009 National Survey on Drug Use and Health: Volume I. Summary of national findings.* Retrieved from http://www.oas .samhsa.gov/NSDUH/2k9NSDUH/2k9ResultsP.pdf.

Williams, D. (2010). Offender gambling behavior and risk during the re-entry process. Los Angeles, CA: Leisure and Deviance Education/Research Services (LEADERS). Retrieved from https://dspace1.acs.ucal gary.ca/bitstream/1880/48141/1/Gambling_Behavior_and_Risk_During _Re-entry.pdf.

Williams, R. , Royston, J., & Hagen, B. (2005). Gambling and problem gambling within forensic populations: A review of the literature. *Criminal Justice and Behavior, 32,* 665–689 Retrieved from http://cjb.sagepub.com /content/32/6/665.abstract.

Chapter 6

A "BIT" OF COMPUTER EDUCATION

When eating an elephant take one bite at a time.
    –Creighton Abrams, American General, 1914–1974

Abrams is right. No one can eat an elephant in one bite. However, even an elephant can be consumed one small bite at a time over numerous sittings. It is so with learning computer technology. Obtaining a basic computer management understanding can be accomplished one "byte"[1] at a time. The only requirement is to be hungry for knowledge. Consider this chapter an appetizer to the meal of basic computer management skills.

TWO BASIC CONCERNS

There are two core computer questions in the forefront for any CCO involved in computer management. The first question is how can a particular computer or specific component be used to commit a crime or violation behavior? Knowing what a device can and can't do is central to understanding how it can be used to commit violation

---

1. The references to bit and byte are a play on words. A bit is the smallest digital unit of measure. It is a value of 1 or 0. A "1" reflects the presence of an electronic charge and a "0" reflects no charge. A computer reads the presence of these charges, which is how data is stored. A nibble contains 4 bits. A byte consists of eight bits. One important thing about the term bytes is they are also used to describe processing speed or storage. Devices will denote how many bytes they can hold or process. The higher the number, the more data that can be stored or processed. It is now common that devices have gigabyte or terabyte storage capabilities, which is measured in one billion and one trillion bytes respectively.

behavior. Some of this knowledge is very basic. For instance, it is pretty apparent that a computer monitor, which is used to display information, is useless by itself without a computer. It only becomes functional when connected to a computer. Other issues are a bit more complex. Unless a computer has some specific hardware, such as an outside modem, modem card, or network interface (NIC) card, it can't usually connect to the Internet. Likewise, without a wireless network interface controller (WNIC) or Universal Serial Bus (USB) Wireless adapter, a computer can't connect to the Internet without a cable or telephone line connected to it. Storage devices, such as flash drives, are useless without a device (a computer) to read the data. Some devices and computers only become a risk when used in conjunction with one another (see Figure 4).

Obviously, as technology keeps advancing, it is getting harder to know all of a device's capabilities and therefore rule out that device poses a threat. For instance, a few years ago, a computer could be isolated rather easily from the Internet. Typically this was accomplished by removing a modem card and making sure it was not reinstalled. Additionally checking to insure the offender did not have Internet ac-

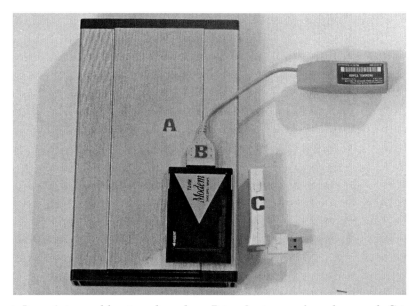

Figure 4. Item A is an old external modem. B is a laptop card modem card. C is a wireless USB modem.

cess at home via a telephone line, digital subscribe line (DSL), or cable connection also was a good added precaution. However, newer laptops come with built in WiFi making it possible to connect to a neighbor's network and the Internet. Even if the neighbor doesn't have WiFi, the laptop can be transported to a local WiFi "hot spot," such as a coffee shop or fast food restaurant, where the user can access the Internet. There are also WiFi adapters that can plug into a USB port providing WiFi network and/or Internet access (see Figure 4, Item C and Figures 5 and 6).

Mobile phones are another example. At one time most mobile phones did not have Internet access. Now it is getting harder to find phones that can't access the Internet. Gaming devices also now permit Internet browsing, chatting, etc. MP3 players, common for playing music, can now also be used to view images or videos. Frequently the only way for CCO to keep up with these newer devices and their capabilities is to examine them and to do online research (Figure 7).

CCO also need to be cautious about apparently damaged or dated computer equipment. They often can be made operational very easily. For example, a check fraudster presented a beat-up old laptop with a missing battery and power cord as the only computer in his posses-

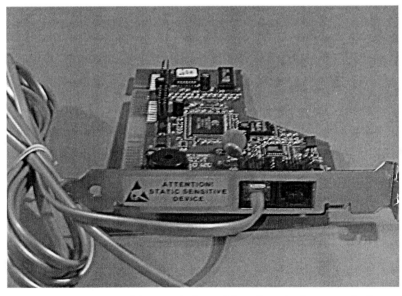

Figure 5. This is a modem card from a desktop. Note the telephone cord plugged into it.

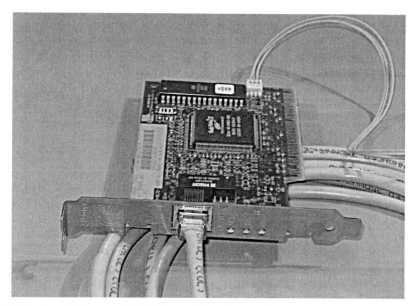

Figure 6. Desktop Ethernet Card. Note cable is larger than in Figure 5. This card allows Internet access through either Digital Subscriber Line (DSL) or cable.

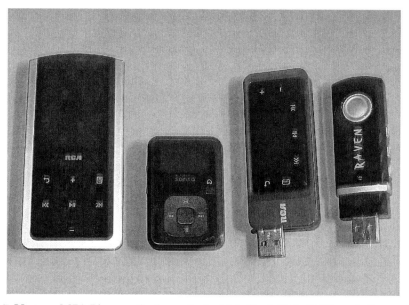

Figure 7. Various MP3 Players, the largest of which (far left) is 3 GB and allows viewing of images and videos.

sion, noting it was also nonfunctioning. Later, this same laptop was found connected to a printer and was being used to print bogus checks. In short, a device in apparent poor physical condition may still be capable of being used to commit violation behavior.

The next question that needs to be addressed is whether a particular device can be searched, monitored, and/or restricted (removed/disabled) by a CCO, so that any risk it presents is either minimized or eliminated. The key point here is whether the CCO can undertake the activity. Just about any device can be searched by someone. But does that effectively manage the risk if the search can't be undertaken in a timely manner and has to be conducted by someone other than the CCO? For instance, a gaming device can be searched. However, it is not an easy task and definitely not something that can be done as a routine computer management component. Few if any correction agencies have a computer forensic expert on call who can drop everything to search an X-Box 360® every few months to insure an offender was not using it to violate his or her conditions. It may be appropriate to prohibit the possession and use of such a device, particularly if the offense involved a high community risk, such as a minor victim.

Oftentimes offenders will have multiple computer components in their possession. Some examples are circuit boards/cards, hard drives, computer cases, and printers. These items are sometimes fully functional and some are just "junk." But checking out each of them is going to involve time and resources. Again a visual inspection can't always determine the device's functionality. Consider hard drives for instance. These devices store data and are needed for most computers to function.[2] It is not unusual for an offender to have several of these devices lying around. They may have upgraded their system and the device is still functioning or it may simply be broken. They can all be searched, unless they are truly nonfunctioning. But it can't always be determined until an attempt is made. Even if they are successfully searched and nothing is found, that does not stop their later use for violation behavior. For instance, one sex offender was recently bragging to an undercover agent that he regularly defeated his parole officer's efforts to search his computer by switching hard drives when a search was anticipated. In this way, the parole officer searched a drive that had no evidence of his illic-

---

2. There are bootable DVD/CDs with operating systems which allow one to operate a computer without a hard drive.

it activities, such as downloading child pornography or arranging with an undercover agent to have sex with a minor. The evidence of this activity was on a hard drive concealed from the parole officer.

Monitoring software may be installed, but that again involves resources. The CCO could seize the hard drive, but it will not take long to overwhelm an agency's evidence storage capability if all extraneous devices on all cases are seized. The offender could be directed to dispose of the device, but that doesn't preclude it returning to the offender's possession undetected at a later date. Leaving the device unsecured means it might have to be searched again.

In such cases, it might be best to take the excess devices, place them in a cardboard box, seal the box with tamper tape, and leave the box for the offender to maintain. A quick check of the box during subsequent field contacts will detect if it has been opened and that the devices maintained within have not been reconstituted for the offender's use. This does not prevent the offender from opening the box. However, they can't use the device without being discovered, which would then necessitate a search. This could have been undertaken with the seemingly damaged laptop that was later used for a bogus check-making operation. It is a simple method to minimize, if not eliminate, the risk excess components may pose. This approach's beauty is the offender maintains the device's possession, has to store it, but is prevented from using it. It does not take computer skills to place these devices in the box or to periodically check the tamper tape to insure they are still secure. Additionally, tamper tape can also be used to secure a computer case to prevent an offender from switching hard drives undetected to defeat search and/or monitoring efforts.

For devices that have to be used by an offender for some legitimate purpose, such as schooling or employment, computer monitoring and/or periodic searches will have to be employed to manage risk. However, some operating systems, such as Linux, are not conducive to using monitoring software.[3] A hardware device can be installed in such cases, provided no other keyboards can be installed on the system. Otherwise the use of this operating system will have to be prohibited or the computer will have to be subject to periodic searches. There is monitoring software for some mobile phones but not all of them. Gaming devices also

---

3. As will be discussed later most software for Linux operating systems emphases filtering and/or blocking as opposed to monitoring.

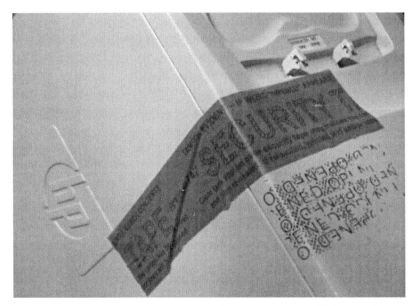

Figure 8. Tamper tape placed over access panel on computer and effects when removed.

Figure 9. Serial Port Hardware Keylogger, plugs between the keyboard and the computer.

can be searched but they can't have monitoring software installed on them. It should be apparent that a basic understanding of computer hardware and software will help CCO understand what is an appropriate course of action to minimize or eliminate risk (Figure 9).

COMPUTER BASICS

The devices that are physical and can be held are called hardware. The major hardware components fall into the following functions: input, output, storage, processing, electrical supply, and communication (Andrews, 2003). Most input and output devices are located outside of a computer case. Storage and processing components are usually inside of a computer. The Central Processing Unit (CPU) is the traffic cop for all other components. It receives, interprets, and/or sends data/instructions to or from other components. Andrews (2003) notes that for each hardware device to operate, the following are required: (1) a method for the CPU to communicate with the device; (2) software to instruct and control the specific device (also known as drivers); and (3) electricity to power the device (Figure 10).

Figure 10. Inside Computer Case. B and/or C are physically where hard drives are usually located.

Considering the process involved in the creation of a simple document will hopefully clarify this information. When someone types on a keyboard they are using an input device. The keystrokes they type send electronic signals to the CPU (processing device). The CPU interprets these signals and sends instructions to the monitor, an output device, which displays what was typed. If keystrokes are typed, which the CPU interprets as instructions to print the document, it sends instructions to the printer (another output device) to perform that function. If the keystrokes typed are interpreted by the CPU as instructions to save the document, the CPU sends instructions to the hard drive, a storage device, to save data to a file, which represents the document that was typed. Prior to the data actually being saved, it often exists in Random Access Memory (RAM), another device that only stores information temporary to make the system run more efficiently. However, data that exists only in RAM will remain only as long as the system's on. Once the system is shut down, the data in the RAM will be lost.[4]

The data and instructions to the CPU are communicated through a motherboard which oftentimes has other smaller cards or circuit boards, attached. Some of these cards also have "ports" which are simply plugs that allow devices outside of the computer case to connect and communicate with the CPU. Examples of such devices are keyboards, mouse, webcams, printers, monitors, scanners, external hard drives, modems, etc. In the past, these devices all required cables to plug into the ports to communicate with the CPU. With WiFi, many of these devices can communicate with the CPU with a WiFi card or adapter through radio waves.

All this communication requires electricity. The CPU receives current through the motherboard, which receives it from a power supply, which reduces the power from an electric outlet to an amount appropriate for computer devices. The power supply also provides electricity to the motherboard so the CPU can communicate with the various components. Some devices, such as printers and scanners have their own power supply.

---

4. Sometimes data that was in RAM will be saved to the hard drive, even if the user never wanted the information saved. The operating system will sometimes do this to allow the RAM to receive more data. The data that was in RAM but gets saved to the hard drive by the system can sometimes be found and recovered. Sometimes such data is overwritten as it was never meant to be saved by the user. It is therefore not a certainty that RAM data of an evidential value will be found.

Instructions that tell these devices how to operate or process information are programs or software. Software which provides a framework for all other software applications and hardware to be accessed by the user are called operating system programs. Examples of operating systems are: Windows, Apple, and Linux. Software that performs a specific user function, such as word processing, is an application program. Software which is very specific to a component and how it communicates with other components is called drivers. A CPU must be able to communicate with a component through this software or the device will not function properly.

For instance, when a new printer is purchased the drivers for that device must be installed on the computer or the CPU will not be able to send it instructions even if the printer has electricity and is plugged into the computer. Some operating systems have "plug and play" functionality, which means the common drivers are already installed as part of the operating system. This process oftentimes occurs when a USB flash drive is plugged into a computer for the first time. The newer operating system will search and usually find the drivers already installed on the system. However, if one tries to plug in a new USB flash drive into a computer with an older operating system, such as Windows 98, the device will not work as the drivers are not on that system. They have to be installed for the CPU to be able to communicate with the device.

This is a very basic overview of how computer components operate. The next sections will hone in on the information that is central for computer management of offenders.

Input and Output Devices

As was noted above, these devices are located, for the most part, outside of a computer case. Input devices include, keyboards, mice, microphones, game controllers/joy sticks, webcams, cameras, and scanners. Output devices include monitors, printers, and speakers. Computers such as laptops, mobile phones, and personal gaming devices will have many of the components built in. Common examples of built-in features are keyboards, mouse, controllers, monitors, microphones, speakers, cameras, and/or webcams.

For a user to interact with a computer, there must be some method to input data and receive it. This is basic and is not always a risk. For instance, a keyboard and mouse do not constitute a risk. However, some input devices in and of themselves constitute a risk for certain offenses. For instance, a webcam possessed by an offender on supervision for communicating inappropriately online with a minor is a risk. Another example is a digital camera possessed by an offender convicted of creating child pornography. A scanner in the possession of someone convicted of counterfeiting or identity theft is another example. Scanners have also been used by some sex offenders to morph or change legitimate images into child pornography.

Some of the risk from these devices can be mitigated rather easily. A webcam has no data retention capability and communication transmitted by the device through a computer cannot always be retrieved during a search. However, some monitoring software will alert when such a device is activated and will record some of the communication. Additionally, the device is not a necessity and it can be placed in a box with tamper tape or removed from the offender's possession rather easily. Monitoring software cannot be installed on a digital camera, but it may be searched rather easily. Additionally, if the risk is significant, it can also be secured or removed.

A scanner may have a legitimate function and may be more difficult to justify removing. It can be used to scan resumes, education materials, and other legitimate records. Additionally, the community risk may not be as serious as the examples of a webcam or digital camera in the possession of a sex offender. A scanning device that requires a computer can be managed as monitoring software will usually record the scanning. However, a stand-alone scanner/printer represents a device that can only be searched and, depending upon the risk, might be something that has to be secured or removed.

Most output devices such as monitors do not usually represent an unacceptable risk. However, they can be informative. One sex offender was found to have a monitor that was well beyond the normal size for a computer monitor. He apparently was using it to view pornography.

Printers usually aren't a significant problem based solely upon risk and frequently are required by the modern day user. Their operation, much like that of the scanner when used with a computer, will be captured. However, if they are combined with a scanner and can be operated independent of a computer, there may be an issue. This is particularly the case where scanning was central to the offense conduct, such as in counterfeiting and check/identity fraud.

Unfortunately, there are some input devices that have been created specifically for adult entertainment (sexual) purposes. These devices are thankfully rare. Obviously, for sex offenders, such devices should be secured or removed.

With the exception of scanner/printers/copiers, the discussion has not touched upon devices in which the various components are built into the computer, such as a webcam built into a laptop computer or a camera that is part of a mobile phone. Such built-in features are becoming more and more commonplace. In the case of a webcam built into a laptop, place tamper tape over the camera lens or rely on the monitoring software to pick it up when it is used. Mobile phones can be searched and images taken with a built-in digital camera can be retrieved. Additionally, some mobile phone monitoring software can alert and forward images taken with a built-in camera. Some mobile phone monitoring software can also disable the camera completely.

Beyond the exceptions noted above for digital cameras, printers, and scanners, there is usually no digital evidence associated with input and output devices. However, there may still be other reasons to seize such devices in a search. For instance, keyboards and mouse might contain DNA or fingerprint evidence. As noted previously in sex offense cases, they may reflect the presence of semen under ultraviolet light. There also may be passwords, significant websites, etc. taped under keyboards. In short, don't rule them out without thinking about why they might be significant to seize.

Storage

There are two kinds of storage, temporary (primary) and permanent (secondary). The CPU uses temporary storage for maintaining data and instructions during processing. As indicated previously, this is data saved in RAM, which only exists while the computer is on. There are components on the motherboard that are used for storing RAM. From a computer management point of view, they are of little concern for risk. However, the size of system's RAM can be an issue for running certain programs, notably bootable forensic CD/DVDs used to preview computers. If the system does not have enough RAM, the programs will not run. This is an issue usually with older systems.

Additionally, older systems may have difficulty running certain newer monitoring software for this reason. RAM can also be collected from a running system, which will be discussed later. However, once the system is off, the RAM storage devices contain no data.[5]

There are also chips that contain Read Only Memory (ROM). The chips contain basic information that is critical for the start-up or "booting" of a computer. In older chips, the ROM can't be altered. However, new chips have "flash" ROM, which can be modified. These instructions, called Basic Input/Out System (BIOS) provide information to the CPU on certain functions, such as accessing the monitor and where to locate the operating system.

Permanent (secondary) storage is very significant for CCO management. Permanent storage devices include internal and external hard drives, optical disc drives,[6] and flash (USB) drives. Older storage devices that might be encountered include 3.5 inch floppy drives, Jazz drives, and Zip drives. Any device which maintains data independent of whether a computer is on is a permanent storage device. The data is either stored on the device itself, such as a hard drive or flash drive or on media that is inserted in the device, such as CD/DVD/BDs. These devices are where the system looks for the operating system to "boot" or start up. The BIOS noted above, will have a device order of where the CPU should look at for the operating system. Usually, the first operating system the CPU finds is the first the computer will start up. If no bootable device is found, the CPU will return an error message and the computer will not function properly (see Figure 11 and 12).

---

5. RAM devices are important for CCO involved in computer forensics. They should seek computers with a large amount of RAM in order to properly operate forensic software, which are oftentimes memory-intensive programs.

6. The types of optical drives that can be found are Compact Disk (CD), Digital Versatile or Digital Video Disc (DVD), and Blu-Ray® (BD). Blu-Ray uses blue-violet lasers to read and write data, as opposed to red light lasers, which are used in CD and DVD drives. Many modern drives have not only the capacity to read data but also save or "burn" data to them. There are two basic types of CDs and DVDs. Those that can have data recordable once, such as CD-R and DVD-R and those that can be save data more than once, (rewritable), as in CD-RW and or DVD-RW. Likewise, BD come in BD-R (record once) and BD-RE (rewritable more than once). CDs typically can store up to 700 megabytes of data. DVDs, depending upon the type can storage anywhere from 4.7 up to 17.08 gigabytes (GB). BD push the storage range to 25 to 50 GB, with new capacity approaching up to 500 GB. Typically, these drives are "backward" capable, meaning they can read information from an older format. For instance, a Blu-Ray device can frequently read data on a DVD or even CD. However, an older device, such as a CD drive can't read data saved in a newer format, such as a DVD or a BD (CD Information Center and Blu-Ray.Com).

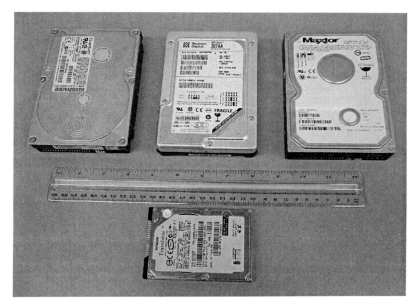

Figure 11. Hard Drives, 30 to 60 GB. The three behind the ruler are from a desktop and the one in front is from a laptop.

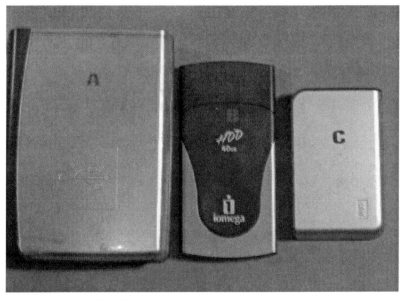

Figure 12. External 40 GB USB Drives. C, the smallest, does not require its own power source.

Computers may have more than one hard drive and some hard drives are divided into more than one "partition" or area. Each hard drive and even each partition may have its own operating system.[7] Additionally, some CD/DVDs can contain operating systems that a computer can start from, such as Knoppix, a Linux operating system. Additionally, there are "rescue" or "recovery" CD/DVDs, which contain basic operating systems to repair the normal operating system or recover data from the hard drive. As such, devices that can read CD and DVD can be in the boot order listing. Newer computers also permit USB devices to be listed in boot order as they can also contain operating systems.

At a computer's start-up, there are function keys displayed prior to the operating system starting up, such as F12, which can be pushed to access the BIOS settings. In these settings, the boot order of these devices can be modified. For instance, the boot order could be changed from look from (1) hard drive, (2) CD/DVD, and (3) USB Device to 1) CD/DVD drive, (2) hard drive, (3) USB device. A device can also be removed from the listing or deactivated as a bootable device.

It is also important to note that the BIOS setting may also include a password option. If activated, a password must be entered to operate the computer and to make changes to the system, such as the order of bootable devices.

The discussion about installed boot order and these devices is important to CCO for several reasons. Operating systems change data. If one can prevent the operating system from starting up and accessing the data with another controlled operating system, they can possibly preview the data without making any changes to it. This is the heart of an on-site preview with bootable disks.

Additionally, monitoring software is installed on the device containing the operating system. It starts up with the operating system. If the offender can bypass the operating system that contains the monitoring software, he or she can bypass the CCO's management efforts. For instance, the CCO installs monitoring software on a hard drive. The boot order for this computer is look for the operating system first

---

7. A single hard drive can have numerous partitions. A computer operating system will denote a partition with a specific letter. Partitions can be used to store data and to separate different operating systems from one another. Some partitions can also be concealed from the operating system. They are oftentimes only detected with the use of forensic software.

on the CD/DVR drive then the hard drive. As there is never a CD/DVR in the drive, the computer goes to the hard drive and starts up. However, if the offender places a bootable disk, such as Knoppix in the CD/DVR drive, the computer will start up with Knoppix and bypass the monitoring software altogether. Additionally, these bootable CDs may not save information to the hard drive, such as web browsing history. As such, there may be no evidence on the hard drive that offender bypassed the monitoring software in this manner.[8]

Thankfully, most offenders are unaware of this or that such a thing as bootable CD/DVR disk exists. Additionally, these bootable operating systems can sometimes be challenging to configure to work with all peripheral devices, such as printers.[9]

Additionally, permanent storage devices are also where the data is saved. Certain monitoring software will record its results to the hard drive. Additionally, this is where documents and images are frequently saved by the user. This is where web browsing artifacts and e-mails are found. Information that is saved by the computer unbeknownst to the user is also saved on the hard drive. In short, this is where evidence of noncompliance is located and therefore these devices are extremely important for a CCO. Permanent storage devices and media therefore constitute a risk as well as an opportunity.

The challenge for the CCO is to determine how significant a storage device is in any given situation. If conducting a search based upon reasonable suspicion, every storage device and media can be significant and should be previewed or seized for later examination. There are exceptions. For instance, numerous CDs or DVDs with legitimate factory labeling reflecting music or games might be appropriate to leave behind. The reason being that the offender can't save contraband to this media. DVDs containing movies can likewise be left behind, provided they are not themes that are contraband in and of themselves, such as pornography in a sex offender case.

Software CD or DVD might be significant if they related to the alleged noncompliance activity, such as check creation software in a check fraud case, or a wiping utility used to defeat monitoring efforts.

---

8. The exception is if a Linux bootable CD is used on certain systems containing specific Linux operating systems. In such cases, the computer will record that the system has been started up with another system.
9. These bootable CD/DVRs will be discussed for the CCO conducting certain preview functions.

Additionally, a CD containing an operating system such as Linux or a bootable operating system, such as Knoppix, is appropriate for seizure or securing, as they can be used to defeat monitoring efforts.

However, does the presence of a CD or DVD present a risk in non-search situations? It is not uncommon for users to regularly back up important legitimate files on a CD or DVD. Hard drives sometimes "crash" and if there is no copy of an important document, such as a tax return, business record, etc., the user is at a loss. Prohibiting blank CD/DVDs therefore may be a bit overkill. If monitoring software is installed on system, it will likely record any viewing or saving of inappropriate matter from the CD/DVD. The concern therefore is the CD/DVD may contain a bootable operating system, which can bypass the monitoring. Check CD/DVDs for hand-written marking or labeling and consider spot checking them as needed during field visits. Also focus on CD/DVDs that are left in the drive or nearby the computer, indicating they are used regularly. Additionally, be suspicious of any CD or DVD found concealed.

During search situations, be aware that the seemingly blank CDs or DVDs may be significant and should be seized or at least checked. In one case, an offender was regularly backing up his system to CDs and then wiping the laptop. A limited on-site preview failed to detect any noncompliance. However, a review of the back-up CDs revealed numerous incidents of noncompliance. Obviously, seemingly blank disks may contain contraband.

USB Flash drives pose the same concerns as CD/DVDs, however, unlike CD/DVDs don't come in packs of 25 or more. In search situations, they are fair game for previewing and/or seizure. In monitoring situations, they should be limited to only one or two, consistent with the requirements of the case. Others should be secured or removed (Figure 13).

Flash media, such as memory cards for cameras, likewise can be used for noncompliance. Some cards can store several gigabytes of data. Coupled with a USB reader, a card could contain a bootable operating system. They can also be used to view and create pornography. Limit excessive possession of memory cards. The number should be limited to that needed for legitimate purposes and that can be reasonably searched as needed (Figure 14).

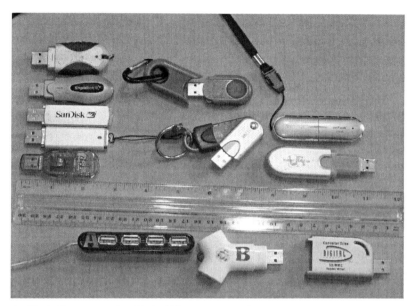

Figure 13. Flash Drives and a Hub (A). B is a combination drive and hub. After B is a USB Card Reader. Size represented range from 64 MB to 4 GB.

Figure 14. Memory Cards and an Adapter. The smaller one is taken from a mobile phone but is the same size, 4 GB, as the larger card.

There are also WiFi hard drives, which can be accessed remotely from a system. These storage devices can even be hidden within walls, ceilings, or floor boards. They are particularly a concern for search situations. There have been cases where a computer is removed for a more thorough search only to discover that the contraband was not saved on the hard drive but on a WiFi device hidden in a wall. Monitoring software will capture the accessing and saving of information from or to a WiFi hard drive (Figures 15 and 16).

Storage devices can be searched and/or monitored. The key is to know what they are and, if possible, to limit the number of such devices and/or storage media to that which can be reasonably searched or monitored. This is one risk that cannot be eliminated. It can only be minimized. A committed offender, with knowledge and a small bootable USB device can defeat monitoring efforts. However, a surprise home visit may detect the device's use. Likewise, it may be discovered from a concerned family member or during a polygraph examination. The point is to manage risk, as it can't be eliminated entirely.

Storage devices are also of important consideration for CCO involved in collecting digital evidence. When a hard drive is imaged, the target drive or media must be the same or larger size. Capturing RAM off a live machine also requires a media with the proper size or not all of the data will be captured.

Processing, Communication, and Electrical Supply

These devices can't be searched and can't be monitored per se by software. Their significance comes from their presence in an offender's possession. A CPU is useless without the the other computer components. However, a very high-speed CPU within a computer provides the offender the ease to view images and videos much easier than with a computer with a slower CPU. Likewise, a computer with a high-speed CPU is a must for any CCO involved in computer forensics because of the amount of data that usually has been processed during imaging or analysis.

A motherboard is needed for a computer to operate. It allows all the components to communicate with one another and it provides power to the internal components. It may contain many additional circuit boards or peripheral cards, which allow the user to have Internet

Figure 15. Wireless Router, which might be associated with the Internet and/or wireless hard drive.

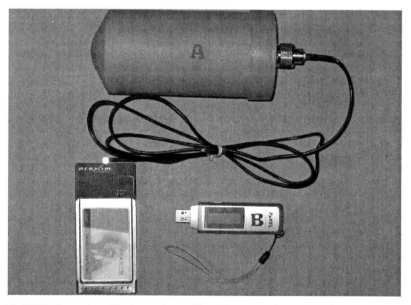

Figure 16. WiFi Detection Devices. A is a Yagi directional antenna for use with a laptop. B is wireless network device. Both devices were provided free during training at SEARCH.org.

connections or access to a cable or WiFi network. Without these additional cards, the computer has limited ability to connect to the Internet or a network. However, these limitations can be overcome if the computer has a USB port. Additionally, if the motherboard still has serial or parallel card[10] the computer may be connected to an external modem using either the serial or parallel port as appropriate.

An electrical supply is required for all computers to operate. For desktop computers, there is a power supply inside the case, which receives an electrical current from a wall plug. Some users will have uninterrupted power supply which provides power in the event the electricity goes off. When seizing a computer, it is recommended to pull the plug out of the back of the computer case and not from the outlet due to concern the user may have an uninterrupted power supply.

Laptop computers will have special cords that plug into the device. However, merely unplugging the cord will not remove a laptop from its power source as there usually is a battery in the device. It is oftentimes recommended to remove the battery during previews or seizures. The presence of a laptop cord is a red flag that there is a computer somewhere nearby.

Software

Software plays a role in computer management in several respects. The first area is the operating system. For instance, the monitoring software must be specific to the operating system that it is installed on. One can't install monitoring software designed for a Windows operating system on a computer running an Apple operating system. Likewise, newer monitoring software for a Windows operating system can't always be installed on a system running an older version of Windows. As was eluded to earlier, some operating systems, such as Linux, do not have monitoring software that can be installed by a CCO.

Additionally, some operating systems, such as those that are in gaming systems, are not easily examined with common forensic software packages. The result is that such systems require tools that are

---

10. Serial connections transfer data one bit at a time while parallel connections transfer several bits of data simultaneously. Serial ports were used for keyboards, mouse, and monitors. Parallel ports were used for printers and later modems. They have been replaced to a large extent by USB and Firewire connections, which have much faster data transfer rates.

sometimes beyond the ability of individuals accustomed to using "off-the-shelf" forensic software.

Mobile phone operating systems and file structure are frequently equally challenging for examiners; the reason being the hardware and software are often changed by the manufacturer or service provider. A forensic technique that worked one week on a mobile phone may not work as well the next week on another phone of the same make and model. It is a constant challenge. These issues thankfully are not as prevalent with desktop and laptop computers. Examiners usually only have to adjust when the new computer operating system comes out every few years with these devices.

Application software is another CCO concern if its presence represents a risk of either noncompliance or defeating management efforts. Software that can be used for counterfeiting or fraud are examples. Software that allows individuals to use peer-to-peer networks or file sharing are problematic for sex offenders involved with child pornography. Software that can be used to defeat management efforts include anti-spy, wiping, and concealment (encryption/steganography) programs. Programs that are antivirus or firewall, however, are legitimate programs that must be accommodated when possible.[11] In short, some of these programs may have to be removed from the offender's system or they will have to be configured to allow computer management efforts.

Software (drivers) that allows devices to communicate with the CPU and other components becomes important for a CCO when it becomes necessary to use a specific device, such as a USB device, on the offender's computer. CCO frequently use USB devices to install monitoring software, preview using forensic software, and save evidence from the offender's computer. However, if the USB device is plugged into an older computer, such as one running Windows 98, it may not function.[12] As a result, CCO doing field installations or exam-

---

11. Antivirus programs protect the offender's computer from malicious attack. However, they also may protect the CCOs devices as well. An officer's USB device plugged into the system for monitoring or a compliance check can be infected if the offender does not regularly run antivirus software. A firewall software prevents the offender's system from being accessed directly or from sending information without the user's knowledge from the system. Exceptions can be made for communication that is occurring due to monitoring software usage.

12. A USB device may still function on an older machine if the computer can boot to a CD containing an operating system, such as Knoppix. This is because the device is communicating through Knoppix, which has the appropriate drivers installed, as opposed to Windows 98.

inations have to be prepared to have their software stored on another media, such as a CD or even a 3.5-inch floppy.

CCO must be aware that their software also has license requirements. For commercial packages, common with forensic and monitoring, the software frequently can't be installed on more than one computer. If this occurs, the user is violating the copyright restrictions. Some software vendors have methods in place to detect if software has been installed on more than one computer without a corresponding license. Some vendors, particularly with monitoring software will disable the software. Frequently monitoring and forensic software are only licensed for use for a year. After the year is up, the vendor will not provide updates and/or support. In the case of monitoring software, it may stop forwarding keyword alerts.[13] In short, follow the license requirements for all software used in computer management.

Other Concerns

Thus far the discussion has centered on stand-alone computers, such as desktops and laptops. Computers can also be connected together in a network. This is common in a business setting, but is occurring in homes as well. Networks can be connected via cables or by WiFi. Small area networks found in homes, small businesses, and small geographic areas are often referred to as a local area network (LAN). A LAN can be connected to a larger network, called a wide area network (WAN). A CCO may confront a LAN although a WAN is not inconceivable in the future. Monitoring software can be installed on a single computer or multiple computers in a LAN. Depending upon how the network is set up, a target computer might be able to boot up an operating system from another computer which is not installed on the target computer. Again, this would bypass the monitoring efforts. Computers on a LAN can likewise be searched.

The important think to remember is a LAN, and particularly a WAN, may include a server, which is a special dedicated computer

---

13. One vendor has the monitoring software first forward the alert to them, which they in turn forward on to the designated e-mail address. During this process they check the licensing information. If the license has expired the alert might not be forwarded on to the designated e-mail. The software frequently will continue to monitor and record activity. However, if a critical update is not made it will also eventually stop functioning.

that services the needs of the entire network. Additionally, there may be a computer specifically for data storage on the network. Special steps may be needed to properly search for an offender's activities. Additionally, there may be very specific instructions for shutting down the network prior to seizure to prevent damage to the system. Thankfully, these issues are not common-place in supervision activities.

CONCLUSION

This chapter was meant to provide a basic understanding of computers and their operations, specifically as they pertain to computer management. There are hundreds, if not thousands, of computer-related text and handbooks available. Likewise, there are numerous computer-related classes. Most individuals, including CCO, as a result, view gaining a rudimentary understanding of computers as an insurmountable obstacle. However, as this chapter demonstrates, it is not an impossible task to understand technology if it is taken one "bit" at a time.

REFERENCES

Abrams, C. Retrieved http://www.brainyquote.com/quotes/quotes/c/creight ona207381.html.
Andrews, Jean. (2003). *A+ in depth.* Boston: Thompson, Boston.
Blu-Ray.Com. http://www.blu-ray.com/info/.
CD Information Center, http://www.cd-info.com/.

Chapter 7

PRINCIPLES OF EFFECTIVE
COMPUTER MONITORING

In preparing for battle I have always found that plans are
useless, but planning is indispensable.
–Dwight D. Eisenhower, U.S. General and President
(1890–1969)

Many argue that monitoring offenders' computer access is next to
impossible. There are computers in almost every home, library,
school, business, etc. Additionally there are small storage devices, such
as flash drives that can conceal image files and Internet browsing.
These same devices are extremely portable and are very easy to hide.
In fact, some can be concealed inside pens or watches (see Figures 1
and 2). Many small devices, such as mobile phones, Palm Pilots, etc.
have the same computer functionality, including Internet access.
Modern laptops coupled with thousands of wireless "hot spots" in coffee shops, hotels, airports, and other public areas, make the Internet
accessible anywhere at anytime. Finally, gaming devices are now
capable of Internet browsing and live chatting. There are also portable
gaming devices that not only connect to the Internet but also to other
nearby users' devices. Theses issues and the continuing development
of technology make managing an offender's computer use challenging.

The task can be daunting, but it is not impossible. Consider for a
moment substance use. Drugs and corresponding paraphernalia, for
the most part, are easily concealed. They are used in situations that are
not usually open to probation/parole or law enforcement officials.

Many offenders are able to continue to use drugs for a time, but eventually they are detected. In short, probation and parole agencies can detect and prevent offenders from using drugs via drug testing, searches, and collateral contacts. It is not 100 percent all the time, but that does not mean we don't try to manage the risks. This is what was previously pointed to in Chapter 2 as the essence of computer management (Tanner, 2007). This chapter focuses on some core principles involved in effective computer management.

PRINCIPLE 1: HAVE A PLAN

The first step in computer management is to have an overall risk management plan. In developing the plan, what do the supervision conditions reflect. Do they prohibit all access to a computer? What about access to the Internet? Are there exceptions to the prohibition, such as employment or school? What do the conditions authorize to manage the risk, such as the installation of monitoring software and search and seizure? Do these conditions align with the cyber-risk identified through steps noted in Chapter 5 and if not, can the conditions be modified to enhance risk management?

Some jurisdictions have developed standard conditions for computer management which frequently include computer restriction and monitoring programs (CRMP). Core conditions provide for specific restrictions, search/seizure, and/or monitoring, with a CRMP being a list of specific requirements to further enhance computer management. Program components usually include requirements to disclose all computer and Internet access, passwords, etc. and restrict hardware and software to only those approved. A sample CRMP is contained in Appendix A. Below are several options for conditions incorporating the use of a CRMP[1]:

Option A: Total Computer/Internet Restrictions

The offender[2] is prohibited from access to any computer, Internet Service Provider, bulletin board system or any other public or pri-

---

1. Obviously, consult legal authorities in the appropriate jurisdiction as some states and/or agencies have approved conditions in place.
2. The term offender can be replaced with child, defendant, probationer, parole, etc. as the supervision type warrants.

vate computer network or the service at any location (including employment or education) without prior written approval of the AGENCY. Any approval shall be subject to any conditions set by the AGENCY with respect to that approval, but shall include at a minimum participation in the AGENCY'S Computer Restriction and Monitoring Program. Any computer found in the offender's possession is subject to seizure and/or search.

Option B: Total Internet Restriction

The offender is prohibited from access to any "on-line" computer service at any location (including employment or education) without prior written approval of the AGENCY. This includes any Internet Service Provider, bulletin board system, any other public or private computer network, or social networking site. Any approval shall be subject to any conditions set by the AGENCY with respect to that approval, but shall include at a minimum periodic computer searches and/or the installation of monitoring software and participation in the AGENCY'S Computer Restriction and Monitoring Program.

Option C: Computer/Internet Access Permitted

The offender shall consent to the AGENCY conducting periodic unannounced examinations of his/her computer system(s), which may include retrieval and copying of all memory from hardware/software and/or removal of such system(s) for the purpose of conducting a more thorough inspection and will consent to having installed on his/her computer(s), at the his/her expense, any hardware/software to monitor his/her computer use or prevent access to particular materials. The offender hereby consents to periodic inspection of any such installed hardware/software to insure it is functioning properly. The offender shall abide by all rules of the Computer Restriction and Monitoring Program.

Besides knowing the cyber-risk present in any case CCO must be aware of the offender's computer or Internet access. This frequently can be a moving target. However, it can be nailed down by requiring the offender at the onset to disclose in writing his or her access to computers and the Internet. This is best accomplished with the use of a prepared questionnaire, which must be completed in a specific number of days. The previously mentioned CMRP mandates this information's submission. A properly developed questionnaire should elicit information on all e-mail and social networking profiles and Internet/computer access, including via mobile phones and gaming devices. It should also obtain information that may pertain to legal issues noted in Chapter 4, such as Privacy Protection Act (PPA), 42 U.S.C. § 2000aa. Appendix B includes a sample Computer Usage Questionnaire which covers these areas of concern.

Requiring the offender to disclose in writing what computer(s) and/or Internet access they have provides CCO with a baseline on how best to monitor the risk. Additionally, it establishes what devices the offender had at supervision's commence. Any devices found later on which were not listed and/or approved could be considered contraband, searched, and/or seized.

A questionnaire can also provide additional insight into the offender's expertise level. For instance, are all items covered and if so, how detailed are the answers? Very detailed answers may be an indication that the offender has a lot of technical expertise. Eventually, the accuracy of questionnaire will need to be verified via an inspection. This means going to the offender's home and/or work site and accounting for the computer(s) and/or components reflected on the questionnaire. It may also require a visual inspection of the inside of the computer.

After obtaining this baseline, are there tools available to the CCO to manage the risk? In some cases, there is no monitoring technology available that will work with either the hardware or the operating system that the offender uses. Remember some operating systems, such as Linux, are not conducive to monitoring software installation. Likewise the options for installing monitoring software on mobile phones are limited. There is no monitoring software for gaming devices. These factors may limit computer management to periodic searches, third-party contacts, and reviewing records, such as mobile phone billing statements.

If determined appropriate, who pays for the installation of monitoring software, the offender, the agency, or is it "shared"? These issues are oftentimes based upon an agency's budget and upon who should own the software at the end of supervision, the agency or the offender.

Additionally, does the agency have the personnel who have the expertise to use these tools? Some tools, particularly monitoring software, require very little training. Others, such as forensic tools, can be more complicated. How will the agency deploy or use these tools to accomplish the computer risk management plan? Equally, important is whether an agency will allow CCO to use these new technologies. Answers to these questions must be obtained before going to an offender's home to install monitoring software or to do a search.

Again, with all these factors considered, are the conditions sufficient for management of an offender's cyber-risk? If not, can the conditions be modified to assist in monitoring? For instance, a sex offender who is allowed Internet access may agree to have monitoring software installed on his or her computer but refuse to give up their X-Box 360 or Wii. In such cases, pointing out the difficulties in managing risk for these devices, coupled with the offender's overall risk may convince the appropriate authority to provide a specific condition prohibiting the offender's possession and/or use. This action will reinforce CCO efforts to manage the cyber-risk.

PRINCIPLE 2: LIMIT ACCESS

One of the easiest ways to defeat monitoring is to use a system that is not being watched. Imagine the futility of installing monitoring software on an offender's home computer and he promptly goes to a friend's home to download pornography on a nonmonitored system. Additionally, purchasing another laptop and concealing it provides an avenue for offenders to avoid periodic computer searches as well as the deployment of monitoring software. Without a prohibition against this conduct, there is no sanction that can be applied when the offender does just that. There must be a condition or program requirement that prohibits nonapproved computer and/or Internet use. Along with this requirement, it must be clear what the offender can use, such as the monitored computer or one subject to periodic searches. Additionally, there must also be a prohibition against offenders obtaining additional hardware or software without advance approval. An offender who obtains an unapproved firewall could stop monitoring information from being forwarded. An offender who obtains wiping utility could erase all evidence of noncompliance, defeating a search. The best method is to provide written approval, clearly delineating what can and cannot be used by the offender. Appendix C provides a form which lists specific programs that can't be used, regardless of whether computer monitoring and/or searches are the management method chosen. The form also provides space for the officer to approve a specific computer.

Frequently the question arises about an offender's school or work computer. Schools do not want their systems used for viewing pornography or downloading pirated music, movies, or games. Businesses also have a vested interest in making sure their computers and systems are not misused. Employees may waste away their working hours on the Internet. More than one business has also been victimized by allowing employees unfettered access to computerized trade secrets or important business records. As a result, many schools and/or businesses may already be deploying monitoring and/or filtering software. The question that remains is how effective are their efforts? This requires the officer to do some investigation to ascertain, the offender's access to computers/Internet; their need for same; and whether monitoring is occurring. Table 5 has some questions to assist in that regard. A similar investigation is warranted if the offender is enrolled in school.

Certain employment opportunities, particularly for high cyber-risk cases, create significant challenges to computer management. For instance, offenders employed as systems administrators can circumvent all monitoring that may normally be present in the employment setting. In fact, they are frequently the ones in charge of the monitoring of the employer's computer system. Additionally, the nature of their position allows them free rein over numerous other employees' computers. Depending upon the circumstances and the risk posed by the offender, a special employment condition such as follows, may be warranted:

Special Employment Restriction

The offender cannot be employed directly or indirectly as a systems administrator, computer installer, programmer, or "trouble shooter" for computer equipment or in any similar position.

Table 5.
EMPLOYER QUESTIONS

Question	Implication
What is the normal work schedule of the offender?	Working odd hours may provide "private" time on computer.
Does the offender have a computer(s) assigned to him or her and if so provide a description?	Creates problems for monitoring and accountability.
Does the offender have access to other employees' computers?	
Does the offender have Internet access at workstation?	No Internet access reduces risk for some offenders.
Is the Internet and/or computer access needed to perform his or duties?	If they don't need computer/Internet can it be prohibited at work without jeopardizing their employment.
Does the employer monitor computer/Internet activity?	If yes, maybe their assistance can be gained to provide notification of problem behaviors. Make sure it isn't the offender who is responsible for monitoring at the work site.
If no monitoring is in place, will the employer authorize monitoring software and/or hardware to be installed on the computer(s) assigned to the offender?	If they authorize installation get their written consent. Appendix D has such a form which can be used for any third party. If they don't other methods, such as getting consent for periodic inspections or searches of work computer or frequent work visits to check on the offender's use will have to be utilized.

Cases not involving a sex offense, such as a computer crime offense (hacking, unauthorized/exceeding access, theft of services) may not require the installation of monitoring software/hardware. These individuals' livelihood frequently depends on their access to computers and a complete employment ban regarding technology may not be warranted, particularly if they are first-time offenders. The following condition may be considered to address third party risk in such cases:

Special Third-Party Notification for Computer Cases

Within 30 days of being directed, the offender shall provide the AGENCY a list of his/her current customers' identities (names, addresses, and telephone numbers) and he/she shall advise all of his/her current customers of his/her conduct in the present case. Prior to gaining any access to other computer systems/data, the offender will notify the AGENCY of the name, address, and telephone number of the person with legal authority over such systems/data and the purpose of gaining such access. Additionally, the offender shall notify the legal authority over such systems/data of his/her conduct in the present case prior to accessing their systems/data. The offender will permit the AGENCY to inspect any records pertaining to his/her customer information on a periodic basis. In the event the offender secures employment with a company, as opposed to self-employment, he/she will be required to notify his/her employer of his/her offense conduct, if he/she is required to perform the duties of system administrator, computer installer, programmer, or "trouble shooter," for computer equipment or any similar position. Finally, the offender will permit the AGENCY to verify his/her compliance with this third party notification condition.

PRINCIPLE 3: ACTIVELY LOOK FOR CIRCUMVENTION

As alluded to above, the easiest way around monitoring software is to get to a system that isn't being watched, such as a friend's house, a library, purchasing a laptop, etc. The possibilities are endless. One of the first steps is to establish how much time they normally spend on the computer or Internet. This information is requested on the Computer Usage Questionnaire contained in Appendix B. Document this information and see if the monitoring process shows a drop in reported use over time. This may be an indication that they have obtained access elsewhere. Traditional field work is also very important. Conduct surprise home visits. Talk to the offender's family. Where are they spending their time when they aren't at home? Are they at a friend or relative's house? Get out and talk to the friend or relative and find out what they do there. An offender's frequent visits to wireless hot spots are also a red flag that an offender may be accessing another computer. A wireless detector may be needed to determine if someone's un-protected wireless network is bleeding into the offender's residence, unknowingly giving them Internet access. Of equal importance are periodic requests for bank and credit card statements. Look for large purchases, indicative of a computer or regular monthly charges for In-ternet Service Providers. Also don't forget to review mobile phone records. These may indicate that an offender is accessing the Internet beyond their monitored desktop via their mobile phone provider net-work. Additionally, periodically require the offender to update infor-mation they have provided on their computer and Internet access. Appendix C includes a form for just such a purpose.

Periodically perform cyberspace investigations to determine if the offender has obtained unauthorized Internet access or additional e-mail accounts or social networking profiles. Some of the techniques for conducting such are discussed later.

Officers should also have the ability to conduct a search of the offender's residence, car, or place of business. It is just too easy to hide a laptop, flash drive, mobile device, etc. and bring it out for illicit use. If the offender's conditions authorize and it is feasible, use periodic polygraph examinations to detect unauthorized access to unmonitored systems.

These efforts serve another purpose besides detection, specifically deterrence. Offenders will obviously become aware of questions with family or friends concerning computer use and may reconsider at-tempts to use others' computers to circumvent their monitoring. Additionally, knowing that a search is possible can be a deterrent to an offender purchasing a laptop or other computer component and attempting to conceal it. Periodic polygraphs, particularly for sex offender cases, also serve as a deterrent to seeking computer or Internet access beyond that which is monitored. The bottom line is, don't be content with waiting for the monitoring results forwarded to detect noncompliance. Be proactive!

PRINCIPLE 4: UTILIZE A RESILIENT METHOD

Whatever monitoring method is deployed must be stealthy and resilient. The characteristic of being stealthy is the first line of defense. If the offender can't find it, he can't easily disable it. Don't alert the offender to the software's name being installed. Don't let them watch while it is being installed. Use tamper tape to prevent the hard drives from being switched. Additionally, the monitoring software should not be readily apparent and show up in the Start-Up Menu or the Task Manager for Windows operating systems. They also should not be readily apparent in Program File Folders for Windows operating systems. Be aware that improper installation of monitoring software will also make them readily detected and disabled by antivirus software and firewalls. These same rules apply when dealing with non-Windows operating systems.

The method should also be resilient. It should not be susceptible to inadvertent deletion or tampering. Obviously anti-spy software is something that should be prohibited. Nevertheless monitoring software should not be easily disabled in the event it is obtained. For particularly difficult cases, it might be appropriate to deploy more than one monitoring method. This makes it harder for the offender to delete one package without being detected and recorded by the other. As an added measure, a hardware device, such as a Key Ghost Logger®, could also be deployed, to record all key strokes typed on the system. Such a hardware device is not susceptible to anti-spy software (see Figure 9).

PRINCIPLE 5: RELIABILITY AND ACCURACY

Most monitoring software uses a variety of methods for recording what it monitors. These methods include screen shots and/or activity databases. Some software also includes built-in features for verifying their monitoring reports veracity. CCO need to be aware of what monitoring software does and doesn't record. Test the software out. For instance, when a particular monitoring software is being considered, request a trial or demo version. Most vendors will allow an officer to use a demo version or a trial test for a brief time. Install it and determine how accurate it records user activity. Document the test and maintain the results. They may be needed in case the monitoring results from a offender's computer come into question.

Computer forensic examiners likewise test forensic software to insure it is reliable and accurate. Although time constraints may limit the opportunity to do so, this practice is strongly encouraged for agencies using periodic searches as the prominent method for managing computer risk.

PRINCIPLE 6: UTILIZE ALERTS

The better monitoring software packages have a method for alerting when a certain behavior occurs. Usually, this alert occurs when a keyword is typed or appears in a web page or document. The alert can also be triggered if a user attempts a specific action, such as chatting or going to a prohibited website. The software will forward a message via the Internet to a specific e-mail account, of the alert's context including the time and date. The feature's utility is obvious for an officer trying to manage an offender's computer use. The only caveat with using alerts is to be careful what terms are used. Select terms that do not normally appear on a web page. It may seem a good idea to use the word "sex" for sex offender until one gets inundated with hundreds if not thousands of false hits as this word comes up in the context of other than sexual activity. In short, be selective. A better word starts with "F" but rhymes with duck. This word will generate less false positives.

The best option is to use software that can alert using multiple factors. For instance, software that will only send an alert when the "F" word appears along with the words girl, boy, etc. will generate far fewer false positives than a single alert scheme. Some software can also trigger alerts based upon the proximity of a target word with another word. For instance, the "F" word might have to be within five words of the word girl or boy.

Additionally, some monitoring software will alert officers if the offender has attempted to delete a component or conduct online research on the software or its processes. These are obviously valuable features to have when managing offenders' computer use.

PRINCIPLE 7: REVIEW NOTIFICATIONS/DATA

The ability to monitor is worthless if no one is reviewing the results. This is frequently the problem that confronts systems administrators who have computers logging all attempted hacks and no one reviews them until it is too late. Someone must go through the notifications and/or data that is produced by the monitoring process. This should be done promptly, on a regular basis, and the results documented, whether or not they were problematic. Equally important is someone needs to be responsible to detect a significant lack of any notifications and/or data. Obviously, this may be an indication that the offender is complying but it also may mean that the monitoring software has stopped functioning. A quick work around when installing software that only generates alert, is to add a specific pattern, which the offender can be instructed to periodically type. For instance, the sentence "I want to test the software now" could be made one word by deleting the spaces. The offender types this "word" and an alert would be generated, thereby confirming that the software is still operating without requiring an in person field contact.

PRINCIPLE 8: ACCESSIBILITY

The results of monitoring must be able to be accessed by more than one staff person. If for some reason, the person becomes permanently incapacitated, the agency must be able to retrieve the monitoring results or turn-off the monitoring at the time a person is off supervision. One method for insuring that no matter what the monitoring process functions properly is documentation. Documentation must start from the very beginning and includes the software installed, date/time of installations; all passwords and hot keys needed to activate the software; the e-mail addresses and passwords for where alerts are forwarded; and any significant other information that may be needed to retrieve information or uninstall the software. Agencies should also develop uniform or standard operating procedures for installing monitoring software so any officer can access monitoring software if they know the approved procedures. As an added measure, it is suggested that at least one other staff member be knowledgeable about how to install/uninstall monitoring software and retrieve monitoring reports.

PRINCIPLE 9: AVOID NEGATIVE IMPACT ON OTHERS

Everyone who uses a "managed" computer must have a clear understanding that the system is being monitored, this includes nonoffenders. Both software and hard copy notices, such as stickers (This Computer Is Being Monitored by AGENCY), serve this purpose. There should be as little disruption of a nonoffender's computer use on the monitored system as possible. Most monitoring software will not adversely affect system performance. However, any disruptions need to be investigated promptly to ascertain if they center around the monitoring process. Once this has been ruled out, the CCO needs to politely inform the offender they are not their "system support person" and they need to contact their normal technical person for assistance. Of course, any changes suggested by their technical person will require approval to insure monitoring is not hampered.

Be aware that there may be occasions where monitoring and/or a search reveals information of a very sensitive nature concerning a nonoffender. Examples include, but are not limited to, acts of infidelity and serious health concerns. Disclosure of this information to the offender is very problematic and not advised without specific agency approval. Legitimate reasons for disclosure should be limited to cases involving serious injury or death if not disclosed.

The question of disclosure oftentimes occurs when monitoring software is installed on a family computer where a parent is the person being supervised. An adolescent will disregard the warning about monitoring and engage in illegal or very risky behavior. Real-life examples include discussing alcohol consumption, arranging drug purchases, and inappropriate sexual communication with an adult. In some cases it may be justified to only disclose to a parent. However, other cases, may warrant disclosure to a law enforcement agency. Seek appropriate agency approval and provide disclosure to the most appropriate concerned party accordingly.

PRINCIPLE 10: MONITORING CAN BE COMPROMISED

By far the easiest method to defeat computer management is to use a undisclosed computer. However, actually tampering with the monitoring process can also be accomplished. One example is the use of a CD/DVD or other media to boot to another operating system which does not have monitoring software installed on it. These operating systems can also be stored and booted from a USB device. This completely bypasses the monitoring software and in most cases, will leave no trace on the computer itself. During home inspections and search-es, look for operating systems, such as Knoppix, a version of Linux, bootable from a CD/DVD or USB device.

Another example is for the offender to wait until the monitoring software is installed on a hard drive. Once installed, that hard drive is removed from the computer and another hard drive, without the mon-itoring software, is installed. The second hard drive is used until the offender's officer is due for his or her visit, at which point the first hard drive is reinstalled. This compromise can be defeated by sealing the CPU case with tamper tape after installing the monitoring software. The tamper tape will physically reflect if the CPU case has been open-ed, which is an indication that changes were made to the computer's internal components. Tamper tape can also be used to secure hard-ware devices, such as a Key Ghost Logger, to insure they are not re-moved after installation (see Figure 8).

It was mentioned that some anti-spy software can disable monitor-ing software. This method can be detected by attempting to access the locally installed monitoring software. If the software can't be accessed, it may have been disabled by anti-spy software. Depending upon the monitoring software, it may also mean that an update occurred to the operating system and the monitoring software is now out of date. Obviously, the new occurrence of the anti-spy program on the com-puter can also be a dead give-away. In such cases, it would be prudent to conduct a preview search of the system.

Some operating systems, starting with Windows XP, also have a feature that appears to wipe out the installation of monitoring soft-ware. By using the Restore feature, the system will reset itself to an ear-lier time. This could be before the monitoring software was installed. This would be detected by checking the last restore dates and also by attempting to open the monitoring program.

Other methods to defeat the monitoring process or a search are more drastic. They include wiping the hard drive, destroying the sys-tem itself, or disposing of components, such as the hard drive. More than one sex offender who has failed a polygraph due to obtaining a computer and Internet access have disposed of a hard drive or laptop in a river.

All of these are reasons and others unnamed, are why any com-puter management program must include a requirement that the offender will not attempt to remove, tamper with, reverse engineer, or in any way circumvent the monitoring software/hardware and will not possess certain software. Again, these requirements are incorporated into the sample Computer Restriction and Monitoring Program Participant Agreement included in Appendix A.

CONCLUSION

These general principles are noted to assist in understanding the major concerns in offender computer management. Knowledge of them will better prepare CCO for the ever-changing area of technology and the methods individuals may use to exploit that technology for their own illegal purposes. The next two chapters will focus on searches and the deployment of monitoring software.

REFERENCES

Eisenhower, D. Retrieved from http://www.brainyquote.com/quotes/quotes/d/dwightdei164720.html.
Tanner, J. (2005). Beyond prosecution: Improving computer management of convicted sex offenders, pp. 1–7. Retrieved from www.kbsolutions.com.

Chapter 8

SEARCH AND SEIZURE

The search for the truth is not for the faint hearted.
—Vincent D'Onofrio, Actor, playing Detective
Bobby Goren, on *Law & Order: Criminal Intent*

One of the most important skills involved in offender computer management is the ability to search a computer and associated media. Palmiotto and MacNichol (2010) note that all but one of six residential searches involving computers, conducted in the Middle District of Florida from 2007 to 2009, discovered violation evidence. Four of the six resulted in new law violations. The resulting imprisonment sentences imposed for the new law violations totaled over 84 years. Most agencies are, however, concerned that they do not have the knowledge or the tools (hardware and software) needed to examine computers. Until recently, search efforts required specific hardware, such as a write-blocker,[1] to forensically preview a computer.

In the past it was almost considered sacrilege for anyone but the most experienced of computer forensics experts to consider conducting any type of examination on a "live" computer running a Windows operating system.[2] Exceptions were limited to life and death situations,

---

1. Hardware write blockers are devices connected between a target media, such as a hard drive, and a laptop, which allow the hard drive to be previewed or imaged without the laptop making any changes to the hard drive's data.

2. In October of 2010, Apple's market share was approximately 10.4% of total personal computer sales (Weintraub, 2010). There are, of course, regional differences in the percentages of Windows to Apple based computer uses. CCO in some areas will therefore have a higher percentage of Apple users who are offenders. Nevertheless, based upon market share, it would seem much of CCO management efforts will involve Windows based computers. As a result, the discussion will center on these computers periodically noting options for Apple computers.

such as a kidnapped or missing child. The rationale was that the act of running any type of program would make changes to the data. This was considered bad as data could be inadvertently destroyed. Additionally, it creates chain of custody issues. For instance, the date a file was accessed might change to the date found by an officer as opposed to the earlier date the offender accessed it. In one extreme case, a computer was seized by law enforcement and while it was in the evidence room, it was examined by a police officer with the best of intentions. The officer had some computer knowledge but no computer forensic training and started searching for child pornography images, which he found. The problem is, he had commenced his activities within the native operating systems, without any forensic software or hardware.[3] The result was important dates on files and the system were changed to the date he did his activities, i.e., while the computer was in the police evidence room. One can readily see the argument made by the suspect, specifically, "I didn't download those images. They are dated when the computer was in police custody."

However, several factors have changed the thinking on conducting limited previews on a Windows-based operating system. The first factor was the appearance of a feature in some Windows Vista® versions that enabled the user to encrypt the entire hard drive. This feature, referred to as BitLocker®, if activated, would prevent the forensic examination of the hard drive if the computer was shut down without the password. If the computer was not previewed or evidence copied before the shutdown, the computer might not be able to be examined.

The next factor was the realization that Random Access Memory (RAM) can contain quite a lot of data or evidence. Recall from Chapter 6 that data that exists in RAM will remain only as long as the system is on. Once the system is shut down, the data is lost. If RAM contained evidence that the system had been hacked, that evidence was gone when the computer was turned off.[4] Additionally, RAM can some-

---

3. Apparently, the police officer used the built in Windows feature that allows the user to search for files. Once he located the files of interest, he proceeded to open them. This activity made numerous changes to the system and the files. No one should be using the native operating system in this manner to search for files on an offender's computer. As this chapter will discuss, there are much better options available that are either completely forensically sound or provide a much less drastic impact on the evidence.

4. Just because RAM was not captured does not make the hacker excuse valid. There are other forensic techniques that can diffuse this claim.

times contain passwords, which might be needed to access a particular system or file. Again, it would be lost with the system being shut down.

As a result, techniques and software were developed that allowed the collection of RAM from a running system by first responders. This obviously requires that someone work on a live computer as opposed to simply pulling the plug.

Additionally, merely shutting down a computer might neglect to collect evidence that the person was saving or working on files via "cloud computing." In a cloud computing environment, applications and data do not have to exist on the offender's computer.

Finally, the reality of waiting for a complete forensic examination, which, depending upon a lab's backlog could be months, is becoming an unacceptable delay for many prosecutors. How can it be justified to seize a computer on a dangerous sex offender and wait several months to examine it to determine if the computer contained evidence of a child's victimization? Imagine, a sex offender being allowed to remain in a home with a child he or she was victimizing, while their computer was waiting to be examined so he or she could be charged. The answer is that increasingly law enforcement agencies are doing quick computer previews or "triages," to determine if there is evidence that someone can be charged.[5]

It is still true that to do a complete computer forensic examination requires proper training and equipment (hardware and software). However, it is no longer an evidence collection sin to work on a live machine, provided one understands what he or she is doing and documents all actions taken. There are now tools available that can allow CCO with a minimum amount of training/experience and equipment to preview many computers on-site. This chapter initially focused on these tools with the understanding that information presented is only a start to any officer seeking to develop this needed skill. This chapter will also discuss other search options as well as proper seizure procedures for electronic media.

---

5. Note, this does not mean the computer will not be forensically examined later. The preview can provide initial evidence that a sex offender is committing a crime and that he or she should be arrested for community protection. Consider a drug case where an offender is caught by police with a bag of suspected cocaine. The police may do a field test, but they do not usually let the offender go pending a lab confirmation that the material is in fact cocaine. The individual is still arrested despite the fact the suspected cocaine has to be tested by a lab.

SEARCH TYPES

CCO searches are conducted either pursuant to a condition, a statute, or consent of the offender or a third party.[6] Searches are supposed to be conducted based upon at least reasonable suspicion. Some times a search warrant based upon probable cause is obtained by a CCO. Additionally, some conditions may specifically authorize random searches be conducted.

CCO may be called to conduct searches under three different scenarios. The first scenario is as a component of offender computer management, either alone or in conjunction with the monitoring software/hardware installation. If the agency requires offenders to fully disclose all hardware and software, such as delineated in Appendix B, the CCO will know what he or she is confronting from the start.

Searches prior to the monitoring software installation are usually conducted to (1) establish if there is any contraband on the system (hopefully, not child pornography); (2) get an understanding of the offender's problem behaviors; and (3) determine if there is anything that might interfere with monitoring. Periodic computer searches conducted as the primary management tool are also looking at items 1 and 2.

One caveat is important for CCO involved in pretrial supervision cases where the individual supervised has not been convicted. Searches for these cases should be narrow to insure only that the computer can be monitored or that no violation of the release or bond conditions has occurred. A general search to undercover evidence of either new criminal conduct or evidence related to the pending case will undoubtedly be frowned upon by the court. However, if evidence, such as child pornography,[7] is found in plain view while conducting a limited search, the computer is still subject to seizure. It is just like a pretrial officer doing a routine home visit and their client allows them into the home to find a bag of cocaine on the floor. Contraband found in plain view is subject to seizure.

---

6. Appendix F contains a written consent form for this purpose.

7. The officer will have to be prepared to articulate how he or she came to know the image was child pornography. Some cases are rather apparent such as those dealing with infants, toddlers, and prepubescents. The only gray area would be images involving the 16- to 18-year-old range. Officers can be aided in this determination looking at the image file names. For instance, a file named, 15-year-old-bj.jpg, is on indication that the file is In fact of a minor. Obviously, asking the defendant about the image can be helpful. Remember this found image is new evidence but consistent with the pretrial function caution is an order.

The second search type will be where the CCO has no knowledge of the offender's computer. This may occur where an offender under computer restrictions has an unknown and therefore unauthorized device. It may also occur when a search is conducted on an offender not subject to computer restrictions. For instance, a case where reasonable suspicion has been established that a drug offender is selling drugs out of his or her home and the computer, or more specifically a mobile phone, has information germane to the investigation. This is the exact situation many in law enforcement face on a routine basis, specifically little or no knowledge about the computer they will search prior to their arrival.

The third scenario is where an offender has used a computer belonging to another party to commit violation behavior. For instance, an offender may have used a parent or employer's computer to download pornography. In this situation, the officer will have to obtain the third party's consent prior to examining the computer. Appendix F contains a written consent form for this purpose. This form can also be used for offenders who do not have search conditions.

The key to conducting searches is to first know what your objective, or more specifically what is being sought from the search. Oftentimes an officer with computer expertise is called upon by another officer to search an offender's computer with the request, "Tell me what is on it." This is the equivalent of telling someone to search an apartment building for something without telling the person what they are looking for in the structure.

Officers doing computer searches must have a specific idea of what they are looking for on the computer, consistent with the needs of the case or the alleged issue. For instance, in a case involving a sex offender, graphic and movie files are frequently the order of the day. However, evidence of Internet browsing is also important. Text pertaining to rape and incest stories can also be important.

However, the files of importance in a case involving a offender suspected of dealing drugs might not involve graphic or movie files.[8] In a

---

8. There are of course exceptions. For instance an offender could change a spreadsheet's file extension containing their drug transaction records to that of a graphic file. The result is the file would appear to be a graphic file from the directory listing. However, this can be overcome with forensic software. Additionally, the offender might be using steganography to conceal the spreadsheet inside of graphic file. This is more problematic for the exam.

case involving an offender suspected of credit card fraud, the information sought would likely be credit card numbers or personal identifiers. A stalking case would likely involve information pertaining to the victim as well as threatening communication.

It is therefore imperative that CCO have a clear understanding of what they are looking for prior to conducting the search, particularly when it is being conducted on-site. Specifics can allow the CCO to focus on areas likely to be most fruitful and to possibly structure search parameters to locate the piece of evidence needed quickly. Otherwise, the on-site search will likely take much longer.

All types of searches can also lead to seizure of the computer. This could occur where the on-site examination was inconclusive but pointed to the need for a more in-depth computer examination.[9] Remember the case *U.S. v. Tucker,* 305 F. 3d 1193 (10th Cir. 2002), noted in Chapter 4. In Tucker, the first responder found that files were recently deleted but could not determine that any involved child pornography. However, he examined Tucker's web browser history and noticed that he had visited newsgroups whose names suggested they contained child pornography. The computer was seized and a full forensic examination found child pornography. The on-site search might also obviously detect clear noncompliance evidence or new criminal activity which would warrant seizure of the computer. Proper seizure or "bag and tag" procedures will be discussed later.

One final note on preview searches needs to be stressed. Officers should not be conducting these searches alone in an offender's home. At least two officers need to be present, even if the search is merely a routine check-up or prior to installing monitoring software on a new supervision case. An officer conducting a search is focused on the computer and may not be aware what an offender is doing at the time. There have been cases of offenders attempting suicide during these searches. As such, one officer needs to be focused on the offender while the other works on the computer. Additionally, if other electronic media needs to be examined or seized, one officer can record and maintain these items while the other looks for additional evidence and insures safety. If there are numerous others in the home, additional officers should be available to insure everyone stays safe.

---

9. The form in Appendix F provides for consent to remove the computer for a more thorough search, even for third party's computers.

BOOT CD/DVD SOFTWARE

There now exist several CCO options for previewing a computer without a hardware write blocker and laptop. The first option is software contained on a CD or DVD, which allows the computer to boot up into another operating system that will not write to the hard drive inadvertently. This is sometimes referred to as a software write block. The other options operate in a Windows or Apple environment but do so in a very limited fashion, which will be covered in the next sections.

In about 2000, Klaus Knopper developed an entire operating system based upon Linux, which could fit on a CD (Rankin, 2008). Many of these bootable CDs, with limited exceptions, do not make changes to a hard drive. Law enforcement and computer forensic versions of bootable CDs soon followed.

Various CDs, such as FIRE (Forensic and Incident Response Environment), PLAC (Portable Linux Auditing CD), and INSERT (Inside Security Rescue Toolkit), are focused primarily on handling intrusion and incident response investigations.[10] Many come with a wealth of forensic software that is useful for those who strive to go beyond onsite previews to full forensic examinations. The additional benefit of all of these CD/DVDs is that they are usually based upon Linux, and therefore free.

There are several caveats to the CD/DVDs. For those provided by law enforcement agencies, one must attend sanctioned training, which is free but for travel expenses. This training is extremely important as it not only demonstrates how the tool works but covers basic evidence collection issues associated with electronic media. Additionally, the programs do have some minimum requirements to operate on an offender's computer. They usually require at least 128 MB of RAM on the target computer. They all require that the computer has a working CD/DVD drive, and at least one hard drive. The RAM requirement is because some or all of the operating systems on the CD/DVDs are loaded and run from RAM. The program obviously can't be loaded if there is no working CD/DVD drive.[11] Lastly, if the computer does not have a hard

---

10. These programs can be obtained for free at (FIRE) http://fire.dmzs.com/; (PLAC) http://source forge.net/projects/plac/; and (INSERT) http://www.inside-security.de/insert_en.html.
11. Knoppix can be used to create bootable USB devices, with the same features as the CD/DVDs. As of this book's creation, law enforcement bootable USB devices have not been made available.

drive, there is nothing to look at on the system. Additionally, these programs frequently only work on PC-based computers, such as those running Windows or be Intel-based Apple computers. Finally, many of these programs require a USB device, which is used either to assist in processing and/or to save copies of discovered evidence.

It is important to stress that these tools are not meant to document or collect every piece of evidence. They are only used to establish a violation and to justify that the computer needs seized for a more through examination. These CDs should not be used instead of conducting a forensic examination. All that is needed is several child pornography images or a document that reflects a fraud is taking place, and the computer needs seized for a complete examination. Once contraband is found on a computer, do not forget to consider the possibility of other evidence contained on other electronic media, such as CD/DVDs, USB flash drives, memory cards, etc. These items will either have to be examined or seized. The CDs that are most useful for CCO are: ImageScan; TUX4N6™; and Knoppix.

ImageScan

ImageScan is a FBI program and as such is only available through their sponsored training. The software is designed to mount the hard drive so it can be read but not written to. It is a recognized first responder tool for law enforcement and is used by many CCO for checking sex offender's computers. It is described as:

> . . . a preview tool developed by the FBI CART Unix Program for the Innocent Images National Initiative to aid field investigators in safely viewing a variety of graphics formats on a subject's computer. ImageScan uses a customized Linux boot CD in conjunction with a mass storage USB device that allows investigators in the field to access the graphics files on a subject's computer while making absolutely no changes to any files. When this system is used for consent searches, it maintains the forensic integrity of the computer viewed for subsequent forensic examination in a laboratory environment. (ImageScan3 Brochure, 2009)

The program will work on most computers manufactured in the past 10 years and has ongoing FBI support. The program's key features are it:

- Can view graphics and movies;
- Creates and saves a directory listing of pictures;
- Allows the viewing and coping of specific files to the USB device for further investigation;
- Permits the easy transfer of the USB device's contents to CD-ROM; and
- Provides a forensically sound method for wiping the USB device after use so it is ready for the next case.

It is very easy to use and it is definitely a must for an CCO involved in computer management of sex offenders. Training is approximately eight hours, at the conclusion of which officers are licensed to use it and provided the software CD and a USB flash drive. Licensed users are provided updated versions at no cost. The training and the program can be obtained by contacting a local FBI office or visiting the Regional Computer Forensic Labs National Program Office at www.rcfl.gov.

TUX4N6™

This program is a live CD created by the Computer Crimes Section of the National White Collar Crime Center (NW3C) for conducting on-site previews. Free training and the program are provided through NW3C's Secure Techniques for Onsite Preview (STOP) course. This program allows offenders to search not only for images but evidence in other cases. Like ImageScan, it mounts the evidence as "read only." It allows officers to browse the directories of the target hard drive. It also has several automated features that will collect graphics and predetermined folders, such as My Documents and copy them to the USB device. The program is very user friendly. The training is approximately two days and is provided through NW3C (http://www.nw3c.org/ocr/courses_desc.cfm?cn=STOP). At the end of the training, individuals receive the CD and a certificate. The program runs with a USB flash drive, which is not provided. As this program can collect a lot of data, a larger USB flash drive is recommended, such as 40 GB. However, these devices are inexpensive.

Knoppix

Knoppix, unlike ImageScan and TUX4N6, was not designed specifically for forensic purposes. It can be obtained without attending any training by downloading an ISO (International Organization for Standardization) image[12] from http://www.knopper.net/knoppix /index-en.html. The ISO image must be converted by CD-Writing software and "burned" out to a CD. This is not hard to accomplish. The converted image, depending upon the version downloaded, will fit nicely on a 700 MB CD.

An important recommendation is in order. Do not use a Knoppix version more recent than Version 5.1. The reason is versions after 5.1. will mount a hard drive and allow the user to make changes to the target media. Newer revisions will allow officers to preview a hard drive. However, without being extremely careful, an officer could inadvertently modify the target media. By default, Version 5.1 and earlier versions mount the media as "read" only. The user has to take several affirmative actions in these earlier versions to make changes to the target media.

In order for Knoppix to run, the computer has to be set to boot first to the CD/DVD drive. This is accomplished through the BIOS. When a computer first starts up, immediately prior to the operating system commencing, instructs will briefly appear reflecting how to access the BIOS. Usually, BIOS are accessed at this junction by pushing the F1, F2, F8, F10, F12,or Esc keys.[13] BIOS contain a series of menus, with boot order or boot device being listed. The menus also provide instructions on how to effect changes to the BIOS. Be careful when changing the BIOS settings. Only change the boot order. Other changes could adversely affect the computer's operation. Once the BIOS settings are changed and saved to first boot to the CD/DVD, restart the computer, placing the Knoppix in the CD/DVD tray before the computer is turned off.

In case the computer was turned off before the Knoppix CD was in the tray, a large paper clip can be used to open the tray without

---

12. An ISO image is an archived file of the entire contents of CD or DVD. It can't be just saved to a CD. It will not boot up.
13. Each computer model can be different. To see a listing of access keys to BIOS settings go to http://www.iomega.com/support/documents/2157.html or complete a Google search on the phrase "BIOS settings."

turning the computer on. Bend the clip so that one end is exposed. The diameter of the large paper clip is the exact size of a hole on the front of the tray. Insert the exposed end into the hole and the tray will pop open.

Turning on the computer with Knoppix CD/DVD in the tray will start the program running. A series of computer actions will then appear on the screen. At some point, the Boot prompt will appear. At that point, type in *knoppix no swap* and push enter.[14] This command will prevent the program from mounting any Linux swap partitions that may be present.[15] If the command is not typed, the program will boot within a few seconds. This command does not have to be used if it is certain that the target drive has only a Windows operating system installed.

Once Knoppix finishes loading, a screen similar to a "Windows" Desktop will appear. The media to be examined will be reflected as an icon, such as "Hard Disk Partition (hda1)." Multiple partitions or hard drives will be numbered hda2, hda3, etc. The target may also be reflected as sda1, etc. for Small Computer System Interface (SCSI) drives. A device that is mounted will have a little triangle at the bottom right of the icon. Devices have to be mounted to be read. Knoppix usually does this automatically for the user (see Figure 17).

Knoppix will auto detect when a USB Flash drive is connected and put an icon on the desktop. These devices can be used to save files of interest. Clicking on an icon will mount a device if it is not already mounted and bring up a program called Konqueror. This program is very similar in appearance to Windows Explorer. As can be seen in Figure 18, it provides a quick look at all of the directories and files on the target media.

Before any media can be saved to the USB Flash Device, it must be mounted and its properties must be changed from "Read Only" to

14. The boot command *knoppix forensic* in Knoppix 6.4 can be used for this and to mount the target media as read-only. However, Knoppix 6.4 is not as friendly for the novice in conducting previews of offender's computers.

15. Ernest Baca, a Special Agent with the Department of Homeland Security, Immigration and Customs Enforcement (ICE), modified Knoppix into a package called Penguin Sleuth Kit (PSK). One of the changes he made was so Knoppix would not automatically mount swap partitions. Baca describes PSK as "no more than Knoppix on steroids" and notes it is just another alternative not a replacement. Baca has done a validation study of Knoppix and its effects on various operating systems. His modified version can be obtained at: http://www.linux-forensics.com. The only caveat is the current PSK revision is based upon a much earlier Knoppix version from approximately 2003.

Figure 17. Knoppix 5.1 Desktop View.

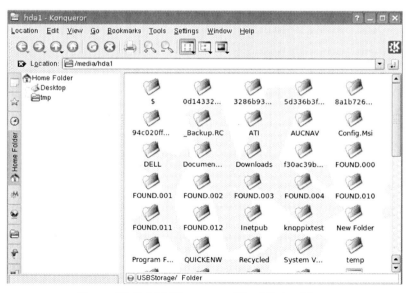

Figure 18. Initial Konqueror Hard Drive View.

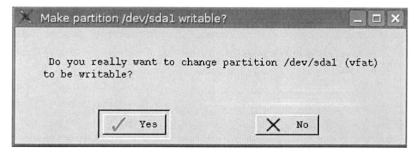

Figure 19. Making Device Writable.

"Write."[16] First click on the device's icon and use Konqueror to double check the properties being changed are for the correct device. Some officers will create folders on the USB device ahead of time, with the offender's name, with sub-folders called images, documents, etc. Make sure the correct USB flash drive is the one with the properties being changed. Once the correct device is confirmed, close Konqueror, and right click on the same icon. This will bring up a menu. Select "Change read/write mode." The question will appear, "Do you really want to change partition /dev/sdb* (vfat) to writeable?" Click "Yes." Files can now be saved to the USB Flash Drive (see Figure 19).

Konqueror can be used to search a system for specific files of interest. It operates very similar to the Windows Search/Find functions. Again, click on the target media, which will bring up Konqueror. On the pull down menu, select "Tools." After selecting "Tools," several options will appear. Select "Find," which will bring up a new screen. For the heading, "Named" type *.*jpg*. Additionally, make sure that the block "Include subdirectories" is checked and "Case sensitive search" is NOT checked. Click the "FIND" button. This will activate the program and will look for all jpg graphics files on the offender's computer and display the results. Be patient. If the thumbnails cannot be seen, pull down the "View" menu and change the icon settings to a larger size. Hovering with the mouse pointer over an icon will also provide a larger file view, with a property listing. Clicking on a file icon will open the file for viewing and/or copying. However, the search will have to be completed over again as Konqueror will close. Files of

---

16. It is worth noting that Konqueror can also safely preview USB Flash Drives as they are write protected as soon as they are detected.

Table 6.
SOME SPECIFIC FILE EXTENSIONS OF INTEREST

Offense/Issue	General Types	File Extensions
Sex	Still Images	BMP, GIF, JPG, JPEG, PNG, TIF
	Movies	AVI, MPEG, MPG, MOV
Sex, Threats, Financial	Documents	DOC, PDF, PWD, TXT, WKS, WP
Financial	Worksheets	WPSPXL, WB (1 or 2) XLS, WK (1, 3, 4, or S)
All	Web based pages	HTML, HTM, MHT
All	Compressed	ZIP, TAR

interest can be copied, saved to the desktop and transferred to the USB Flash Drive. The copy and paste feature is very similar to Windows® based operating systems. This same search can be used to find gif, bmp, or any other file extensions (see Table 6 and Figure 20).

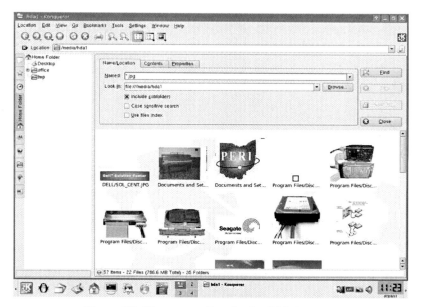

Figure 20. Konqueror Results for JPG Images.

Table 7.
SOME FOLDERS OF INTEREST*

Windows NT, 2000, XP

\Documents and Settings\Administrator (or User Name)

\Desktop

\Favorites

\My Documents

\My Pictures

\ My Videos

\Recent

\Local Settings

\Cookies

\History

\Temporary Internet Files

Windows Vista and 7

\Users\[user]\AppData\Local\VirtualStore and sub-folders

Additional Issues

Look for Interesting Folders (e.g., Downloads, My Stuff, Porn, Secrets, My Shared Files/Folder, etc.)

*Note: Look under drive root of hda1, sda1, as appropriate

Konqueror can be used to also look at specific folders of interest. Once in a specific folder, select Edit from the pull down menu. This allows the user to select and copy all or just certain files. As noted previously, these commands are very similar to a Windows environment. Some suggestions for folders to look at under the root of the drive (hda1, scda1, etc.) are reflected in Table 7. Finally, it is very important to document the process. Appendix G has a form for this purpose when conducting a Knoppix preview.

NTA STEALTH™[17]

NTA Stealth™ hit the market in approximately 2004 and was developed by New Technologies, Inc. (NTI). This forensic program boots

17. For more information see New Technologies, Inc. at http://www.forensics-intl.com/nta.html.

up outside of a Windows operating system with a CD and USB devices. It then searches the hard drive for Internet browsing and e-mail address artifacts and past porn site visits. The hits are then viewed by another program, NTA Viewer (this program is free). Along with flagging porn sites, it will also note threat and foreign country sites. NTA Stealth™ was developed in part with probation and parole officers in mind. It does not require advanced forensic training and works on DOS, Linux, and Windows operating systems 95, 98, NT, 2000, XP, and Linux. Several caveats are in order. The program notes that it identifies "computer usage leads." The computer will have to be seized and examined forensically if more specific information concerning those leads is needed. The other caveat is that this program has not moved beyond Windows XP. Although there are obviously still Window XP systems out there, we now have Windows Vista and 7. NTA Stealth™ is relatively inexpensive but agencies need to consider how effective it will be on newer systems. Other noted options may be more prudent.

Discussion

All the above are tools provide for quick computer preview in the field. But, they are not the only tools available. One tool, Storage Media Analysis Recovery Toolkit (S.M.A.R.T.), by ASR Data Acquisition & Analysis, LLC (www.asrdata.com), is another great bootable CD that provides the ability to preview a system. It actually has very cool search features built into the program. Many of these features are functional from the downloaded version. However, others require it to be registered; licensed properly with ASR Data Acquisition Analysis, LLC; and use a dongle.[18] Additionally, S.M.A.R.T. is designed to be a fully functioning forensic acquisition and analysis program, which is installed on a computer. First get accustomed to Knoppix and the other tools and use that knowledge to try out S.M.A.R.T. and any other such bootable CD/DVDs as they come available. Additionally, CCO will want a variety of bootable media as sometimes one program will not function as needed where another will. Obtain these programs

---

18. A dongle is usually a special USB device that has a token on it that installed software must detect for it to operate. It is commonly used in conjunction with forensic software as an added protection against pirating the software.

either from attending the appropriate training or downloading them. Then try them out on computers that are not offenders, such as CCO personal computers, or excess agency computers, to get a feel for how they operate.[19] The practice will pay off in the field.

WINDOWS-BASED SOFTWARE

The mere start-up of Windows operating systems has been known for years to change computer data. During a recent review of a hard drive after the start-up and shutdown of a Windows operating system, it was observed that approximately 1,250 files were accessed; modified and/or created. These numbers only increase with the complexity of newer Windows® operating systems. Vacca (2002) noted:

> . . . potential evidence can also reside in file slack, erased files, and the Windows swap file. Such evidence is usually in the form of data fragments, and can easily be overwritten by something as simple as booting the computer and/or running of Microsoft Windows. When Windows starts, it potentially creates new files and opens existing ones as a normal process. This situation can cause erased files to be overwritten and data previously stored in the Windows swap file can be altered or destroyed. Furthermore, all of the Windows operating systems (Windows 95, 98, 2000, and especially XP) have a habit of updating directory entries for files as a normal operating process. As you can imagine, file data are important from an evidence standpoint. (pp. 143–144)

However, there are other considerations in computer management that mitigate these impacts. One has to boot into Windows to install monitoring software, which will create countless system changes. Officers should be able to document the system and what actions they have performed while installing monitoring software. Using specific tools in a systemic method will provide officers with supporting docu-

---

19. Make sure that proper approval is granted before running these programs on excess agency computers. It is not that they will damage the computer. It is the possibility that something unpleasant and/or improper, such as pornography, might be discovered from trying out these programs. This obviously may cause problems for the one trying out the software as well as the one who last used the computer. Accordingly, supervisor approval is strongly encouraged before honing these skills on agency computers.

mentation that they did not place contraband on the system during the installation process. This approach insures not only integrity in the overall monitoring process but also that officers can answer any questions that may arise if illegal contraband is discovered. Data collected can also assist in correcting any technical problems that may arise later in the case. The alternative of manually exploring a target drive, i.e., opening directories and files, in a Windows environment is a far greater potential for system contamination.

The tools that will be discussed are executed but not installed on the offender's computer. Although these programs are not installed on the system, they will nevertheless make changes to the target system. Plugging in USB flash drive, which sometimes contains the tools to be used, will create and modify entries in the Registry[20] and other files on the target system. Even if the tools are run from a CD, there has to be some method to preserve the results and a USB flash drive is the most likely solution for today's computers.

These tools will not install contraband on a system or create changes that indicate someone has violated their supervision or criminal law. Additionally, these programs will usually not change the modified, creation or access dates for most files of interest. The key in their use is to document what was run and when and note anything unusual. CCO and their agencies are encouraged to develop standard operating procedures that are used in every case working with these tools, particularly during monitoring software installation. Appendix H contains a form that can be used to document these tools used in a Windows environment.

Field Search

This program was developed with assistance of the National Law Enforcement Corrections and Technology Center (NLECTC) specifically for probation and parole officers' use. It targets areas of interest in sex offender management, specifically, Internet history records, image and media files; and text searches. The program is free to use but is only available to law enforcement and corrections. It can be ob-

---

20. The Registry is a Windows hierarchical database that stores configuration settings and various options on a computer system. It can be a treasure trove of forensic information as it frequently contains data concerning user actions on a computer.

tained from http://www.justnet.org/Pages/fieldsearch.aspx. There is a very detailed manual that comes with this program and training is also available on its use. Prior to running this program, one should at a minimum be familiarized with the operational manual.

The program is run from an executable file and is menu driven. There are options for selecting what drive(s) to examine and to input specific keyword searches. Once the program is executed, it will gather data that can be reviewed. However, be patient reviewing results while the program is running. Additionally, be cautious opening image files found to get a better view as this may open the associated application program, which might make additional changes to the target system.

The program will create a log file in a directory on the flash drive from where it is run. This log file will contain information about all instances where Field Search has ever been run. Additionally, the program allows the user to export the results in a report format to a USB flash drive. This tool also comes in a version that can be run on an Apple computer. Field Search is a must for the CCO computer management arsenal. It should be utilized in all installing monitoring software situations and for compliance checks. It also should be considered in situations, such as where encryption might exist, to get evidence off of a live machine before shutting it down. One caveat is that the current version of this program will not recover deleted files (files located in unallocated space). However, its "RAW scan" will search a drive's free and slack space for orphaned Uniform Resource Locator (URL), or website addresses[21] (see Figure 21).

---

21. Free space is also another term for unallocated space. Typically, in a Windows XP system, data is saved at 4,096 bytes per cluster on a hard drive. If a file has 8,000 bytes or is approximately two kilobytes (KB) in size, the data will have to be saved to two clusters. It is just two big to fit in one. However, two clusters hold 8,192 bytes, leaving 192 byes left unused in one cluster. This 192 byes could be empty or it could be residual data from another file that was deleted or moved from the cluster. This space between what the file uses and what is left over in a cluster is referred to as file slack. It can contain a wealth of forensic information. At the time this book was being written, significant updates were anticipated to greatly enhance Field Search's usefulness for CCO as well as law enforcement.

Figure 21. Field Search Operation.

Digital Evidence and Forensic Toolkit (DEFT)

DEFT is an Italian program based upon Linux,[22] which also has a Window side. The ISO image can be downloaded for free from deftlinux.net. All programs on the CD can be freely used.

This CD should be run prior to Field Search as it will document the system's condition nicely before a search is completed for contraband. The Windows side of the CD will auto run and start the program. It first asks the user where to save the audit report, which is a record of all programs run from the CD and the time they were executed. The program will not record executables run from other than the CD.

---

22. The Linux side is not for the novice and can result in someone inadvertently altering target media. For this reason, it was not listed as a must have bootable disk. However, feel free to try it out. They have recently published a draft operational manual in English. Additionally, consider C.A.IN.E (Computer Aided INvestigative Environment), a similar Italian bootable CD which can be obtained for free at caine-live.net. Their English operation manual is not yet available. Both websites are in English.

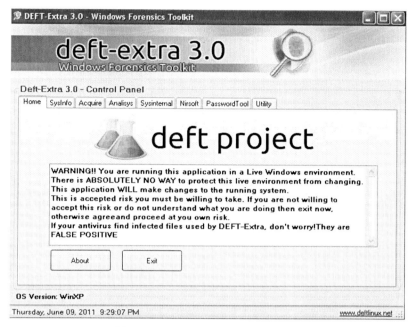

Figure 22. DEFT Start-Up Menu.

After this information is entered the program will then display tab menus for Home, SysInfo, Acquire, Analysis, Sysinternal, Nirosoft, Password Tool, and Utility (see Figure 22). The CD is literally loaded with programs that can be used, under the right circumstances.[23] The program's log file makes it easier to justify using but does not mitigate changes that may occur. The programs recommended for use prior to installing monitoring software are as follows: FTK Imager, WinAudit, and USBDeview. Each of these will be discussed below. Once the program activates the menu, do not close the program until all programs needing run are completed.

---

23. Presearch, the image viewing program developed by former Naval Criminal Investigative Service Special Agent, Paul Bright, is on the Windows side of this CD. Additionally, there are numerous Internet history viewers. However, the purpose of running many of these individual programs is negated if Field Search is used. There are tools for capturing RAM from a live machine. Again, try out the CD.

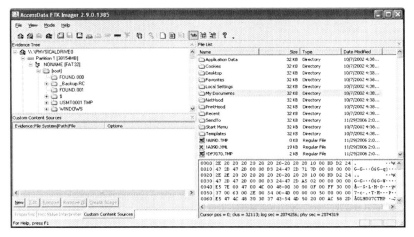

Figure 23. FTK Imager.

FTK Imager

This program is made available by AccessData®, one of the premier computer forensic software companies. It is free for download from them, but it is included in this CD. The program is accessed from the Acquire tab. Once the program starts, the user will see a tab menu at the top. Select File and Add Evidence. This will pop up a menu selection from which the user can select several different options. Selecting Physical Image will allow the user to view all data on the hard drive. Figure 23 displays this option completed.

Having done this, the user will be able to browse the directories and see files, include those deleted (located in unallocated space). From the File menu, click Export Directory Listing. This will capture the directory and file listing for the drive and export it to the flash drive. The user will be asked to provide a location for the export file, which is an excellent way of documenting the file and folders contained on a system before installing monitoring software. If another drive or partition exists on the computer, the same process will have to be undertaken to get a listing of files and folders on that drive or partition. Once the directory listings files are created, locate them on the flash drive. Right click on each file to show its properties. Change the properties on the file to "Read Only." This is an added measure to preserve the file. The file itself can be searched on-site or later for evidence of troubling file names or programs.[24]

FTK Imager is a very powerful tool, as are all of AccessData products. It will allow one to explore a hard drive and make copies of files, along with hash values[25] of those files. It will also allow a user to capture Registry files and memory from a live system. Try the tool out and get trained on it. As it is a free tool, its abilities are limited compared to other software sold by this vendor.

WinAudit

This program audits Windows-based personal computers and can be accessed through the tab called SysInfo. Just about every aspect of computer inventory is examined. The report is displayed as a web page, which can be saved in a number of standard formats, including Adobe Acrobat®. It provides a listing of hardware, programs installed, and numerous system configurations for the target computer. Also, it will collect, if requested, information on files on the entire target computer, with various extensions, such as exe, jpg, etc. Once executed, click on the menu tab, "Options." The menu reflected in Figure 24 will appear.

Selecting too many items may cause the program to hang. Under find files, at a minimum, identify exe. This will give you a listing of all files with this extension regardless of where they are located on the target computer. It will display an executable file even if it is not located in the Program File Directory. Once satisfied, click Apply. This will return the start screen, which reflects to Audit Your Computer. Select "Here." Clicking "Here" will activate the program, which may take several minutes. Once completed a screen similar to Figure 25 will appear. This is the results which can be explored for troubling programs and/or files. To save the file, click on Save. There are several formats that it can be saved in. Adobe Acrobat is the best as it can be made so

---

24. This can be accomplished with either the program Word or Note Pad, found under All Programs, "Accessories." Once the program opens the file, select "Edit" and then "Find." Type in text, such as anti-spyware, porn, etc. and the program will search file names containing the text. This is less impact on the target media compared to either using Windows Find/Search or manually searching folders.

25. Hash values are a numeric representation of a file. If one bit of information is changed on the file the hash value will likewise change. There are several different hash value schemes, such as MD5 and SHA1.

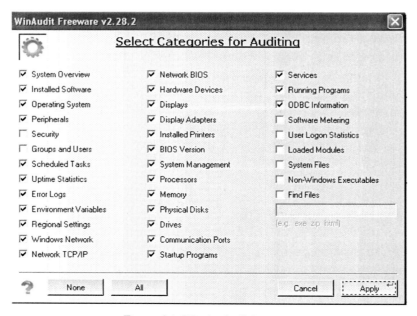

Figure 24. WinAudit Selections.

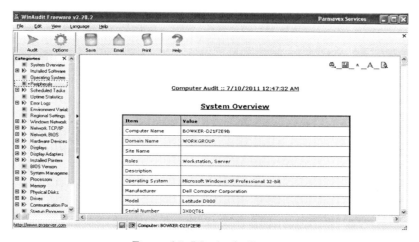

Figure 25. WinAudit Report.

it cannot be modified. Make sure the file is being saved to the flash drive. Additionally, make sure the box, "Allow document to be edited" is NOT checked. Click Save. When using the PDF format, it will create a large file quite possibly in excess of several MB. One final caveat: this program will capture the presence of the flash drive being used in the process.

USBDeview

This program is run from the Nirosoft tab. It lists all USB devices that are currently connected to a computer, as well as all USB devices that have been previously used. For each USB device, the following extended information is displayed: Device name/description, device type, serial number (for mass storage devices), the date/time that device was added, VendorID, ProductID, and more. The data can also be sorted and arranged by type, connected, etc. Note the flash drive being used for collection will be listed as well. The listing can be used to identify unaccounted USB devices that might be used to store pornography or other contraband or software to tamper with monitoring efforts. Figure 26 is a screenshot of this program's results.

On the top menu, select "File" then "Select All." This will highlight all devices. While the devices are highlighted, select the disk icon at the top. This will pop up a screen requesting input of where the user

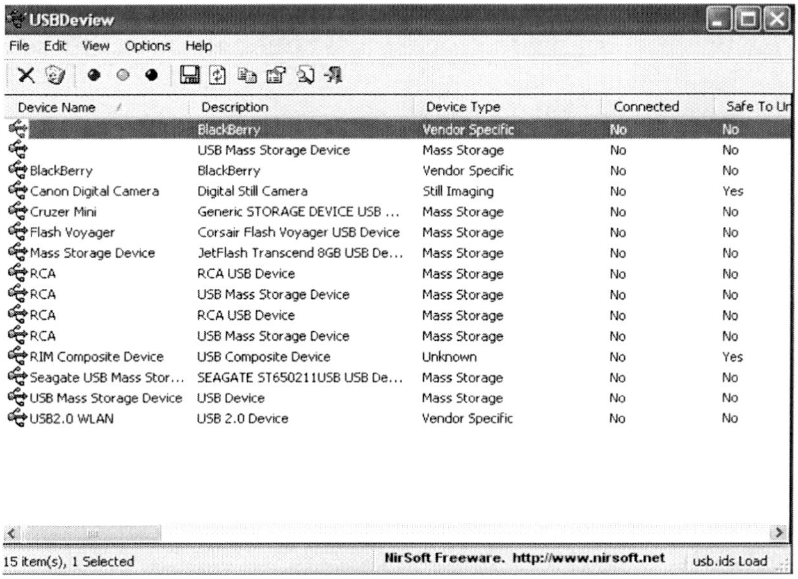

Figure 26. USBDeview Results.

```
auditlog - Notepad
File  Edit  Format  View  Help
#################################################################################
####                                                                         ####
####                           DEFT-EXTRA 3.0                                 ####
####                      Windows Forensics Toolkit                           ####
####                                                                          ####
####                       Report File Generation                            ####
####                                                                          ####
#################################################################################

Report creation: 7/10/2011 1:11:42 AM

=================================================================================

-> 7/10/2011 1:11:49 AM - launch program: FTK Imager Lite

=================================================================================

-> 7/10/2011 1:11:59 AM - launch program: WinAudit

=================================================================================

-> 7/10/2011 1:12:21 AM - launch program: USBDeview.exe

=================================================================================

Report close: 7/10/2011 1:12:30 AM
```

Figure 27. DEFT Log File.

wants a text file listing of the results saved. Select the flash drive being used for data collection and save.

DEFT can now be closed. All programs run from the CD will be recorded on the log file previously noted (see Figure 27).[26] These programs provide a good snapshot of the programs, files, and devices associated with a managed computer. The search results should be maintained in digital format in case issues arise later, such as a question that the offender had some file, program, or device prior to the installation of monitoring software or other management efforts.

Triage Tools

It was previously noted that one reason for venturing into live examinations was the examination backlog in many computer labs. One way to deal with this backlog was to focus on computers that contained potential evidence so they could get quick attention by the forensic examiner. In the last few years, vendors have developed tools for this

---

26. All of these programs can be copied to a USB drive and run from it as well. However, the nice thing about running them from the DEFT CD is a log file is created of when the programs were executed and in what order.

purpose. These tools allow law enforcement first responders, with very little training or expertize, to capture information from a live machine.

The program protocol is usually an experienced officer pre-configures the vendor program on a flash drive, which is then provided for a first responder's use in the field. The flash drive is plugged into a target computer and with very little interaction by the first responder, sets to collect and analyze data from the computer. The first responder can the review the results on-site with many of these programs. Additionally, the programs will save relevant data to the flash drive. The data can then be provided to an experienced examiner for further review with forensic software. The tools also provide for easy exportation of the results as needed. The kind of information obtained with these programs is obviously very germane to those involved in computer management of offenders. Evidence found with these devices can be used in violation proceedings as well to justify seizure and probable cause for a warrant. These programs will usually perform many of the following functions:

- Search and view files, particularly images;
- Internet searches/browsing;
- Recently accessed files;
- Recently accessed media play files;
- General system information/installed applications;
- RAM collection
- Identify anti-forensic programs, such as encryption

Individuals can be trained to run these program rather easily. Microsoft has created a free law enforcement version called Computer Online Forensic Evidence Extractor (COFFEE). This program allows on-the-scene responders "to run more than 150 commands on a live computer system." The program will collect data and save it to a USB device. However, the data must be viewed by another computer containing the parent program. COFFEE can be obtained by law enforcement or CCO for free through NW3C at www.nw3c.org or by contacting INTERPOL at COFEE@interpol.int (COFFEE, 2011).

Additionally, there are several vendors who offer similar or enhanced programs at less than purchasing a full forensic software package. Some of the vendors offering these programs are: AccessData

(AD Triage and Live Response®); ADF Solutions (Triage-Examiner®); Encase® (Encase Portable); and Wetstone (US-Latt™).[27]

Advanced Computer Examination
Support for Law Enforcement

The Advanced Computer Examination Support for Law Enforcement (ACES)[28] program is congressionally funded to provide forensic software to qualifying state and local law enforcement personnel, including CCO. The computer forensic tools and techniques are provided to qualifying personnel free of charge. ACES utilities are currently implemented for the Windows® NT, Windows® 2000, and Windows® XP. ACES has software utilities which block all system-initiated attempts to write to any user-specified blocked computer media. For instance, installing their software on a computer running Windows XP®, would allow that computer to be used to examine other computer media without concern the operating system would alter the data. In this way, a CCO could review a targeted external USB drive; flash drives, and even a hard drive. One caveat is in order. Menz and Bress (2005) note that software write blockers can fail, noting only a properly configured hard write blocker can accomplish full protection.[29] ACES also have an iPhone® utility for looking at these mobile devices.

ProDiscover

Technology Pathways, LLC, is another leader in computer forensics and has a tool called ProDiscover®. A freeware edition of their product is available for use.[30] This program can be run from a flash drive for preview and imaging files, etc. It will show deleted files. The edition is quite a capable forensic tool and includes all the tools nec-

---

27. See AccessData (accessdata.com); ADF Solutions (adfsolutions.com; Encase (guidancesoftware.com) and Wetstone (wetstonetech.com) for more specifics. It is noted that AccessData's Live Response only collects information. Like COFFEE, it can not be viewed on-site by the first responder without the use of the originating program.
28. ACES is operated through the FBI. To obtain more information and to register, go to www.acesle.com.
29. It is noted that Mark Menz and Steve Bress are from MyKey Technology Inc., a company that manufactures and sells write blockers (NoWrite™). Menz and Bress, however, are very knowledgeable and respected in the computer forensics field.
30. For more information about this company and to download a copy of ProDiscover go to techpathways.com.

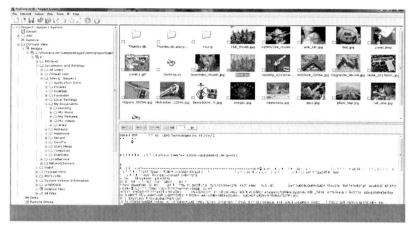

Figure 28. ProDiscover Preview.

essary to work the vast majority of computer management cases. Coupled with ACES software write blockers, it would be an inexpensive method to conduct many forensic examinations.[31] More complex examinations, involving memory collection or Volume Shadow Copy[32] analysis requires the purchase of their product, which is priced very reasonably (see Figure 28).

ComputerCop

This program has been around for years and was one of the earlier tools marketed to probation and parole officers.[33] The program works entirely from a CD. Once loaded the program searches for words/phrases from 21 crime categories including sex, drugs, weapons, gang, hate crimes, fraud, and terrorism offenses. The program also will search for images. Unlike the current Field Search version, this program will find deleted files. Like Field Search, it will not alter file-related dates (Created, Modified, Accessed) and can export de-

---

31. FTK Imager can also be used in this manner to image and examine media.
32. Microsoft's (Volume Shadow Copy, or Volume Snapshot Service) (VSC) was first introduced in Windows XP as a nonpersistent backup for software distribution creating what is referred to as restore points. This feature allows the user to revert their system back to an early time. VSC can contain a wealth of information for the forensic examiner (Volume Shadow Copy with ProDiscover).
33. For more information, see computercop.com.

tailed reports. ComputerCop also sells a USB write protector, and when coupled with the software provides for forensic previews.

As this program operates in an Windows environment, it was not embraced by many in the field due to forensic concerns. For those concerned about the forensic implications of working in Windows there were other software options that were more acceptable for the cost. As working in Windows is now at least discussed without revulsion by the forensic community, this program may be an option for some agencies. However, for those agencies operating in a tight budget, the other options noted, such as Field Search, ProDiscover, and FTK Imager make more sense.

Remote Examination Agents (REA)

REA are offered by many vendors[34] as a method to examine computers over a network, including the Internet. Basically, an individual installs an agent associated with the forensic software, which allows the computer to be examined remotely through a network or the Internet. The forensic software connects to the remote computer via the agent and allows searching, RAM collection, hard drive imaging, etc. These tools are increasingly being deployed by corporations. They also may be used by large correction agencies, such as those running prison systems, to monitor their employee's computer activities. At present, few if any community correction agencies are using REA in offender supervision.[35] However, it is not inconceivable that their use will increase, particularly with offender cyber-conduct on the rise and faster Internet connections. However, they should not be used as a substitute for regular field work. Officers on-site for a field visit or to complete a search could install the agent, while someone familiar with computer forensics examines the offender's computer remotely to determine if seized. However, there must be a live Internet connection present for the exam to be completed remotely. Obviously, installing this agent

34. Examples are: AccessData (AccessData Enterprise), at accessdata.com; EnCase (EnCase Enterprise) at guidancesoftware.com; F-Response (F-Response TACTICAL and F-Response Consultant) at f-response.com; and ProDiscover (ProDiscover Incident Response) at www.tech-pathways.com.
35. RemoteCOM, is a notable exception. This company is not a corrections agency. However, they provide services to probation and parole agencies. One of those services includes the remote collection of data, which is likely being accomplished through a REA. RemoteCOM will be discussed in greater detail in the next chapter.

will also cause changes to the system. Cost though may initially prohibit this option for CCO as opposed to other mentioned alternatives.

FORENSICS SOFTWARE AND HARDWARE

Thus far, the discussion has centered on tools to complete a quick preview or to gather some key pieces of data for examination by experienced forensics professionals. Additionally discussed was the use of an agent which can provide remote access to an offender's computer. There are tools that can be purchased by CCO to complete forensics in-house. Use of these tools should only be undertaken after obtaining a basic understanding of computer forensics. This will greatly enhance these tools' usefulness and insure that the CCO can explain the actions they took to find important evidence. The top providers of complete forensic software packages, AccessData, EnCase, and ProDiscover have already been mentioned. Several other vendors, for use on and with Apple operating systems warrant mentioning. SubRosaSoft.com Inc. has a computer forensic suite, MacForensicsLab™.[36] Additionally, Black Bag™ also has a forensic package for use with Apple® operating systems.[37] What about hardware though? What is needed to do computer forensics?

One thing that should be avoided is relying on an agency's excess or surplus equipment to save money. This is not a good option for several reasons. Excess equipment is frequently outdated. The hard drives are smaller than newer models. The operating systems are also frequently outdated. More importantly, they do not usually have sufficient RAM or processing speeds to run many of the advanced computer forensic programs. The programs may run but very slowly. It is quite possible they also will crash at the most inconvenient time, losing data as well as wasting time. Using an older machine to run new computer forensics programs is like trying to pull a new mobile home up a steep hill with a 1969 Volkswagen Beetle. It just doesn't make sense.

All forensic software vendors will provide minimum product specifications for running their programs. Many also have agreements with various companies to package their software with forensic desktop or

---

36. See macforensicslab.com for more information.
37. See blackbagtech.com for more information.

laptop computers. Even if an agency decides to purchase their own computer, they need to rely on the software vendor's specifications to ensure the programs run as intended.

The next decision is to decide between purchasing a desktop or laptop computer. Many law enforcement agencies are opting for laptops because they can be used in the field as well for quick previews. Also what about their operating system, i.e., Apple or Windows? Many advocate for Apple laptops, however, just as many are noting the advantages to using Windows-based laptops. Along with cost, it important to consider what operating system the end user will be most comfortable with starting out in forensics. Most CCO work on Windows machines at work and this may be initially the most appropriate.

After a computer, there are two other pieces of hardware that must be considered. The first is a hardware write-blocker, which guarantees that data can be previewed and/or imaged without any alterations to the data. The second is a hard drive duplicator, which is a device specifically for making an exact bit-for-bit copy of a drive, without altering the target media. As they are focused on making a copy, they frequently are extremely fast compared to using other methods of drive imaging. The decision of what to purchase is going to be based upon not only cost but volume. If CCO are going to regularly be making images of a lot of hard drives, then they will need to consider a hard drive duplicator. However, if they are not going to be doing a lot of forensic drive imaging on a regular basis, a hardware write-blocker is the way to go. It will allow the CCO to preview a hard drive or image a drive.

Companies that specialize in providing forensic hardware include Digital Intelligence, Intelligent Computer Solutions, Logicube, MyKey Technology Inc., Silicon Forensics, and WiebeTech. Some companies provide numerous hardware devices, including forensic laptops or workstations and others specialize in hardware write-blockers or hard drive duplicators.[38]

---

38. For more information on these vendors and their products visit: Digital Intelligence (digitalintelligence.com); Intelligent Computer Solutions(ics-iq.com); Logicube (logicube.com); MyKey Technology Inc. (mykeytech.com); Silicon Forensics (siliconforensics.com); and WiebeTech (wiebetech.com).

SEIZURE

A CCO's seizure of a computer may occur under the following scenarios: the offender is prohibited or otherwise unauthorized by his or her conditions to have a computer; a preview search has detected contraband; or seizure is necessary to complete the examination. The paramount concern is for officer safety. The scene needs to be secure. Individual CCO should not attempt to seize a computer unless it is clear they can do so safely. The next concern, to paraphrase a Dirty Harry quote, "A man (or woman) has got to known their limitations." If it looks like a very complicated system is running involving a server, seek expert advice, before pulling power cords and cables. Next, be prepared to document everything. Take photos if possible, log and record what was where, and label everything. The following is an example of what not to do:

> Two inexperienced officers seized two computers from a sex offender with a request to examine the offender's wife's computer first as she needed it returned. They provided a property receipt merely reflecting two computers were taken. When asked which computer was which, the officers responded that the offender's was the "icky looking one."

This is obviously not the proper method of identifying a seized computer. Also be prepared to record and account for all miscellaneous digital media, such as CDs, taken. In the same case, the officers had seized numerous CDs and did not bother to count or record how many had been taken on the property receipt. This creates a chain of custody issue as the offender could easily say the CD containing contraband was not his or hers. Not knowing how many items were seized is not a proper accounting for chain of custody.

The National Institute of Justice's *Electronic Crime Scene Investigation: A Guide for First Responders, Second Edition* (2008) and the Secret Service's *Best Practices For Seizing Electronic Evidence (Version 3): A Pocket Guide for First Responders* (2006) are excellent free publications on the various issues involved in seizing electronic evidence. In most cases, CCO will be confronted taking either a stand alone desktop or laptop.

As such, the Secret Service (2006) recommends the following procedures:[39]

- Do not use computer or attempt to search for evidence.
- Photograph computer front and back as well as cords and connected devices, as found.
- Photograph surrounding area prior to moving any evidence.
- If computer is "off", do not turn "on".
- If computer is "on" and something is displayed on the monitor, photograph the screen.
- If computer is "on" and the screen is blank, move mouse or press space bar (this will display the active image on the screen). After image appears, photograph the screen.
- Unplug power cord from back of tower.
- If the laptop does not shut down when the power cord is removed, locate and remove the battery pack. The battery is commonly placed on the bottom, and there is usually a button or switch that allows for the removal of the battery.
- Once the battery is removed, do not return it to or store it in the laptop. Removing the battery will prevent accidental start-up of the laptop.
- Diagram and label cords to later identify connected devices.
- Disconnect all cords and devices from tower.
- Package components and transport / store components as fragile cargo.
- Seize additional storage media. (CD/DVDs, flash drives, etc.)
- Keep all media, including tower, away from magnets, radio transmitters and other potentially damaging elements.
- Collect instruction manuals, documentation and notes.
- Document all steps involved in the seizure of a computer and components. (p. 4)

Packing for seized items must be such that static electricity is not a problem. Don't use Styrofoam peanuts as they can build up a charge as well as small pieces may find their way into computer cases. If anti-static bags are not available, paper over plastic is better. Appendix I

---

39. Be aware these guidelines predate the appearance of many triage tools. These tools, with proper training and procedures in place, can be used to collect "volatile" evidence prior to shutdown of the system.

includes a form for use in the seizure of electronic evidence, including mobile phones, which are discussed next.

MOBILE PHONE AND DEVICE SEARCHES AND SEIZURES

These devices are different in many ways from desktop and laptop computers. Much of the information they contain may be lost if power is not maintained to the device. Additionally, mobile phones are frequently receiving data from other sources, such as updates from service providers or messages from other phones. This incoming data will overwrite data that is not saved on the device. There is also software that can be activated remotely to lock or destroy data, to make evidence collection more difficult.

Additionally, the operation and structure of devices are frequently being updated by the manufacturer and/or service provider. As a result, forensic examination can be trying. However, there are software and hardware available to forensically retrieve data from these devices. Notable vendors are Cellebrite; Micro Systemation (MSAB); Oxygen Software; Paraben®; and Susteen®, Inc. Another company, Fernico®, provides a system in which camera shots are taken of the mobile phone and all areas of interest, such as Address Book, Text Messages, My Pictures, etc. The camera shots are maintained in a software package, making the documentation of the mobile phone much easier.[40]

Another solution that is available is through the FBI and the Regional Computer Forensic Laboratory (rcfl.org). At select FBI offices and all regional RCFLs, there are Cell Phone Investigative Kiosks. These Kiosks are free and allow users to extract data from a mobile phone, put it into a report, and burn the report to a CD or DVD. The only requirement for using these Kiosks is users should have familiarity with computers and must take a one-time hour training course.[41]

Secret Service (2006) provides the following suggestions for seizing mobile phones and Personal Digital Assistants (PDA):

---

40. Cellebrite (cellebrite.com); Fernico (fernico.com); Susteen, Inc. (mobileforensics.com); Micro Systemation; (msab.com); Oxygen Software (oxygensoftware.com); and Paraben (paraben.com)
41. For more information on these kioks, visit http://www.rcfl.gov/DSP_P_CellKiosk.cfm.

- If the device is "off", do not turn "on".
- With PDAs or cell phones, if device is on, leave on. Powering down device could enable a password, thus preventing access to evidence.
- Photograph device and screen display (if available).
- Label and collect all cables (to include power supply) and transport with device.
- Keep device charged.
- If device cannot be kept charged, analysis by a specialist must be completed prior to battery discharge or data may be lost.
- Seize additional storage media (memory sticks, compact flash, etc).
- Document all steps involved in seizure of device and components. (p. 7)

Preventing mobile phones from receiving signals (data) can sometimes be accomplished temporally with two arson or clean paint cans. The device is placed in a quart can sealed, which is then placed in a gallon can, which is also sealed. There are also special bags that can be purchased, called Faraday Bags or boxes, which will prevent signals from getting to the device. These bags can also be used while the phone is being examined. One vendor who supplies these bags and similar devices is Teel Technologies (teeltech.com).

EVIDENCE STORAGE

Digital evidence has to be stored pending examination or prior to transfer to the person doing the examination, who will then have to secure it. Storage must be secure. Tampering and/or theft must be prevented. No one who is not the evidence custodian or the examiner should have access to the evidence. Some small evidence may be secured in a safe or locked cabinet. However, many items, such as a desktop computer, may require a large cabinet or small room.

The storage area must be free of dust, moisture, static electricity, and extreme temperatures. These all can have a negative impact on electronic evidence. Additionally, storage must be not only secured but provide a chain of custody. Items must be logged in and logged out. Property receipts reflecting what was seized must match up with the property and be accounted for on the logs. For more information on proper storage procedures, go to the International Association for Property and Evidence, Inc. (iape.org).

EVIDENCE DISPOSAL

Eventually, evidence will have to be removed from storage and either returned to the owner (if not contraband) or destroyed. This is going to occur after the evidence is no longer needed for a violation or new case. It could also occur when the item seized is not illegal per se to possess, such as a computer. The only reason it was seized is because the offender was on supervision and that has ended. These are usually somewhat expensive property to replace and some offenders might actually want them back.

Examples of contraband that can't be returned include child pornography and pirated movies, music, and software. What if these electronic files are saved on a computer? Some courts will just order forfeiture of the computer or the offender will agree to abandon it. Obviously, such actions need documented and then the property can be destroyed.

However, can't the offensive material just be deleted and the computer returned? The answer is maybe. Someone who has downloaded a lot of child porn will have those images saved in folders as well as in Internet cache. They literally can be all over the place. To surgically remove those files is going to take time and even then some might be missed. In these cases, the preferred method for removing child pornography is to wipe the entire drive. This obviously will erase all other information on the drive as well, including the operating system. Prodiscover has a wiping tool as part of their freeware program. Many of the forensic packages likewise have wiping capabilities. The hard drive could also just be removed from the computer case and destroyed. The rest of the computer could then be returned.

What about removing adult pornography? Can't that just be returned to the offender? After all, it is not illegal to possess adult pornography. It may or may not be a supervision condition. Common sense, however, indicates that it is not a good idea to give a sex offender a hard drive full of adult pornography, particularly while he or she is on supervision. In this case, one is going to have to make a judgment about how "infested" the computer is with adult pornography. If it requires wiping, get either the offender's consent or the appropriate authorization. However, if it is one folder or even just Internet browsing, it can probably be removed without wiping the entire hard drive.

Oftentimes during the first compliance check with Field Search or prior to installing monitoring software, adult pornography or troubling websites will be found.[42] Document what was found and consistent with an agency's policy delete the file(s), and if necessary, remove the files by emptying the Recycle Bin. After this is done there are programs that can help make sure the problem images or troubling websites are gone. These free programs run from a USB flash drive and can accomplish this objective: Eraser Portable (http://portableapps .com/apps/utilities/eraser_portable) and CCleaner Portable (http: //download.cnet.com/ccleaner/?tag=pop). Again, this is only for images which are not normally illegal to possess. Child pornography images and the computer gets seized.

CONCLUSION

This chapter has presented search options, ranging from previews, triage, up to and including full forensic examinations. Many of the tools presented are free, with the exception of having to expend one's time to learn to use them properly.

The financial investment for software/hardware can range from a few dollars up to the cost of creating a small computer forensic lab ($15,000 and up). Proper training also requires an additional investment, cost, staff salary, etc. Unfortunately, these are not one time expenses. Training and equipment must be kept up to date. Many agencies will be frightened by these costs. But the price of farming out even basic services may be much greater. However, the cost of doing nothing may very well be the death of an innocent person, excessive negative media coverage, and a civil suit with damages. At a mini-

---

42. One of the issues with only doing compliance searches is that one has to do a good cleanup job. Otherwise those images and/or websites will keep showing up. Accordingly, one has to pay attention to Modified, Access, and Creation (MAC) dates on files. However, monitoring software will only capture user activity. So if there is a missed image or two somewhere on the drive, it will only capture it if the offender views it, which would clearly be new behavior.

mum, CCO must have the skills to conduct on-site previews and the ability to seize electronic media so it can be forensically examined.

REFERENCES

AccessData. Retrieved from http://accessdata.com/.

ADF Solutions. Retrieved from http://adfsolutions.com/.

Black Bag. Retrieved from https://www.blackbagtech.com/.

Cellebrite. Retrieved from http://www.cellebrite.com/.

Computer Aided INvestigative Environment (C.A.IN.E). Retrieved from http://www.caine-live.net/.

Computercop. Retrieved from http://computercop.com/.

Computer Online Forensic Evidence Extractor (COFFEE). Retrieved from http://www.microsoft.com/industry/government/solutions/cofee/default .aspx.

Digital Intelligence. Retrieved from http://digitalintelligence.com/.

D'Onofrio, V. Retrieved from http://www.brainyquote.com/quotes/quotes /v/vincentdo409862.html.

EnCase. Retrieved from http://www.guidancesoftware.com/.

F-Response. Retrieved from http://www.f-response.com/.

Fernico. Retrieved from http://fernico.com/.

Field Search. Retrieved from http://www.justnet.org/Pages/fieldsearch.aspx.

Forensic and Incident Response Environment (FIRE), Retrieved from http: //fire.dmzs.com/.

ImageScan3 Brochure. (2009). Retrieved from http://www.rcfl.gov/down-loads/documents/IS3_Brochure.pdf.

Inside Security Rescue Toolkit. (INSERT). Retrieved from http://www .inside-security.de/insert_en.html.

Intelligent Computer Solutions. Retrieved from http://www.ics-iq.com/.

International Association for Property and Evidence, Inc. Retrieved from http://www.iape.org/index.php.

Knoppix. Retrieved from http://knopper.net/knoppix/index-en.html.

Logicube. Retrieved from http://logicube.com/.

Menz, M., & Bress, S. The fallacy of software write protection in computer forensics. Retrieved from http://www.mykeytech.com/SoftwareWrite Blocking2-4.pdf.

Micro Systemation. Retrieved from http://www.msab.com/.

MyKey Technology Inc. Retrieved from http://mykeytech.com/.

New Technologies, Inc. Retrieved from http://forensics-intl.com/.

Oxygen Software. Retrieved from http://oxygensoftware.com/en/default.asp.

Palmiotto, M., & MacNichol, S. (2010). Supervision of sex offenders: A multi-faceted and collaborative approach. *Federal Probation,* September, 2010.

Paraben. Retrieved from http://paraben.com/.

Penguin Sleuth Kit. Retrieved from http://penguinsleuth.org/index.php.

Portable Linux Auditing CD (PLAC). Retrieved from http://source-forge.net/projects/plac/.

ProDiscover. Retrieved from http://techpathways.com/DesktopDefault.aspx.

Regional Computer Forensic Labs National Program Office (RCFL). Retrieved from http://rcfl.gov/.

Silicon Forensics. Retrieved from http://siliconforensics.com/.

Storage Media Analysis Recovery Toolkit (S.M.A.R.T.). Retrieved from http://www.asrdata.com/.

SubRosaSoft.com Inc. (MacForensicsLab). Retrieved from http://macforensicslab.com/.

Susteen, Inc. Retrieved from http://mobileforensics.com/.

Teel Technologies. Retrieved from http://teeltech.com/tt3/.

U.S. Department of Homeland Security, United States Secret Service. (2006). *Best practices for seizing electronic evidence (Version 3): A pocket guide for first responders.*

U.S. Department of Justice, National Institute of Justice. (2008). *Electronic crime scene investigation: A guide for first responders* (2nd ed.).

U.S. v. Tucker, 305 F. 3d 1193, (10th Cir. 2002).

Vacca, J. (2002). *Computer forensics: Computer crime scene investigation.* Hingham, MA: Charles River Media.

Volume Shadow Copy with ProDiscover. Retrieved from http://toorcon.techpathways.com/uploads/VolumeShadowCopyWithProDiscover-0511.pdf.

Wetstone. Retrieved from http://www.wetstonetech.com/.

WiebeTech. Retrieved from http://www.wiebetech.com/.

Chapter 9

DEPLOYING MONITORING SOFTWARE

> I believe in having each device secured and monitoring
> each device, rather than just monitoring holistically on the
> network, and then responding in short enough time for
> damage control.
> —Kevin Mitnick, Security Consultant
> and reformed hacker

Monitoring software has been used in offender management for almost 14 years. Initially software was adopted by CCO from programs designed to monitor kids, spouses, and employees. Later, several companies ventured into software and services specifically for community correction agencies, the most notable United States companies being Internet Probation and Parole Control, Inc. (IPPC) and RemoteCOM.

Harrold (2005) indicates there are four basic approaches to managing offender computer use with monitoring software. The first approach is using filtering software, which blocks access to certain websites and also logs a user's activity. Harold refers to the next two as "system resident" approaches. The first of these, Type I, is installed on the offender's computer but an officer has to retrieve the results directly from the offender's computer. The second "system resident" approach, Type II, also involves the software being installed on the offender's computer. However, it then sends periodic reports and e-mails to the officer. Harold describes the last type as a "forced gateway" software, where the offender's online activity is remotely viewed by an officer, after software is installed on the offender's computer. Keep Harrold's observations in mind as this chapter explores monitoring software development and its use as a component in computer management.

EVOLUTION OF MONITORING SOFTWARE

Ever since corporations started using computing resources, there have been tools or programs utilized to monitor systems. However, these tools were used not to watch the employees per se but how the systems were functioning. There obviously were logs of who logged into what system and when. However, this was not the same as using monitoring software to watch individual user activity. No doubt hackers also developed tools to capture user activity, such as passwords typed. At least as early as 1983, keyloggers were discussed as just such a security problem (Kivolowitz, 1983). It is also very likely that three letter government agencies were using monitoring software. However, nothing similar was available to the general public or even CCO until the 1990s.

In 1991, WinWhatWhere (TrueActive) was founded (Bloomberg BusinessWeek, 2011). WinWhatWhere developed and started selling a powerful monitoring software capable of capturing most computer activity and providing the results in an easy to interpret format. This was followed with the founding of other companies, such as SpyTech in 1998 and Spectrosoft, Inc. in 1999, which are still in operation today. The tools were marketed then as today to parents, spouses, and employers as a way to monitor computer activity.

In approximately 1998, several federal probation officers[1] began to realize these same tools could be adapted to managing the risk posed by cyber-offenders. However, it was not until approximately 2002 that IPPC appeared on the scene. In about 2007, MyMobileWatchdog, a company focused on mobile phone monitoring for parents, appeared. Only a few companies have ventured into mobile phone monitoring. As previously occurred with desktop and laptop monitoring, the focus

---

1. Notables in this group were Lanny L. Newville, Electronic Monitoring Specialist, Texas Western Pretrial Services and Dan Wieser, Jr., Senior U.S. probation Officer Middle District of Florida. Dan passed away in 2002. Lanny is still working as of this writing and is also an FBI ImageScan instructor.

has been on the noncorrections market.

In approximately 2007, RemoteCOM began operations, focusing on probation and parole officers' needs in offender computer management. In 2008, Surrey Police, United Kingdom, in conjunction with the Lucy Faithful Foundation, deployed Securus Software to monitor sex offenders as a special project (Securus, 2011). This software is still available to United Kingdom law enforcement.[2] Options are therefore limited to a few companies or using off-the-shelf monitoring software.

CONSUMER MONITORING SOFTWARE

Let's start the discussion with looking at the products that were initially used by officers, specifically, off-the-shelf or consumer monitoring software. These programs were and continue to be designed to monitor kids, spouses, and employees. They are very good at it as a whole. As they are being marketed to nontechnical folks, they are also easy to install. There can be minor configuration concerns, but they are few and far between. They also are relatively inexpensive, the most costly being $99.00 per license. Licenses are usually good for one year. Besides these factors, there are other issues that must be considered prior to adapting them to managing an offender's computer use.

Original Focus

As previously noted, these products were initially developed for an entirely different market. This market collectively had three consumer groups, specifically, parents, spouses, and employees. Parents needed a product that could help keep their children safe online. Troubled spouses wanted some tool they could use to check if their relationship problems might be the result of a partner's infidelity. Employers concerns centered on making sure their employees were not wasting resources or causing sexual harassment issues by viewing Internet pornography on the job. Additionally, they were concerned about prevent-

---

2. It is noteworthy the the FBI also started using monitoring software, including WinWhatWhere and similar programs, to catch Russian computer hackers and an alleged mobster Nicodemo Scarfo Jr. (Brainerd Dispatch, 2002). In 2009, law enforcement started using MyMobileWatchdog as a tool to document undercover stings involving mobile phones (Pontz, 2009).

ing the theft of their intellectual property. Each consumer group wanted to protect either their children, their relationships, or their property. Contrast these goals with that of a CCO, which is to protect the entire community and one can see the first consideration in using off-the-shelf monitoring software.

Authority

The second consideration has to do with authority. Each of these consumer groups has some degree of authority over the target computer and the person being monitored that a CCO does not possess. Let's start with the target computer aspect. Parents and employers have complete ownership of the target computer. The spouse, at the very least, has shared ownership in the computer, unless, of course, the computer is completely owned by the other spouse.[3] As a result of these ownership interests, the person being monitored can't just make wholesale system changes that would negatively affect monitoring. Parents and employers have total control of the target computers. If they wish, they can invoke administrative privileges[4] on the computer, preventing the removal or installation of any program. Spouses have shared administrative privileges and any changes made by the other would likely be mentioned or at the very least noticed almost immediately. All three groups likewise can remove the computer, without waiting for "reasonable suspicion" and approval to do so.

Familarity

Additionally, each of the groups has a familiarity of sorts to the computer they wish to monitor. They are aware of the operating system and the computer's "quirks." For instance, they are aware the mouse is configured for a left-handed person as opposed to a right-handed person. They know the monitor display is larger or smaller, as they are likely the ones who set it. They also are aware that the CD drive doesn't always work and to use the DVD drive. The list can be endless. The point is they know the computer and are familiar with it.

---

3. A spouse installing monitoring software on a computer he or she does not own or at least have a shared interest in is probably on shaky legal ground.
4. CCO could force and receive administrative privileges, but then they would likely also take on the role of systems administrator for the offender's computer. Such a role would likely greatly increase time and supervision resources spent on a case and is not recommended.

Time/Access

Parents, spouses, and employers also spend a significant amount of time on a daily basis with the person they wish to monitor. Parents and spouses live with their "targets." They not only have total access to the computer but also to the rest of the living space. Employers have total access to the computer and work area during and after business hours. This access allows these consumer groups to check on the monitoring software and review its results regularly whenever they want. Additionally, if they choose, they can physically watch the person using the monitored computer.

Volume

With the exception of employers, these groups are not likely to be monitoring numerous computers and/or individuals. A parent might be focused on one or two computers. A spouse would likewise be limited to monitoring a small number of computers, but no more than one individual. An employer could be involved, in monitoring numerous computers. However, the more computers involved the more likely the company has its own Information technology (IT) staff to assist in monitoring. As a result, many employers would likely have the capacity to put more technical staff on the monitoring.

Comparison

Compare these factors to that of a CCO, whose authority comes from the conditions imposed in a case. A parent or employer could deem a website or activity unaccepted and prohibit it without concern their decision might be appealed. A CCO has to have some justification for denying access or their decision will be overturned. Even the most intensive supervision does not involve sleeping in the same house, like a parent does with a child or spouse does with his or her partner. Nor does a CCO spend eight hours a day, five days a week at the same location with an offender, like an employer.

Every CCO installation is different. Even with details about the system being provided by the offender, those "quirks" don't always come out. Think about trying to perform basic point and click tasks with a mouse configured totally different than what one is accustomed to. Sure the mouse's configuration could be changed temporarily. But how many settings have to be changed just to make installing the software easier? What about the monitor resolution: too dark, too bright, too small, etc.? At some point, the CCO has to install monitoring software and then go back and return all those settings to their "original" state. Sometimes it is just easier to deal with it. Additionally, CCO can be confronted with a vast array of computers, such as a laptop with a touch pad mouse one day, a "home-made" desktop the next, and a touch screen computer the day after. Few IT staff, with the exception of the Geek Squad™, face the technical diversity involved with offender computer management.

Finally, a CCO, depending upon his or her agency, might be involved with computer management of ten or more offenders, dispersed over a wide geographic area. Some offenders may be sex offenders, but others might be cyberstalkers or fraudsters, each requiring a different focus and reflecting a different risk. Finally, CCO are installing the monitoring software in situations where someone may have been previously incarcerated and/or could very well end up going to prison based upon the monitoring software's operation. No parent, spouse, or employer faces these challenges when they install monitoring software.

These programs are inherently designed for a different purpose and user group. This is not meant to imply they cannot be adopted, only that these issues must be taken into account when using them. However, the tools will work. The more they are used, the easier installations become as well as comprehension of the results. Think of car mechanics. They work on different makes and models all the time. However, the cars, like computers, all function basically the same. Additionally, they don't go out and get needed tools for each car. Adopting a monitoring software program and getting accustomed to it will greatly assist the process. The first task in that regard is picking a program, unless, of course, the CCO adopts a company approach, which will be covered later.

Features

Many of these consumer monitoring programs will record: websites visited; online searches; username/passwords; social networking site activity; chats/instant messages; e-mail, including web-based; keystrokes typed; applications run; and screenshot captures of images displayed on the computer screen. Many also have filtering/blocking capabilities to include: certain websites and social networking sites; keyword blocking (bad word comes up and the site is blocked); or category blocking (material determined to contain violence, sex, drugs, etc.). Some also can block Internet use during certain times of the day or completely. Many of these programs will also generate e-mail alerts for keywords detected. The program results can be replayed on-site from the monitored computer; received in a report format via e-mail; or by logging into the vendor's website for remote viewing. Depending upon the vendor, the results can be displayed in a report format or played back similar to a video. The programs also usually have a stealth mode so it can't be discovered easily by a user. However, they do not always provide an electronic warning banner. If they do, the banner sometimes identifies the software, which can lead to a tamper. Again, this is a reflection of their normal market needs. Parents don't need a banner, as they own the computer. Spouses don't want their partner to know about the monitoring. Employers though should be concerned about this issue.

One final issue needs to be pointed out. This is particularly a concern for pretrial service officers but can be an issue for all CCO. Specifically, can the software be remotely uninstalled when supervision ends? Some offenders get committed to prison with little notice and unless prior arrangements are made, such as a family member agrees to provide access, the software will remain on the computer. IPPC and Remote COM do allow for remote uninstalls. Table 8 provides a listing of some of the better consumer monitoring packages, many of which have been adopted for offender computer management.

THE COMPANY APPROACH

Both IPPC and RemoteCOM are companies that were created specifically to meet the needs of offender computer monitoring. IPPC has over ten years experience working with probation and parole officers from around the country monitoring computers. Although RemoteCOM started in 2007, the company stresses that its staff have extensive law enforcement experience. These companies focus on monitoring offender behavior, not on software designed to monitor

Table 8.
CONSUMER MONITORING PACKAGES

Program	Type	Cost Per License Per Year	Company Website	Notes
CyberSentinel®	FG	$39.99	cybersentinel.co.uk	A
eBlaster®	II	$99.95	spectorsoft.com	B
Spector Pro®	I	$99.95		
SpyAgent	FG	$69.95	spytech-web.com	
WebWatcher 7	FG	$97.00	webwatchernow.com	C

Notes

FG are packages referenced by Harrold (2005) as Forced Gateway and Type I and II refer to "system resident" I and II approaches.

A and B: Both programs are also as considered "passive monitoring" for sex offender computer management (Brake & Tanner).

A: This company is located in the United Kingdom. Price is in dollars.

B: Spectrosoft® has a product Spectrpo 360® which requires a server, that would fall under forced gateway type. Only this company of those listed has software that will function with Apple computers.

B and C: Both of these companies have ventured into mobile phone monitoring.

The Securus program, mentioned at the start of the chapter, is only available to law enforcement in the United Kingdom and therefore is not listed. It is, however, a forced gateway approach.

All programs, with the exception of CyberSentinel, a UK Company, have received top rankings by Top Ten Reviews (http://monitoring-software-review.toptenreviews.com/) and/or PC Magazine (PCMag.com).

children or catch unfaithful spouses. IPPC provides the monitoring results to the officer to review via a secure website as in Harrold's forced gateway type. RemoteCOM analyzes the monitoring data and forwards alerts and summaries to CCO.

Both companies are familiar with the needs of collecting evidence so that it can be presented for violation proceedings. One concern in using consumer monitoring software with a forced gateway approach is this issue. For instance, commercial software is installed on a sex offender's computer. The officer checks through the vendor's website and sees the offender has been viewing child pornography, which is illegal for anyone to possess. The evidence is now on a website controlled by a private company. This company is not in the business of preserving evidence and is focused on another market, such as parents. They are just as likely to inadvertently delete the material, particularly as it is illegal for anyone to possess. There are also issues with evidence authentication, which commercial monitoring companies are not designed to consider. This is particularly important if the monitored offender disposes of the hard drive and the only evidence is that which is maintained off-site with the commercial monitoring company. With companies like IPPC and RemoteCOM, these issues have already been ironed out and they know how to react.

Each provides monitoring approaches that are resilient to tampering and to alert if a tamper is attempted or made. Monitoring software designed for consumer groups does not notify if there has been a tamper. Additionally, both companies use methods that aren't easily detected. Consumer monitoring software regularly appears as threats on antivirus software lists. These companies also provide support specific to the needs of someone monitoring offenders. Consumer monitoring software does have support, but it is designed for someone not protecting a community. Although consumer monitoring software is relatively easy to install, there are configurations that must be considered, such as keywords, what to monitor, how long to maintain data, where to forward alerts, etc. These configuration concerns are, for the most part, already built into the services provided by these two companies.

The company approach does have some shortcomings. Neither company currently monitors Apple systems or mobile phones.[5] Pricing varies between the two companies. However, a small agency, with less than ten offenders subject to computer monitoring, may be better off with individual purchases of consumer monitoring software.[6] Both companies focus on monitoring of online behavior and rely heavily on Internet access.[7] IPPC does have some programs that will capture off-line usage. RemoteCOM appears to offer direct access to the offend-

---

5. RemoteCOM is expected to begin monitoring mobile phones soon.
6. Be cautious in buying commercial monitoring software in bulk to get a discount. It may be out of date by the time it is installed. Remember the licenses are typically only for a year.
7. IPPC does have a tool that will lock all Internet access by the offender's computer.

204 The Cybercrime Handbook for Community Corrections

er's computer probably via a REA, which was discussed in Chapter 8, but that again requires on-line access.[8]

Some CCO may develop a misconception that a company is handling monitoring and therefore the need for them to make regular in-person visits and computer inspections is somehow negated.[9] Software installed and monitored by an officer tends to focus CCO into making those in-person inspections. Additionally, officers usually have very detailed case knowledge. They have presentence reports as well as psychological or sexual offense assessments/evaluations and treatment reports. Unless this information is communicated to the monitoring company, they will not have the same insight into problem behaviors. IPPC does not have this issue as the officer is in charge of reviewing the actual results. RemoteCom first reviews the data and sends a summary of the results. As such, unless there is good communication between RemoteCom and the assigned officer, troubling behavior might fester and get out of hand. Obviously, it would be detected, but CCO are suppose stop behavior before it rises to noncompliance. The next two sections will individually discuss each company approach.

Internet Probation and Parole Control (IPPC)

As was noted, IPPC has been around for almost ten years. Its software and services have been used by countless state and federal officers, in all types of cases. IPPC provides officers with the capability to remotely view data on a monitored offender's computer use, almost instantaneously. Additionally, it will send e-mail alerts for problem behaviors and can capture screenshots when keywords appear. Some of the features Berejka and LaMagna (2009) state that IPPC provides are:

- Internet usage by type of activity and websites visited;
- Web search activities, including those triggered by a keyword;
- A record, including screen shots when fantasy role-playing software is running;
- Images accessed via the Internet or other external devices;

---

8. This is not to mean RemoteCOM could not physically receive a seized hard drive or mobile phone for forensic examination from a CCO.
9. This could be an issue if the offender removes a hard drive with monitoring software installed and uses one without the software to avoid detection. Using tamper tape deters this from occurring.

- Chat room dialogues, which may include outgoing (and when permitted incoming); and
- Use of peripherals, such as flash drives or external drives.

Berejka and LaMagna (2009) also note that IPPC has the ability to block websites and to restrict Internet access to certain times. IPPC also has a tool that will prevent all Internet access for those cases not permitted to be online. Along with the ability to review the data as it is received, IPPC also prepares various reports, which are described by Berejka and LaMagna (2009) as:

- Top 100 Internet Activities—broken down by web, chat, news, email, and file transfers;
- Web Search Terms Report—listing keywords and phrases used by offenders to search the Internet;
- Summary of Web Activities by Category Report—reflecting the offender's Internet usage;
- Time at Category Report—reflecting the duration of time an offenders spends on each Internet by type of activity;
- Daily Internet Use—an hourly breakdown of when the offender's Internet activities are occurring; and
- Use of External Removable Media.

As was previously noted in this book, IPPC also has a biometric device which connects to the computer and limits monitoring to the offender's use. IPPC can also do online preinstall checks to make sure there are no configuration issues with an offender's computer. They also provide direct and timely assistance in the unlikely event the software stops working. One area IPPC does not provide is forensic examinations.

RemoteCOM

As indicated, this company started in 2007 and has a strong law enforcement background. It focuses on reducing offender monitoring costs and to serve "as an invaluable tool for the Probation Officer, allowing them more time to monitor their caseloads instead of looking through mounds of paperwork on computer-related activity" (Remote .COM, 2007). Unlike IPPC, it takes a direct role in analyzing and reviewing data. After identifying important areas of concern, it forwards the results to the CCO for their action. Its monitoring activities include:

- Recording User Log-on/Log-off dates and time;
- Capture of e-mails sent or received;
- Capture of both sides of chats and instant messages;
- Captures of all keystrokes typed;
- Websites visited and how long;
- Applications run and how long;
- Capture of Peer-to-Peer file sharing activity;
- Keyword alerts, including screen shot captures; and
- Blocking websites as needed.

One major area that differs between RemoteCOM and IPPC is the latter also offers computer forensic services, using many of the tools noted in this book. Their services specifically include acquisition, imaging, and analysis of electronic evidence. As noted previously, they also appear to have REA capability.

The ability to conduct computer forensic services is a plus. However, anyone contemplating services by any private company needs to be aware of the computer forensic vs. private investigations license issue. According to the American Bar Association (ABA, 2008), many states are looking to require individuals performing computer forensic work to be licensed as a private investigator in their state. Ironically, Texas, where RemoteCom is located, was one of the first states in which this became an issue. The solution is for either the company to obtain a license to operate in a state or, if permitted, subcontract with a person who has a license. There is no national private investigation license, and the license requirements are specific to each state. Failure to obtain a license can be extremely detrimental to getting evidence admitted in criminal court and at least in Texas, subject the person illegally performing computer forensic services to up to one year of jail time and a $4,000 fine plus a $10,000 civil penalty (ABA, 2008). Agencies contemplating contracting for private computer forensic services need to be cognizant of this issue in their state.[10]

---

10. Computer forensics performed as part of one's duties as a CCO is not impacted by the private investigation issue. Neither would forced gateway monitoring, employed by IPPC and some consumer monitoring programs.

Discussion

The decision to go with a consumer monitoring software package, IPPC or RemoteCom, is in the end going to come down at least initially to volume and cost. How many cases is an agency supervising? How many of those cases involve online computer access? Additionally, how many cases involved Apple computers or mobile phones, both of which are not currently monitored by either IPPC or Remote Com?[11] Does it make fiscal sense for an agency to go with a consumer monitoring product or opt for a company approach? Costs for consumer monitoring products can be shifted entirely to offenders. Computer Investigation Resources LLC (CIResources), at http://www.cire sources.com, provides a service for offenders and CCO that facilitates this option. CCO must register at the website, which is free. Offenders register at the site and provide funds for the monitoring software purchases. CIResources does not disclose the name of the software purchased to the offender. They, in turn, advise the CCO who registered that their offender purchased the software and it is available for download by the officer. In this manner, the officer never handles funds and the offender has no idea what software is being used to monitor him or her. Cost ranges from $100 to $200, depending upon the software selected, which mirrors Type I, II, and forced gateway options discussed earlier.

However many offenders can't afford even $100 for monitoring software. Prohibiting their computer use altogether may limit their ability to find and obtain employment. Both IPPC and RemoteCOM have options which allow the agency to assume all the costs, including those routinely assessed to the offender.

There are also costs outside the actual software or service. Specifically, will the use of a company over commercial monitoring software save agency time and resources? Those indirect costs add up. In the end, the decision is like eating. We can choose a full course meal or maybe just a sandwich. What we select in large part is based upon what we have in our wallet and how much time we have. However, we have got to eat to survive. Agencies also have to make some kind of decision. They can't just ignore it. Those hunger pains due to doing nothing will come, just like bad media press or a large civil suit.

---

11. RemoteCOM is expected to begin monitoring mobile phones soon.

MOBILE PHONES

Mobile phone monitoring is currently limited to consumer monitoring software. New companies are starting to get into the mix. However, some are strictly going after the corporate or employer market, which is huge. These vendors' pricing usually will not match well with a community correction agency's budget. Additionally, these are frequently based on large volumes of mobile phones being monitored. This leaves those vendors who are marketing to parents, spouses, and small employers. Pricing for these packages is usually consistent with agency budgets and/or offender's financial ability.

However, there is another catch. Mobile phone monitoring software only works with specific phones, usually the higher-end models, commonly referred to as "smartphones." Even then, not all smartphones are covered. Either the program will not work at all or only certain monitoring features will function. Currently, MyMobileWatch Dog is leading the pack with models covered and monitoring features. Specifically, depending upon the mobile phone, the following features are possible:

- Monitoring of: Text Messages (SMS) and Photos/Videos (MMS) including viewable content for both, E-mail, Logs all mobile Internet activity, Contact List Changes, and Calendar Updates;
- Application Blocking, such as Social Networking Apps (Facebook, Twitter, MySpace, YouTube), Instant Messaging Apps, web browsers, and camera;
- Website Blocking: Any mobile site and an alert is received for any attempts made to access;
- Time Blocking: Restrict calls during certain times exception for emergency and other important numbers;
- Authorized Contact List: Only calls on the approved list are allowed; and
- Easy access to online monitoring results via computer.

MyMobileWatchdog monitor Android®; Blackberry®; Windows; Mobile 5 & 6; and Brew®. As of this writing, monitoring software for Symbian is pending. Again, monitoring features vary by model and specific phone. Conversely, eBlaster® Mobile by Spectrosoft® Inc., and

WebWatcher Mobile by WebWatcher currently work only on Android and Blackberry phones. Monitoring features again vary by mobile phone and by vendor. It is noteworthy that many of these mobile monitoring packages will work on refurbished or rebuilt phones, which many more offenders can afford as opposed to a new phone.

MONITORING OTHER SYSTEMS

As was noted previously, Linux is one system that poses challenges for CCO. There is no consumer monitoring software for Linux. Additionally, neither services offered by IPPC or RemoteCOM cover Linux systems. The logical monitoring solution seems to be just to prohibit Linux use, which is by far the preferred option. However, there are two possibilities as a last result if this can't be done. The first is the use of a hardware KeyGhost® logger (see Figure 9). This hardware device will record up to 2,000,000 keystrokes, which is about 12 months worth of typing. There are models compatible with all keyboard interfaces. The device's cost is comparable with monitoring software noted previously. This option does not require computer experience to install, but to interpret the results, such as monitoring a hacking offender, would require expertise.

The other option requires the CCO or other person to take over the offender's Linux system as an administrator or Root user. As a Root user, Gnome Nanny could be installed. This free program is really for a user to monitor his or her children's activities. It focuses on filtering and blocking and setting time limits on computer use. Again, this would be an extreme option and not recommended unless the CCO has Linux skills or knows someone who can configure it (Gnome Nanny, http://linuxers.org/article/gnome-nanny-parental-control-system-linux). Again, the preferred option is to just say no to Linux.

CONCLUSION

Deploying monitoring software, either through using commercial monitoring software or a company, provides an additional and frequently needed dimension to computer management. It is particularly needed when supervising sex offenders. Its advantages have been noted previously throughout this book. The following additional thoughts are worth noting, regardless of which monitoring approach is adopted:

- Try them out and see which works best before making a decision;
- Consider deploying more than one method, such as Type I, II, and/or forced gateway approaches, as well as a hardware device for those technically sophisticated offenders;
- Do not rely solely on the alerts or noted trouble areas. Periodically check all the results to make sure nothing is being inadvertently overlooked. Offenders can find new ways to get into trouble online and CCO should constantly be willing to look outside the box for those occasions.
- For Type I methods, make sure data collecting settings allow sufficient time to retrieve results.
- Finally, do not check monitoring results on a nonagency computer, such as one's personal computer. This can place contraband on the computer. Agencies should provide a laptop with wireless Internet access or be content to wait until the assigned officer is at a work computer. An assigned laptop with wireless Internet access can also be used to safely conduct online investigations, the topic of the next chapter.

REFERENCES

American Bar Association (ABA). (2008). *ABA adopts resolution regarding computer forensics.* http://www.americanbar.org/groups/science_technology /pages/forensicresolution.html.

Berejka, M., & LaMagna, R. (2009). Remote computer monitoring: Managing sex offenders' access to the Internet. *Journal of Offender Monitoring,* Volume 21, No. 1: 11–29.

Brake, S., & Tanner, J. *Determining the need for Internet monitoring of sex offenders.* Retrieved from http://www.kbsolutions.com/MonitoringNeed.pdf.

Bloomberg BusinessWeek. (2011). TrueActive. Retrieved from http://invest ing.businessweek.com/research/stocks/private/snapshot.asp?privcapId= 8081897.

Brainerd Dispatch. (2002). Software snags crooks, sneaking spouses, but alarms privacy advocates. Retrieved from http://brainerddispatch.com /stories/030202/tec_0302020041.shtml.

Computer Investigation Resources LLC. (CIResources). Retrieved from http://www.ciresources.com.

CyberSentinel. Retrieved from http://www.cybersentinel.co.uk.

Gnome Nanny. Retrieved from http://linuxers.org/article/gnome-nanny-parental-control-system-linux.

Harrold, M. (2005). Computer searches of probationers: Diminished privacies, special needs & 'whilst' quiet pedophiles plugging the Fourth Amendment into the virtual home visit. *The Mississippi Law Journal*, 75: 273–365.

KeyGhost Logger. Retrieved from http://www.keyghost.com/.

Kivolowitz, P. (1983). Security digest archives. Retrieved from http://securitydigest.org/unix/archive/006.

Mitnick, K. Retrieved from http://www.brainyquote.com/quotes/quotes/k /kevinmitni234035.html.

Monitoring Software–Top Ten Reviews. Retrieved from http://monitoring-software-review.toptenreviews.com/.

MyMobileWatchDog. Retrieved from http://www.mymobilewatchdog.com.

Pontz, Z. (2009, April 20). Parents, police monitoring kids' cell phones. CNN. Retrieved from http://articles.cnn.com/2009-04-20/tech/monitor ing.kids.cellphones_1_sexual-predators-cell-phones-mobile-watchdog?_s =PM:TECH.

RemoteCOM. (2007). Promotional brochure. *Remote-Com_brochure.pdf.*

Securus Software. Retrieved from http://www.securus-software.com/benefits /police.html.

Spectorsoft, Inc. Retrieved from https://www.spectorsoft.com.

SpyAgent. Retrieved from https://www.spytech-web.com.

Webwatchernow. Retrieved from http://www.webwatchernow.com.

Chapter 10

ONLINE INVESTIGATIONS

This is just the beginning; the beginning of understanding
that cyberspace has no limits, no boundaries.
–Nicholas Negroponte, American Businessman and founder
of the One Laptop per Child Association (OLPC)
(http://one.laptop.org/)

This book has covered actions that cannot be undertaken without specific legal authorization. CCO can't do computer searches, without a condition, statute, or consent. Additionally, "reasonable suspicion" must exist or search results are likely to be inadmissible for new criminal charges. CCO also can't install monitoring software on an offender's computer without some legal authority. These supervision activities are also usually associated with offenders who have committed an offense with a computer and/or are sex offenders. This next area, online investigations, requires no special condition or reasonable suspicion. They can be conducted on any offender, regardless of their conviction offense or even if they have yet to be convicted. The only requirements are a live Internet connection, a computer, and the desire to conduct what Kentucky Parole Office Sharon Blalock (2007) refers to as "virtual home visits."

SOCIAL NETWORKING

In 1997, SixDegrees.com appeared on the scene, which was followed by Friendster® in 2002 and MySpace in 2003 (Boyd & Ellison,

2007). Facebook came along in 2004 and Twitter in 2006, which significantly changed the online social networking world (Boyd & Ellison, 2007). Individuals, including offenders, are "tweeting" every minute about everything. The small sampling of "tweets" below represents why CCO need to be aware of an offender's online activities (Bowker, 2011):

ScottiePiffin15: *itch im on probation so my nerves bad

.cchellahandsome: Sitting in the probation place like I don't have *hit to do today.

Lil_CrYs420: Ughhhhhh who knew you needed a whole cup of *iss . . . grrrrr hates probation soooo much!!! I need to smoke badly.

Shedd2009: Damn . . . Gotta see the Probation Officer today. . . . Just another #Mutha*uckaIHateButWontEverKnowIt.

Stickileaks: #thingsthat*issmeoff My parole officer . . .

xADRiZZy: I need to get alway frm my parole officer! Smh; All up on my business."

So what is this phenomenon associated with social networking sites (SNS)? What does it mean for the CCO and supervision of their cases? SNS create a network of "friend" connections. Through these networks, individuals can define their likes and dislikes and find others with similar interests. They also allow individuals to search for past acquaintances and to make new ones. They provide a method for individuals to share and market ideas and to advance their careers. Individuals are increasingly turning to them to also do their own investigations about prospective employees, students, "blind" dates, and in some cases, their supervision officer. Many allow individuals to share photos, music, and videos with one another. The online dating scene reflects that they are clearly being used to expanding dating options. Boyd and Ellison (2007) define social network sites as:

. . . web-based services that allow individuals to (1) construct a public or semi-public profiles within a bounded system, (2) articulate a list of other users with whom they share a connection, and (3) view and traverse their list of connections and those made by others within the system. The nature and nomenclature of these connections may vary from site to site.

SNS can become a very important window into who the offender is and how he or she is progressing or regressing in the supervision process. Access to an offender's SNS profile frequently reveals his or her personalities, including motives and personal relationships. Offenders have been found to be associating with one another and committing other violations, such as drug use and even weapon possession. Some offenders have used SNS to publicly identify an informer and to relay threats. For those CCO involved in fugitive apprehension, they can provide valuable location information. Law enforcement has also been known to use SNS to help prove or disprove alibis, to establish a crime or criminal enterprise, and to document instrumentalities or fruits of crime. SNS information can also be used to establish reasonable suspicion for a probation/parole search or probable cause for a search warrant.

Getting Started

CCO have a wealth of information resources at their disposal. They usually have presentence reports which include numerous offender details. They hopefully receive timely monthly supervision reports to keep current on their offenders. They also can interview their offenders, their families, and other third parties to obtain additional information, including their specific SNS profiles. These sources provide the following identification data which can be used to conduct effective SNS investigations: (1) SNS profiles; (2) names and nicknames; (3) past/current addresses; (4) telephone/mobile numbers; (5) current and past e-mail addresses/screen names; (6) their family/known associates; (7) schools they have graduated from or attended; and (8) past and current employers. Obviously, getting the actual SNS profile is the first step. However, all of the other information can be used to locate those unknown offender SNS profiles. Searching by name might not reveal anything. Oftentimes name searches, particularly with common names, will result in too many hits. However, searching with an e-mail, usually the key SNS identifier, will readily produce an offender's profile. Frequently SNS allow searches by zip code, schools, and employer, all of which narrow the search area significantly.

Unless the SNS profile is initially known, the first step is to try a Google search. This can often quickly locate the offender's profile. Plug in the offender's name, trying both first, last name and last, first name order, using quotation marks around the names. Add their location to the mix. Also don't be afraid to try other search engines. Here are a few: bing.com, Yahoo.com, dogpile.com, webcrawler.com, Ice rocket.com, Blogs.com, yoname.com, brbpub.com, and Zoominfo .com. Additionally, do a Google inquiry for the top ten search tips to make these efforts more productive.

SNS Profiles

Once an offender's profile has been located, it will frequently require logging on to the SNS to view it, which requires a profile. Never use a personal SNS profile to attempt to locate or view an offender's profile. This can lead to the officer's personal information being inadvertently disclosed to the offender. However, some sites, such as Facebook, will terminate a profile that is entirely bogus. Some sites will make exceptions for law enforcement agencies, if they are notified in advance. Creating a SNS profile with accurate information on an adult-oriented dating site will subject officers to numerous "offers." However, these sites usually have no prohibition against profiles that contain less than accurate information.

Therefore, officers are encouraged to review a SNS's user agreements to make sure their actions do not violate the site's rules. The penalty for violating the rule on providing fictitious information is frequently only account deletion, which can be frustrating if significant time was spent creating the profile. As a general rule of thumb, create fictitious profiles for accessing adult dating sites, which sex offenders often frequent. For others, create a profile that is accurate but for business purposes only. Individuals can create several accounts (one personal and one or more business) using different e-mail addresses. The e-mail addresses can be created for free on numerous sites, such as Google and Yahoo! Create a Facebook account, with an accurate name, but little or no personal identifiers. Additionally, reflect that it is being used for supervision purposes. This profile then can be used to search and, when needed, to connect with an offender's profile.

If a Google or other search is not productive, it will require CCO to search a SNS directory. This is where the offender's e-mail address can be particularly helpful. Again, the key to making these searches successful is to have the information noted previously readily available. CCO also are strongly encouraged to obtain Kentucky Parole Officer Blalock's (2007) *Virtual Home Visits: A Guide to Using Social Networking Sites to Assist with Offender Supervision and Fugitive Apprehension*. This free law enforcement only guide is a must for CCO.

SNS are very easy to navigate. Sometimes an offender's wall space is set private, but their friends are public. Checking out the friends may reveal one where their wall is public. This can sometimes be used to help establish a rough time-line for when the offender opened the account and how they are posting. For instance, the friend's wall space might have a date when the offender connected with them. The friend's wall space might also give insight into what the offender is using to post. For instance, some posts might reflect they were made by a mobile device. This information may be important for sex offender supervision as well as considering the need to do a search to locate a computer. Try expanding the friend's posts and then conducting a word search by the offender's profile name using the pull down edit feature in the browser (Edit then Find). This will allow a quick search for references to the offender's postings and information.

Two law enforcement tools that will allow CCO to graphically map profile connections are Facebook Visualizer 1.11 and MySpace Visualizer 2.8. These tools were developed by Lococitato (https://www.lococitato.com/). Facebook Visualizer 1.11 is restricted to law enforcement. There are limited feature versions which can be downloaded for free. However, the pay versions are inexpensive and worth the investment. These tools are particularly helpful in investigating gang offenders' profiles.

At some point, a CCO may need to request the offender approve him or her as a friend. Getting access provides the officer a chance to review their posts, friends, and/or photos. Standard conditions are frequently worded to require the offender to either follow instructions and/or permit visits at home and "elsewhere." A SNS is "elsewhere" and this is the authority to get access. However, do not give a lot of warning or allow a significant amount of time to lapse before access is granted. Doing so allows the offender to remove troubling posts or photos. Also be prepared to capture and document any significant findings as they will likely later be gone. Sometimes an offender will simply delete the account to avoid complying with the request, which depending upon the supervision conditions, is noncompliance.

SNS Monitoring

One thing that is of constant concern is an offender prohibited from online access obtaining a profile, undetected, or posting troubling messages on blogs, news sites, etc. Additionally, there is always that high-profile offender who can't seem to stay out of the news. It is time consuming to constantly do Internet searches for this activity. One method to avoid this is to use free tools which constantly monitor the Internet for references to specific terms, such as an offender's real name, profile, or screen name. These tools will forward the results via e-mail on a periodic basis, such as daily or weekly. Google has a built-in feature called "Alerts," located at http://www.google.com /alerts?hl=en for this purpose. Socialmention at http://socialmention .com/alerts/ is another monitoring tool for this purpose. These tools can also be used to stay current on correctional topics.

Another tool is SafetyWeb Online Tracking (SWOT) by SafetyWeb (http://www.safetyweb.com/swot), which is free to law enforcement. It is designed to help parents keep up on their kid's online activities and to aid law enforcement looking for missing children. This tool searches the Internet for a minor's social networking profiles and their activity associated with those profiles. The program uses the minor's e-mail address to conduct the Internet searches. It can also use mobile phone numbers as an added element. This program can be adopted for offender supervision. CCO can set up a "parent" account and create profiles belonging to their offenders to monitor. The program searches constantly for new profiles and activity. It provides that information in an easy to read format accessed via their website. The format provides a listing of all identified SNS profiles and their activities. Periodically logging in will help officers stay on top of what profiles their offenders have as well as their activity associated with those profile. This alleviates the need to constantly check each individual profile or doing Internet searches to find them. Again, this tool should be reserved for use on those with the highest cyber-risk or high-profile cases.

WEBSITES

From time to time, offenders will start up a website. There is nothing wrong with this, provided they are not precluded by their conditions. However, sometimes the website is created to lend an air of legitimacy to fraudulent activity. To obtain information about a website, take the uniform resource identifier (URL) and conduct a Whois search (https://www.arin.net/resources/whoisrws or use any Whois search website. For instance the registration information available on the High Technology Crime Investigation Association at htcia.org is as follows:

Registrant:
High Technology Crime Investigation Association
3288 Goldstone Drive
Roseville, CA 95747 US
Domain Name: HTCIA.ORG
Administrative Contact , Technical Contact:
High Technology Crime Investigation Association
carol@htcia.org
3288 Goldstone Drive
Roseville, CA 95747 US
Phone: 916-408-1751
Fax: (916) 408-7543
Record expires on 05-Oct-2014
Record created on 02-Oct-2002
Database last updated on 06-Aug-2009

A caution is in order. This information can sometimes be fictitious, but it is a good starting point to checking out a website. Another useful website to find out how a site looked in the past is the Internet Archive's Wayback Machine at http://wayback.archive.org. This site has website archives from past years. Some websites will have code placed on their site that will prevent its collection in the archive but many sites do not. It is further noted that this site could also be used to bypass some website filtering as it has archived pornographic websites as well.

Be aware that websites often collect the Internet Service Provider address being used to visit their site. So if a CCO uses an agency provided service, or worse their personal service provider, that address will show up in the website's log. However, one can anonymously surf online with use of websites such as http://hidemyass.com/ and other advanced methods, such as using Vidalia, https://www.torproject.org /projects/vidalia.html.en. Again, this is another reason why CCO should not use their personal computers and have adequate safeguards (antivirus, firewalls) in place.

SEARCH and Vera Software provide free tools to law enforcement to aid in online investigations. These tools have investigative websites, useful search engines, and resources. SEARCH's tool is SEARCH investigative Community Toolbar at http://searchinvestigative.our-toolbar.com/. Vere Software's two tools are Internet Investigator's ToolKit and Vere Software Internet Investigator's Toolbar, both available at http://veresoftware.com/index.php/webcase_overview/down loads.

DOCUMENTATION

CCO are required to document their supervision activities. Online investigations need special care as they can change or be deleted in a heartbeat. Some may argue that all that is needed is a hard copy print-out of a web page or site. There at least four problems with this approach. First, hard copies do not capture web links or video audio media. Second, hard copies can't be electronically searched for text, unless they are scanned and converted to electronic data. Third, printing hard copies is labor intensive. It takes time to print out each web page or location on a SNS. Finally, they are paper intensive. For instance, try printing out an offender's 100 or more friends and see how much paper is involved.

It is possible to save a web page to a "mnt"file, using the File, then save option in some web browsers. This creates an electronic version of the web page. The problem is the saved copy can be easily altered. Additionally, video and audio files are not captured. Additionally, this is very labor intensive. Another approach is to hit the Control (Ctrl) key and Print Screen when viewing a web page and paste the results into Paint Shop. This takes a screen shot of the web page. The problem again is this can be altered. Additionally, web links and video and audio files are lost. Finally, this is also labor intensive.

A somewhat better approach is to use a specific screen capture tool. Hooverdesk is a free tool located on the Windows side of the DEFT CD, mentioned in Chapter 8. This program allows the user to capture screen shots, with time and date information included in the file name. Additionally, there is a setting that allows each shot to be sequentially numbered as well. This makes capturing the evidence much faster. A shortcoming to this approach is the entire web page is not captured. Only the portion that is being viewed is captured. Additionally, web links, videos, and audio are not captured. Finally, unless the files created are hashed, with a tool such as FTK Imager, they can be altered without detection.

TechSmith® (www.techsmith.com) has several commercial products, such as Snagit for screen captures and Camtasia Studio for video captures that can be used to more fully collect a websites physical appearance. However, these products will also not capture web links. Acrobat (not the reader) can be used to capture a website, not only preserving the links but also providing a version that can be electronically searched for text. For instance, using Acrobat one can capture the wall postings on a Facebook profile, save it, and later search the text for troubling postings. However, Acrobat will not capture video and audio files themselves.

There is one commercial tool that CCO involved in online investigations should consider getting. It is Vere Software's WebCase®. This tool will do screen/video/chat captures, web page archiving, hash files for evidence authentication, date/time stamp files, preserve and secure evidence properly, and provide customizable report formats of the evidence collected (Figure 29).

TRAINING RESOURCES

There are resources available to become better at online investigations and to learn to capture online evidence effectively. SEARCH has the following free publications for CCO use at http://www.search.org/programs/hightech/publications/: "How to Capture a MySpace Page

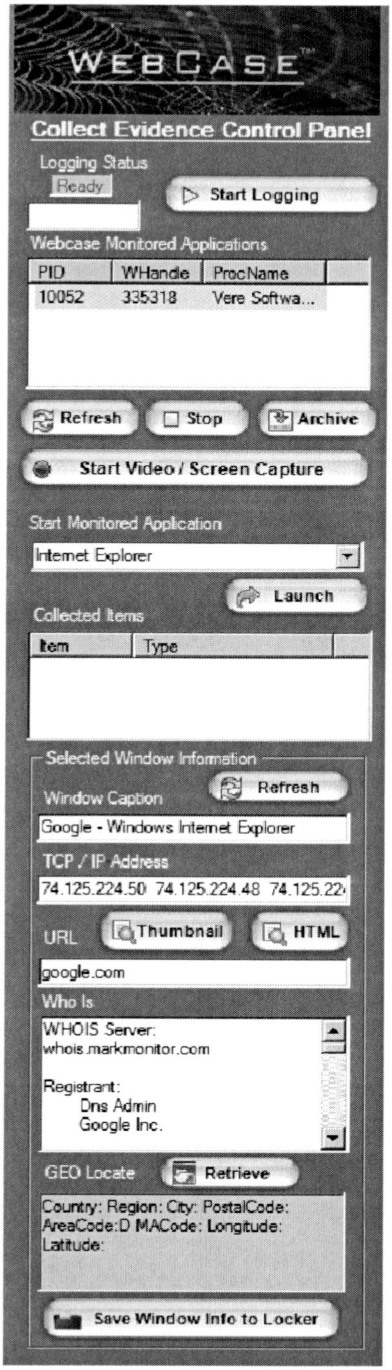

Figure 29. Webcase Control Panel.

for Investigative Purposes and The "SEARCH Investigative Toolbar and Other Mozilla Firefox Investigative Extensions." Additionally SEARCH has a course specific to SNS, "Social Networking Sites: Investigative Tools and Techniques" (http://www.search.org/programs /hightech/courses/). Finally, Vera Software has webinar classes, frequently which are free, pertaining to online investigations (http://vere software.com/index.php?page=webinars.

CONCLUSION

It should be clear from this chapter that individuals are posting a wealth of information on the web, particularly on SNS. This information can be of great assistance in determining what an offender is up to in the real world. It should also be apparent that CCO need to be careful what they post on their personal profile. The same tools they use to search for offenders information can also be used to search for them and their families. As a result, CCO need to be extremely careful about posting information as well as making sure their SNS profiles have the strictest privacy settings. Additionally, they need to be mindful to inform their immediate family and significant others to show the same diligence in their postings and settings. Otherwise, someone with evil intent may use the online information to get at the officer and his or her family. Welcome to cyberspace, a place with "no limits, no boundaries."

REFERENCES

Blalock, S. (2007). *Virtual home visits: A guide to using social networking sites to assist with offender supervision and fugitive apprehension.* District 1, Division of Probation and Parole Kentucky Department of Corrections.

Bowker, A. (2011). Twitter and probation and parole. Retrieved from http://www.corrections.com/cybercrime/?p=174.

Boyd, D., & Ellison, N. (2007). Social network sites: Definition, history, and scholarship. *Journal of Computer-Mediated Communication, 13*(1), article 11. Retrieved from http://jcmc.indiana.edu/vol13/issue1/boyd.ellison.htm.

Internet Archive's Wayback Machin, Retrieved from http://wayback .archive.org.

Lococitato. Retreived from https://www.lococitato.com/.

Negroponte, N. Retrieved from http://www.brainyquote.com/quotes/quotes/n/nicholasne381691.html.

SafetyWeb Online Tracking (SWOT). SafetyWeb. Retrieved from http://www.safetyweb.com/swot.

SEARCH. Retrieved from http://www.search.org/.

Techsmith. Retrieved from http://www.techsmith.com/.

Vera Software. Retrieved from http://veresoftware.com/.

EPILOGUE

The only source of knowledge is experience.
—Albert Einstein, scientist, 1879 to 1955

No longer can community correction agencies ignore the cyber-world. As this book hopefully demonstrated, it is becoming more and more intertwined with the real world. Offenders, like the rest of society, are embracing computers and the Internet. CCO and their agencies must therefore be willing to face the challenges of managing cyber-risk head on. CCO are encouraged to seek out training opportunities with one or more of the following groups listed below to obtain, expand, and hone the needed skills for this task. This book was only a beginning. In the end, only with developing knowledge through experience can CCO hope to be effective in supervising offenders in the 21st century and managing cyber-risk.

- National Computer Forensics Institute (NCFI)
  (http://www.ncfi.usss.gov/overview.html)
- The National Law Enforcement and Corrections Technology
  Center (http://www.prod.justnet.org/Pages/fieldsearch.aspx)
- The National White Collar Crime Center
  (http://www.nw3c.org/)
- The Federal Bureau of Investigation's Regional Computer
  Forensic Labs (RCFL)
  (http://www.refl.gov/index.cfm?fuseAction
  =Public.P_trainingCourses)
- The American Probation and Parole Association
  (http://www.appa-net.org/eweb/)
- SEARCH (http://www.search.org/)

- The High Technology Crime Investigation Association (http://www.htcia.org)

REFERENCES

Einstein, A. Retrieved from http://www.brainyquote.com/quotes/quotes/a /alberteins148778.html.

APPENDICES

A. Computer Restriction and Monitoring Program Participant Agreement
B. Computer Usage Questionnaire
C. Hardware/Software Restrictions
D. Computer Monitoring Release
E. Computer Usage Update Questionnaire
F. Authorization to Search/Seize Computer Equipment/Electronic Data
G. Knoppix Evidence Inventory Worksheet
H. Preview In Windows
I. Property Receipt

Appendix A

COMPUTER[1] RESTRICTION AND MONITORING PROGRAM PARTICIPANT AGREEMENT

I,_____have been placed in the Computer Restriction and Monitoring Program. I understand that this agreement is by reference part of the order setting conditions and that failure to comply with its provisions or my officer's instructions will be considered a supervision violation and may result in an adverse action. I agree to comply with all rules set forth in this agreement and my officer's instructions. I agree to call my officer immediately if I have any questions or if I experience any problems that may hinder my compliance with this program.

I understand that I must provide accurate information on my computer and Internet access, including passwords used, within seven days.

I shall possess and/or access only approved computer hardware or software. I will not install new hardware or software or effect repairs on my computer system without receiving prior permission from my officer.

I shall only use an Internet Service Providers(s) (ISP) approved by my officer. I also shall only use e-mail and/or social networking profiles approved by my officer. I further agreed to provide my officer access to all areas of my social networking profile.

I understand I must have written permission prior to accessing or obtaining any additional computers; ISP; e-mail account; and/or social networking site profiles.

Defendant/Offender   Date   Officer   Date

---

1. The term computer encompasses any electronic, magnetic, optical, electrochemical, or other high-speed data processing device performing logical, arithmetic, or storage functions, and includes any data storage facility or communications facility directly related to or operating in conjunction with such device. This definition covers all desktop and laptop computers, mobile phones, gaming devices, or any devices that meets the above criteria. If you have a question concerning a particular device ask your officer.

I shall not create or assist directly or indirectly in the creation of any electronic bulletin board, ISP, or any other public or private network without the prior written approval of my officer, which may include additional conditions with regard to that approval.

I agree to allow a search of my computer as deemed necessary and to the installation of software/hardware designed to monitor computer activities on any computer I am authorized to use. I understand that the software/hardware may record any and all computer activity, including keystrokes typed, application information, Internet use history, email correspondence, and chat conversations. I agree not to attempt to remove, tamper with, reverse engineer, or in any way circumvent the software/hardware.

I understand that measures may be used to assist in monitoring compliance with these conditions such as placing tamper resistant tape over unused ports and to seal my computer case.

I will notify all individuals that have access to my computer system that it is subject to monitoring and/or search/seizure. I further understand that a notice will be placed on the computer to warn others of the existence of any installed monitoring software.

I will provide copies of credit card billing records or other financial records as directed and will not open any new lines of credit without authorization. I understand that my officer has the authority to request my credit history information to confirm my compliance with the supervision conditions and these program rules. My signature on this document signifies my consent for the release of the credit history information.

  Defendant/Offender   Date   Officer   Date

Appendix B

COMPUTER[1] USAGE QUESTIONNAIRE

DEFENDANT/OFFENDER	
OFFICER	

A requirement of the Computer Restriction and Monitoring Program is you are to provide accurate information about all of your e-mail accounts; all of your social networking profiles; your entire computer system and software; all passwords used by you; and your Internet Service Provider(s). To facilitate your compliance with this requirement you are to complete this form in full and return to your officer within seven days. If you need additional space, write on a separate sheet of paper referencing the item. If an item does not apply, mark not applicable or "N/A." If you are unsure about what to report, ask your officer.

For purpose use following codes:
Work=W, School=S; Personal=P; Other=O.

1. List all e-mail accounts you have. If none, mark N/A. Attach additional sheet if necessary.

	Full E-mail Address	Password	Purpose	
A				
B				
C				
D				
E				
F				
Are you attaching an additional sheet for this item?			Yes	No

1. The term computer encompasses any electronic, magnetic, optical, electrochemical, or other high speed data processing device performing logical, arithmetic, or storage functions, and includes any data storage facility or communications facility directly related to or operating in conjunction with such device. This definition covers all desktop and lap top computers, mobile phones, gaming devices or any devices that meets the above criteria. If you have a question concerning a particular device ask your officer.

2. List profiles with any social networking site[2] (SNS) you have. If none, mark N/A. Use additional sheet if necessary.

SNS	Profile Name	Associated E-mail From Above	Password	Purpose

Are you attaching an additional sheet for this item?	Yes	No

3. List all mobile phones you use or possess. If none, mark N/A. Use additional pages providing the same information, if necessary.

Mobile Phone No.		1 of	

Account No.	Purpose:

Carrier:	Name of Account Holder:

Brand:	Model:

Password:

Please circle all features enabled on this mobile phone:

Camera	Instant Message	Internet	GPS	Removal Storage
Video	E-Mail	WiFi	Blue Tooth	Others (Describe)

List any and all electronic communication accounts accessed via this device (e-mail, IM).

Provider/SNS	Screen Name/E-Mail Address	Password

2. Some examples of SNS include Facebook, MySpace, Bebo, LinkedIn, and Twitter.

4. List any gaming devices you use or have access to. If none, mark N/A. Use additional pages providing the same information, if necessary.

Make/Model	Serial No.	of

Please circle all features with this gaming device	
Camera	Webcam
Instant Messaging/Chat	Internet
WiFi	External Memory

List any and online profiles you have associated with this device. Attach additional sheets if more space is needed.

Site (Game)	Profile	Password

If this device has Internet access, who is the provider and how is it connected (cable, WiFi, etc.)

5. Do you have access to any other computer, Internet Service Provider (ISP), Bulletin Board (BBS), or any other private computer network or service at any location, including but not limited to employment, education, family or friends? (Legitimate financial transactions, such as ATM/DEBIT are not included?)

No, You may stop here and sign below. If Yes, go to next page.

Important Notice: You are to immediately contact your officer prior to accessing any computer or service at any location.

To the best of my knowledge and belief, the information I have provided on this form is true, correct and complete. I understand that a false statement on this form may result in a supervision violation or new prosecution as warranted.

| Defendant/Offender   Date | Officer   Date |

COMPUTER USAGE

1. Where do you use a computer?

    a. Home

    b. School

    c. Work

    d. Other (Explain)

2. Estimate how many hours a week you access computer(s)?

Location	Hours Per Week or N/A
Home	
Work	
School	
Mobile Device	
Other (Specify)	

3. Estimate how many hours a week you are on the Internet?

Location	Hours Per Week or N/A
Home	
Work	
School	
Mobile Device	
Other (Specify)	

4. Do you or someone you share use of a computer with operate a website, electronic bulletin board, list serve, or e-mail service? Explain, all affirmative responses.

5. Do you or someone you share use of a computer with write or publish material for distribution to the public? Explain, all affirmative responses.

COMPUTER ACCESS		
Employment		
1. Do you have Internet access at employment?	No	Yes
2. Do you have remote access to your employer's computer system?	No	Yes
3. Must you use unique passwords to gain access to your work computer, your employer's network, and/or the Internet?	No	Yes
4. If so, does your employer monitor your use? (Note: This information may be verified.)	No	Yes
5. How do your duties at work require computer and/or Internet access?		
6. Name and Telephone No. of person responsible for computer issues at your employment:		
Education/Training		
1. Are you currently enrolled in an educational or vocational program?	No	Yes
2. As a result, do you have Internet access through the program's system?	No	Yes
3. Must you use a unique password to gain access to the program's computer, network, or Internet?	No	Yes
4. Do they monitor your use? (Note: This information may be verified.)	No	Yes
5. What requires you to have access to the programs' computer and/or Internet access?		
6. Name and Telephone No. of person responsible for computer issues at your education/vocational program:		

Note: All e-mail accounts must be reported on page 1.

INTERNET ACCESS

1. List all Internet Service Providers (ISP) you have and indicate which screen names/email addresses correspond with the appropriate ISP. If additional space is needed, attach a separate sheet.

ISP	Account Name (Screen/E-mail)	Password	Who has access?	Cost and How Paid

2. Chat Room/Internet Relay Chat/Instant Messages, etc.: List any and all forms of electronic communication not reflected previously. If additional space is needed attach a separate sheet.

Located	Screen Name	Password

3. Websites: List any and all websites and/or locations, you have privileges to receive, send, and/or store information. If additional space is needed, attach a separate sheet.

Name/URL/IP Address	Domain Registered to:	Password

4. Remote Storage: Provide complete details regarding any storage locations that are not reflected above. Information to be included: Where located (be specific), how much storage space you have, method for paying for space, purpose of having this storage space, and password to access location.

COMPUTER COMPONENTS
In the following sections, you are to provide full information regarding all computers and accessories you can access. If your computer system is networked, you will need to provide all information on all computers on the network and complete a Network Shutdown Procedures Form. If you are unsure about what to report, ask your officer. If you need additional space, write on a separate sheet of paper referencing the item. If an item does not apply, mark not applicable or "N/A."
1. Complete for each computer you have or use:

Computer, of		
Brand:	Model:	Serial:
MHZ:	RAM:	BIOS:

Any user names and passwords associated with this computer:
Where is this computer maintained?
What is the primary purpose of this computer?
Who has access to this computer besides yourself and why?

Is this computer set to boot first from a hard drive?	No	Yes
Is this computer networked?	Yes	No

If so, indicate assignment on network:
How many hard drives does this computer have? Complete Item 2 for each hard drive.

2. Provide information for each hard drive in each computer.
Hard Drive _____ of _____ located in Computer ID. As:

Model#	Serial #

Identified by operating system as drive letter(s):
Drive Size:
Password associated with this drive:
Can your computer boot from this drive?, , Yes, , No
If so, what is the name and version of the operating system(s)?

Windows:	Unix:	Linux:
Apple:	BeOS:	Inferno:

Netware:	Other:

Is this drive a: Primary   Slave
Is this drive partitioned?   Yes   No
If so, how many partitions?   Provide following information for each partition:

Partition	Size and Format (Fat 16/32 NTFS, etc.)	Operating System Designation	If bootable, Name of Operating System
____of ____			
____of ____			
____of ____			

Use additional pages in same format if necessary
What is the configuration of all IDE/SCSI slots in this machine?
Do any of the settings permit the "hot" swapping of hard drives or external drives?,   Yes, , No
3. Additional Hard Drives Not in Use:
List all hard drives to which you have access that are not installed. Use additional sheets as necessary to provide full information.

Serial No.	Size	Where Maintained

4. Removable Media Storage Drives

Provide the following information pertaining to all drives that use removable media, examples of such devices: CD/DVD/BD and those that can be save data more than once (rewritable), as in CD-RW and or DVD-RW. Additionally, report ZIP, JAZ, SCSI,3.5, etc. Use additional sheets as necessary to provide full information.

Serial No.	Size	Where Maintained

5. USB/Firewire Drives

Provide the following information pertaining to all drives that use either USB or Firewire. Examples of such devices: Flash drives (thumb drives), USB external drive enclosures, external USB drives, etc. Use additional sheets as necessary to provide full information.

Serial No.	Size	Where Maintained

6. Modems

List all modems or modem cards, whether internal or external to the above computers. Use additional sheets as necessary to provide full information.

Internal/External	Model/Serial/Speed	Where Maintained

7. Other Accessories		

List all peripherals and expansion cards that you own/possess, that are not listed previously. Examples are: memory sticks; memory cards; WiFi hard drives, palm pilots; digital cameras; scanners; printers; SCSI; NIC; or video cards, etc. Use additional sheet as necessary to provide full information.

Device	Model	Serial

Networks		

8. Do you have a network?   Yes   No
9. If so, have you attached a Network Shutdown Procedure Form?   N/A   Yes   No

---

SOFTWARE

1. Provide the name of all operating system(s) you possess, regardless of whether they are installed:

2. List all major application software you possess:

3. Provide the name of any antivirus or firewall software you have:

4. List all browser software installed on your computer. Include software version number (Internet Explorer 7.0, 8.0, 9.0, Firefox 4, Netscape Navigator 6.0, etc.).

Browser Name	Version

5. Do you have licenses for all copyrighted software on your system(s)?

   Yes   No   If, no explain

6. Please circle any of the following you possess and provide complete details and the reason for possessing on a separate sheet:

   a. Encryption or steganography or similar software/hardware
   b. Monitoring or similar software/hardware
   c. Anti-monitoring or similar software/hardware
   d. Password cracking utilities
   e. Wiping/erasing or similar utilities
   f. Peer-to-peer or file sharing programs
   g. Virus, worms, Trojan horse, logic bombs, sniffer programs, or any other similar programs
   h. Any pirated software (software for which you do not have a license for, which is not shareware or freeware)
   i. Any software, hardware, and/or website that can be used to spoof, conceal, and/or hide your identity.

7. List any passwords that are not reflected above that have access to systems, files, storage, e-mail accounts, etc.

Password	For

8. Note any additional information that you feel is important in regards to your computer/Internet access that is not previously addressed on this form.

To the best of my knowledge and belief, the information I have provided on this form is true, correct, and complete. I understand that a false statement on this form may result in a supervision violation or new prosecution as warranted.

Defendant/Offender Date	Officer Date

Network Shutdown Procedures
1. Provide a written diagram that accurately reflects your particular network. Use a separate sheet for each network you control. Include location of all computers, router(s), server(s), hubs, etc. and advise your network connection media (wireless, coaxial, etc).
2. Provide specific details on how to shutdown all networks. Again, use a separate sheet for each network you control.   To the best of my knowledge and belief, the information I have provided on this form is true, correct and complete. I understand that a false statement on this form may result in a supervision violation or new prosecution as warranted.
Defendant/Offender   Date   Officer   Date

Appendix C

HARDWARE/SOFTWARE RESTRICTIONS

DEFENDANT/OFFENDER	OFFICER
Hardware/Software Requiring Advanced Approval	
The following is a list of items you may not possess or use without advanced written permission:	
Any encryption or steganography or similar software/hardware	
Any monitoring or similar software/hardware	
Any anti-monitoring or similar software/hardware	
Any password cracking utilities	
Any wiping/erasing or similar utilities	
Any file sharing or peer-to-peer network programs	
Viruses, worms, Trojan horse, logic bombs, sniffer programs, or any other similar programs	
Any pirated software (software for which you do not have a license for, which is not shareware or freeware)	
Any software, hardware, and/or website that can be used to spoof, conceal and/or hide your identity.	
OTHER (Defined)	
Hardware/Software Approval	
The Computer Restriction and Monitoring Program Participant Agreement reflects that you will only possess and/or access approved computer hardware or software. In accordance with that agreement you have been approved to possess and/or access the following:	
Defendant/Offender Date Officer Date	

Appendix D

COMPUTER MONITORING RELEASE

The computer owner's signature below indicates they swear to be the owner(s) or duly authorized representative of the owner(s) of the computer(s) covered by this agreement and hereby acknowledge and agree to the following:

We hereby consent and give full access to our personal computers by the AGENCY in accordance with their supervision of:

_____

We, hereby consent to having monitoring software/hardware installed on our computers and any measures used to insure the integrity of monitoring.

We understand that the monitoring software/hardware captures all computer activity of anyone using the computer. We understand that we will have no expectation of privacy when using these machines.

We understand that this computer use is being monitored by the AGENCY and information received will be shared with the appropriate legal authority in accordance with the supervision of above individual.

We understand that the AGENCY will periodically retrieve the information gathered by the monitoring software/hardware, and we give consent to this retrieval of information. We also give consent to the AGENCY periodically inspecting our computers to insure the monitoring software/hardware is functioning properly

_____
Owner Representative   Date   Officer   Date

Appendix E

COMPUTER USAGE UPDATE QUESTIONNAIRE

On _____ you provided the Computer Usage Questionnaire, which provided information on your e-mail accounts; all of your social networking profiles; your entire computer system and software; all passwords used by you; and your Internet Service Provider(s).

Have there been any changes to the information that you provided?

        No   Yes

If yes, contact your officer immediately. You will be required to update the information in writing.

To the best of my knowledge and belief, the information I have provided on this form is true, correct and complete. I understand that a false statement on this form may result in a supervision violation or new prosecution as warranted.

_____   _____
Owner Representative   Date   Officer   Date

Appendix F

AUTHORIZATION TO SEARCH/SEIZE
COMPUTER EQUIPMENT/ELECTRONIC DATA

I,_____ understand that I may refuse to allow a search/seizure and such a refusal would not be grounds for a violation of my supervision, if applicable. With this understanding I hereby authorize:

_____

who has identified themselves as an officer of AGENCY, and any other person (s), including but not limited to a computer forensic examiner, they may designate to assist, to remove, take possession of and/or conduct a complete search of my computer system, any electronic data storage device, media storage (USB Flash drives, memory cards, CD/DVD/BDs, 3 1/2 diskettes, tapes, zip disks, etc.), or any other electronic device capable of storing, retrieving and/or accessing data or necessary to assist in the accessing of said electronic data. The following is a list of items that I hereby give consent to search and seize (Attach additional sheet if necessary and and initial):

_____

_____

_____

This consent shall remain in effect for a period of _____ business days, during which time the aforementioned property will be subject to a forensic analysis for any data pertinent to an investigation concerning a possible supervision violation and/or criminal law violation. I give this consent to search/seize freely and voluntarily, without fear, threat, coercion, or promises of any kind and with full knowledge of my constitutional right to refuse to give my consent for the removal and/or search of the aforementioned property. I am also aware that if I wish to exercise this right at any time during the seizure and/or search of the equipment/data, it will be respected. This consent to search is given by me this _____day of _____at_____ am/pm.

_____

| Person | Date | Witness | Date |

Appendix G

KNOPPIX EVIDENCE INVENTORY WORKSHEET

Original Media Access Worksheet								
TO DOCUMENT EACH ACCESS TO ORIGINAL MEDIA		Accessed by:						
		Computer ID:						
Location of Computer:								
BIOS Settings								
Date Accessed:		Time Accessed:						
System Date:		System Time:						
BIOS Set To Boot to CD/DVD		Yes			No			
BIOS Setting Modified to Boot to CD/DVD		Yes			No			
Search,								
Following files extensions were searched for:								
JPG	JPEG	GIF	BMP	PNG	MPG	MPEG	AVI	
Following text and/or file names were searched for:								
During search the following directories were reviewed:								
Search revealed following:								
Results documented to storage media		Yes			No			
Computer Seized		Yes			No			
Special Notes:								
Time Search Ended:								

Officer Signature   Date

Appendix H

PREVIEW IN WINDOWS

TO DOCUMENT EACH ACCESS TO ORIGINAL MEDIA RUNNING WINDOWS OPERATING SYSTEM	Offender:
	Accessed by:

Computer Location/ID:			
System is:	On/Off	NOTE: Turning on or accessing media without write protection will change data	

Check Purpose of Preview	
Monitoring Software Installation	
Compliance Check	
Check of Public Access/Third Party Computer	
Other (Explain):	

Date Accessed:	Time Accessed:		
System Date:	System Time:		
USB Device being used to access and/or save data?		Yes	No
Does device contain pre-configured "triage" tools, such as AccessData AD Triage or ADF Triage-Examiner?		Yes	No
If so, name of tool and who configured:			

Identify All Tools Run During Exam and Note Order			
	Triage Tools:	Field Search:	FTK Imager:
Prodiscover:	Winaudit:	USBDeview:	Other:
Contraband Found:		Yes	No
Contraband Removed:		Yes	No
Computer Seized:		Yes	No
Notes:			
Exam Ended:			

Officer Signature   Date

Appendix I

PROPERTY RECEIPT

The following items were seized from the person, residence, or automobile of _____as a result of an authorized search by the AGENCY.

_____

The items listed on the attached___worksheet(s) were received from the person, residence, or automobile of the above-named individual as a result of an authorized search by AGENCY.

Time:_____

Date:_____

Location:_____

_____
Witness/Owner   Date

_____   _____
Officer/Date   Evidence-Custodian/Date

Initial Inventory For Each Computer and All Associated Peripherals				
Tag No.	Descriptions	Manufacturer	Serial	Special Markings
	CPU			
	Monitor			
	Keyboard			
	Printer			
	Scanner			

Where located:			
State of computer		On	Off
Connected to Internet		Yes	No
Networked		Yes	No
Photos Taken		Yes	No

Notes:

INDEX

A

AccessData, 176, 181–2, 184–185, 193
AD Triage, 182, 248
ADF Solutions, 182, 193
adult pornography, 31, 72, 191–192
Advanced Computer Examination Support
    for Law Enforcement (ACES), 182
America Online (AOL), 7, 73
American Bar Association (ABA), 206, 210
American Probation and Parole Association,
    11–12, 89, 224
Android, 208
anti-spyware, 17, 177
antivirus, 137, 219, 240
Apple, 7, 27, 125, 136, 155, 185–186, 237
ASR Data Acquisition & Analysis, LLC, 170

B

banners, 70, 76, 79, 201
BIOS (Basic Input/Out System), 128, 130,
    164, 236
BIOS settings, 130, 164, 247
bit, 116
Black Bag, 185, 193
Blackberry, 208
blacklisted websites, 18
blocking software, 18
bootable CDs, 131, 161, 170
botnets, 97
bulletin board system, 45–46, 141–142
bytes, 116

C

California, 58, 70, 89

Camtasia Studio, 220
Captain Crunch, 4
card skimmers, 98
CCleaner Portable, 192
Cell Phone Investigative Kiosks, 189
Cellebrite, 189, 193
Central Processing Unit (CPU), 123–125,
    127–128, 134, 137, 153, 250
Child Exploitation and Obscenity Section
    (CEOS), 8, 14
child pornography, 8, 12, 25–26, 28, 31, 33,
    43, 46–48, 59–63, 66–69, 103–106,
    126, 158, 160, 191
cloud computing, 75, 157
Compact Disk (CD), 128, 130–132, 137–138,
    152–153, 161–164, 172, 174–176, 180,
    183, 187–189, 247
companies, commercial monitoring, 203
components, internal, 134, 153
computer
    employer's, 70, 102, 159
    family, 70, 152
    offender's wife's, 187
    public, 85
    term, 15, 228, 230
Computer Aided INvestigative Environment
    (C.A.IN.E.), 174, 193
computer crime, 7, 12, 60, 91–94, 97, 114
computer forensics, 59, 128, 134, 182,
    184–185, 193–194, 206, 210
Computer Investigation Resources LLC,
    207, 211
Computer Monitoring Release, 227, 244
Computer Online Forensic Evidence
    Extractor (COFFEE), 181–182, 193
computer searches, 17, 26–29, 33, 58–59, 63,
    66, 70, 72–73, 102, 159, 212

Computer Usage Questionnaire, 147, 227, 245
Computer Usage Update Questionnaire, 227
Computercop, 183–184, 193
concealment programs, 17
Condor, 4
CyberSentinel, 202, 211

D

Dark Dante, 4
Department of Justice, 8, 12, 14, 73, 90, 103, 109, 114, 194
devices, bootable, 128, 130
Digital Evidence and Forensic Toolkit (DEFT), 174, 180
Digital Intelligence, 186, 193
Digital Subscriber Line (DSL), 105, 118–119
Digital Versatile Disk (DVD), 4, 18, 128, 130–132, 161, 164, 189
Disk Operating System (DOS), 7, 170
Draper, John aka Captain Crunch, 4
Drug Enforcement Administration (DEA), 111, 114

E

e-mail, 20, 28, 32, 36–37, 43–44, 49, 64, 73–75, 77–78, 84, 150–151, 200–201, 214–215, 228, 230–231
eBlaster, 202, 209
eBlaster Mobile, 209
Eighth Amendment, 37
Eighth Circuit, 40
Eleventh Circuit, 40, 45, 48, 67, 71
Encase, 182, 184–185, 193
Encase Portable, 182
encryption, 17, 50, 99, 137, 173, 181, 240, 243
Eraser Portable, 192

F

F-Response, 184, 193
Facebook, 5, 14, 51, 73, 82, 213, 215–216, 220, 231
Faraday Bags or boxes, 190
Federal Bureau of Investigations (FBI), 42, 46–47, 182, 189, 197
Fernico, 189, 193

Field Search, 108, 172–175, 183–184, 192–193, 248
Fifth Amendment, 37, 81–83, 89
file extensions, 103, 168
file slack, 171, 173
files
    deleted, 60, 173, 182–183
    graphic, 159
    movie, 159
    windows swap, 171
filtering software, 18, 63, 145
Firefox, 18, 240
First Amendment, 36, 45, 52
flash drive, 29, 128, 148, 173, 176, 178, 181–182
Florida, 38–39, 76–77, 196
Forensic and Incident Response Environment (FIRE), 161
forensic software, 25, 27, 128, 130, 137–138, 156, 159, 161, 170, 181–182, 184
Fourteenth Amendment, 36, 38
Fourth Amendment 36, 44, 46, 58, 63, 71, 73, 86, 89, 211
Free space, 173
FTK Imager, 175–177, 183–184, 220, 248

G

gambling, 93, 97, 110–115
gaming devices, 15–16, 19–21, 27, 45, 118, 120–121, 140, 143, 228, 230, 232
gang, 4–5, 183
gang members, 5, 10, 29
gigabytes 29, 116, 119, 128–129, 132–133, 163
Global positioning (GPS), 31–32, 231
Gnome Nanny, 209, 211
Google, 19, 75, 215, 217
graphical user interface (GUI), 7
Griffin v. Wisconsin, 483 U.S 868 (1987), 43, 58, 89

H

hacking, 6–7, 96–98, 146
hard drive, 21–22, 60–61, 76, 120–121, 124, 130–131, 134–135, 153, 155–156, 161–164, 170–171, 176–177, 191–192, 203–204, 236–237

hard drive duplicators, 186
hardware write-blockers, 186
Hash values, 177
Health Insurance Portability and
    Accountability Act (HIPAA), 85, 89
High Technology Crime Investigation
    Association (HTCIA), 218, 225
history, computer's Internet, 68
Hooverdesk, 220

I

I-Pods, 27
identifiers, personal, 99, 160, 215
image files, 105, 140, 173
ImageScan 162–164, 193
information, credit history, 229
input devices, 124–127
Inside Security Rescue Toolkit (INSERT),
    161
Intelligent Computer Solutions, 186, 193
International Association for Property and
    Evidence Inc. 191, 193
Internet, 5, 7–15, 18–21, 23–24, 27–29,
    31–32, 35–38, 42–43, 45–49, 67–68,
    82–85, 109–115, 117–118, 143–148,
    231–234
Internet Crimes Against Children (ICAC), 8
Internet Explorer, 18, 240
Internet Probation and Parole Control
    (IPPC) 22, 78, 195–196, 201–207, 209
Internet Service Providers (ISP), 18–19, 65,
    72–75, 103, 105, 141–142, 148, 219,
    228–230, 232, 235, 245
Interstate Compact Adult Offender
    Supervision, 39
ISO image, 164, 174

J

juvenile sexting, 109
juveniles, 12, 104, 106–107, 109

K

Keylogger, 122, 196
keywords, 150, 201, 203–204
Knopper, Klaus, 161

Knoppix, 130–132, 137, 153, 161–162,
    164–166, 170, 193
Konqueror, 165, 167, 169
Kyllo v. U.S., 533 U.S. 27 (2001), 86, 89

L

laptop, 9, 17, 28, 68–69, 85–86, 96, 118, 120,
    125, 127, 129, 135–136, 147–148, 155,
    187–188
law enforcement, 6, 8, 16, 25–26, 37, 58, 69,
    71, 75, 77–78, 161–162, 172–173, 181–182,
    216–217
Legion of Doom, 4
Linux, 121, 125, 130–132, 136, 143, 153, 161,
    170, 174, 209, 237
Live Response, 182
local area network (LAN), 138
Logicube, 186, 193
Lucy Faithful Foundation, 197

M

MacForensicsLab, 185, 194
Maryland v. Buie, 494 U.S. 325 (1990), 69,
    89
Masters of Deception, 4
M.F. v. State of New York Executive
    Department of Parole, Case No. 10-
    2074-CV, (2011), 40
Micro Systemation (MSAB), 189, 193
Minnesota Sex Offender Screening Tool-
    Revised (MnSOST-R), 107
Minnesota v. Murphy, 465 U.S. 420 (1984),
    81, 89
Miranda, 60, 66, 82
Mitnick, Kevin aka Condor, 4, 20, 34, 195
mobile phones, 5, 19–20, 118, 121, 125, 127,
    133, 137, 140, 143, 189, 203–204,
    207–209, 230–231
Modified, Access, and Creation (MAC)
    dates, 192
monitoring software, 16–19, 22–23, 25,
    27–28, 72, 77–79, 121, 126–128,
    130–132, 136, 138, 141–144, 149–153,
    195–196, 207–209
    commercial, 203, 207
    consumer, 197, 203, 208–209

Morris, Robert, 4
Mosaic, 7
motherboard, 124, 127, 134, 136
MSAB (Micro Systemation), 189, 193
Multnomah County, Oregon, 4
MyKey Technology Inc., 182, 186, 193
MyMobileWatch Dog, 208
MySpace, 4–5, 10, 12–14, 51, 208, 212, 231

N

National Computer Forensics Institute
    (NCFI), 224
National Conference of State Legislatures, 9,
    13, 38–39, 55
National Drug Intelligence Center (NDIC),
    110, 114
National Law Enforcement Corrections and
    Technology Center (NLECTC), 172,
    224
National White Collar Crime Center
    (NW3C), 163, 181, 224
New Technologies, Inc. (NTI), 169, 193
Ninth Circuit, 20, 46
NoWrite, 182
NTA Stealth, 169–170

O

O'Brien v. O'Brien, Case No. 5D03-3484,
    (2005), 76, 89
Office Juvenile Justice and Delinquency
    Prevention (OJJDP), 8, 14
online activities, offender's, 103, 195, 213
operating systems, 7, 25, 27, 61, 120–121,
    124–125, 128, 130–132, 136–138, 149,
    152–153, 161, 170–171, 185–186, 237
    bootable, 131–132
Orange County, CA, 11–12
Oxygen Software, 189, 194

P

Paraben, 189, 194
Peer-to-peer file sharing programs, 17
Penguin Sleuth Kit (PSK), 165, 194
Pennsylvania Bd. of Probation and Parole v.
    Scott, 524 U.S. 357 (1998), 57

People v. TR, Cal: Court of Appeals, 4th
    Appellate Dist., 1st Div. 2010, 55
Personal Digital Assistants (PDAs), 189–90
phishing, 99
phreaker, 4
polygraph 31, 82, 134, 153
pornographic files, 104
pornography, 10, 17–18, 22, 60, 96, 102–103,
    107, 126, 131–132, 171, 179
Portable Linux Auditing CD (PLAC), 161,
    194
Poulsen, Kevin aka Dark Dante, 4
Presearch, 175
printers, 8, 27–28, 45, 120, 124–127, 131, 136,
    239, 250
privacy, reasonable expectation of, 22–23,
    29, 66–67, 70–71, 76, 86, 244
Privacy Protection Act (PPA), 73, 79–81, 90,
    143
ProDiscover, 182–5, 194, 248
ProDiscover Incident Response, 184

R

Random Access Memory (RAM), 124,
    127–128, 134, 156–157, 161, 175, 185,
    236
Read Only Memory (ROM), 128
Recycle Bin, 61, 192
Regional Computer Forensic Labs (RCFL),
    194, 224
Regional Computer Forensic Labs National
    Program Office, 163, 194
Remote Examination Agents (REA), 184
RemoteCOM, 184, 195, 197, 201–207, 209,
    211
Routine Activities Theory (RAT), 94, 97
Rapid Risk Assessment for Sex Offense
    Recidivism (RRASOR), 107–108

S

SafetyWeb Online Tracking (SWOT), 217,
    223
Samson v. California, 547 US 843, (2006), 58
script kiddies, 97
SEARCH investigative Community Toolbar,
    219

Second Circuit, 40, 43–44, 61, 63
Secret Service, 80–81, 187–189
Securus Software, 197, 211
Serial, 117, 122, 136, 179, 232, 236–239, 250
sex offender treatment program, 68
sex offenders, 4, 8–10, 17, 24, 26, 29, 31, 40, 48–49, 77–78, 82, 98–100, 102–105, 107, 126–127
Silicon Forensics, 186, 194
Sixth Amendment, 37
Sixth Circuit, 69
Small Computer System Interface (SCSI), 165, 238–239
Snagit, 220
social networking sites (SNS), 4–5, 10–11, 17–19, 23, 29, 36, 55, 73–74, 82–84, 111, 142, 213–216, 222, 231
space, unallocated, 61, 173, 176
Spector Pro, 202
spouses, 22, 70, 76, 80, 195–201, 208
SpyAgent, 202, 211
spyware, 17, 97
STABLE/ACUTE, 107
stalking horse, 61
State of New Hampshire v. Steven Merrill, Case No. 2009–811, 50, 55
states, two-party, 77–78
STATIC-99, 107
STATIC-2002, 107
steganography, 17
Steve Jackson Games, Inc. v. Secret Service, 816 F. Supp. 432 (W.D. Tex. 1993), aff'd on other grounds, 36 F.3d 457 (5th Cir. 1994), 80
storage, temporary, 127
storage devices, 92–94, 117, 124, 131, 134
permanent, 128, 131
Storage Media Analysis Recovery Toolkit (S.M.A.R.T.), 170, 194
Stored Communications Act, 18 U.S.C. §§ 2701-2712 (SCA), 73, 75–76, 79, 87, 90
SubRosaSoft.com Inc., 185, 194
suicide, 110, 112–114, 160
Supreme Court, 51, 57–58, 67, 70, 81
suspicion, reasonable, 22, 37, 43, 58–63, 66–72, 102, 131, 158–159, 198, 212, 214
Susteen, 189, 194
systems administrators, 145, 150, 198

T

tamper tape, 121–2, 126–127, 153
Technology Pathways, LLC, 182
Techsmith, 220, 223
Teel Technologies, 190, 194
Temporary Internet Files, 169
Temporary Internet Folders, 104
Tenth Circuit, 62–63, 71
terabyte, 116
Third Circuit, 42, 46, 82
training 24, 27–28, 87–88, 135, 144, 157, 161, 163–164, 173, 181, 188, 192
Triage-Examiner, 182
TUX4N6, 162–164
Twitter, 208, 213, 222, 231

U

ultraviolet light, 87, 127
Uniform Resource Locator (URL), 173, 218
United Kingdom, 197, 202
Universal Serial Bus (USB), 27, 117, 128, 132, 184, 238
US-Latt, 182
U.S. v. Antelope, 395 F. 3d 1128, 9th Cir. (2005), 82, 90
U.S. v. Fields, 324 F. 3d 1025 (8th Cir. 2003), 37
U.S. v. Gallo, 20 F.3d7, 11 (1st Cir. 1994), 20
U.S. v. Herndon, 501 F. 3d 683 (6th Cir. 2007), 68, 90
U.S. v. Kevin Mitnick, 145 F.3d 1342, 1998, WL 255343 (9th Cir.) (Cal.), 34
U.S. v. Knights, 534 U.S. 112 (2001), 43, 58, 61–62, 67–69, 90
U.S. v. Lee, 315 F. 3d 206, 3rd. Cir. (2003), 82, 90
U.S. v. Lifshitz, 369 F.3d 173, 175, 190–92 (2d Cir. 2004) 43, 55, 63
U.S. v. Love, 593 F. 3d 1 (DC Cir. 2010), 41, 47, 55
U.S. v. Paul, 274 F.3d 155 (5th Cir. 2001), 41–42, 55
U.S. v. Poehlman, 217 F.3d. 692 (9th Circuit, 2000), 83
U.S. v. Reyes, 283 F. 3d 446, 2nd Cir. (2002), 61, 90

U.S. v. Sales, 476 F.3d 732 (9th Cir. 2007), 41, 45, 55
U.S. v. Scott, 316 F. 3d 733 (7th Cir. 2003), 41
U.S. v. Stoterau, 524 F. 3d 988, 9th Cir. (2008), 82, 90
U.S. v. Tome, 611 F. 3d 1371 (11th Cir. 2010), 41, 48, 55
U.S. v. Tucker, 305 F. 3d 1193, (10th Cir. 2002), 59, 90, 194
U.S. v. Voelker, 489 F.3d 139, 154 (3d Cir.2007), 41, 46, 56
U.S. v. Yuknavich, 419 F. 3d 1302, (11th Cir. 2005), 63, 90
U.S. v. Zinn, 321 F.3d 1084 (11th Cir. 2003), 41, 56
USB device, bootable, 161
USBDeview, 175, 179, 248

V

Vere Software, 89, 219
Vere Software Internet Investigator's Toolbar, 219
Vere Software's WebCase, 220
viruses, 98, 243
Volume Shadow Copy, 183, 194

W

webcams, 17, 24, 46, 98, 124–127, 232
website spoofing, 99
WebWatcher 7, 202
WebWatcher Mobile, 209
Wetstone, 182, 194
wide area network (WAN), 138
WiebeTech, 186, 194
WiFi, 85, 118, 124, 134, 138, 231–232, 239
WiFi Detection Devices, 135
Winaudit, 175, 177, 248
Windows Mobile 5 & 6, 208
wiping, 17, 131–132, 137, 144, 153, 163, 191–192, 240, 243
wireless Internet access, 210
wireless network interface controller (WNIC), 117
worms, 4, 98, 240, 243

Y

Yahoo, 18–19, 215
YouTube, 5, 208